YOUR
Perfect
PORTFOLIO

YOUR Perfect PORTFOLIO

The ultimate guide to using the world's most powerful investment strategies

CULLEN ROCHE

HARRIMAN HOUSE LTD
Website: harriman.house

First published in 2026 by Harriman House, an imprint of Pan Macmillan
Associated companies throughout the world
www.panmacmillan.com

Copyright © Cullen Roche 2026

The right of Cullen Roche to be identified as the author has been asserted in accordance with the Copyright, Design and Patents Act 1988.

Paperback ISBN: 978-1-80409-192-0
eBook ISBN: 978-1-80409-193-7

All rights reserved. No part of this publication may be reproduced, stored in a retrieval system, or transmitted in any form or by any means (including without limitation electronic, mechanical, photocopying, recording, or otherwise) without the prior written permission of the publisher. This book is sold subject to the condition that it shall not, by way of trade or otherwise, be lent, hired out, or otherwise circulated without the publisher's prior consent. This work is reserved from text and data mining (Article 4(3) Directive (EU) 2019/790).

Harriman House does not have any control over, or any responsibility for, any author or third-party websites (including without limitation URLs, emails and QR codes) referred to in or on this book. This book is for informational purposes only. Readers are advised to consult an appropriate professional in light of their relevant circumstances and requirements before acting on any information in this book.

No responsibility or liability for loss occasioned to any person or corporate body acting or refraining to act as a result of reading material in this book can be accepted by the publisher, by the author, or by the employers of the author.

01

Printed in the United States of America.

This book is dedicated to all the portfolios I have divorced over the course of my life. They say divorce is expensive because it's worth it. They are right.

CONTENTS

The Goal Of This Book	ix
Introduction: Does The Perfect Portfolio Exist?	1
Part 1: The Ten Essential Principles For Portfolio Construction	7
Essential principle #1: You are a saver, not an investor	11
Essential principle #2: You are your portfolio's worst enemy	15
Essential principle #3: Beating the market is hard. Really hard.	19
Essential principle #4: Diversification is the only free lunch	22
Essential principle #5: The cost matters hypothesis	27
Essential principle #6: Real, real returns are all that matter	30
Essential principle #7: Risk is uncertainty of lifetime consumption	32
Essential principle #8: Asset allocation is a temporal conundrum	35
Essential principle #9: Past performance is not indicative of future returns	39
Essential principle #10: Set realistic expectations and stay the course	41
Part 2: The Portfolios	43
Chapter 1: The Warren Buffett Portfolio	47
Chapter 2: Why Not 100% Stocks?	65

Chapter 3: T-Bill And Chill (Or Why Not 100% Cash?) — 79

Chapter 4: The Gold Standard Of Portfolios – The 60/40 Stock/Bond Portfolio — 89

Chapter 5: The Global Financial Asset Portfolio — 102

Chapter 6: The Factor Investing Portfolio — 115

Chapter 7: The Forward Cap Portfolio — 140

Chapter 8: The Risk Parity Portfolio — 157

Chapter 9: The Permanent Portfolio — 170

Chapter 10: The Flying Ladder Strategy — 183

Chapter 11: The Boglehead Three-Fund Portfolio — 194

Chapter 12: The Countercyclical Rebalancing Portfolio — 203

Chapter 13: The Bernstein No-Brainer Portfolio — 217

Chapter 14: Dividend Investing And Anti-Dividend Investing Portfolios — 230

Chapter 15: The Trend Following Portfolio — 246

Chapter 16: The Vice And Virtue Portfolio — 258

Chapter 17: The Endowment Portfolio — 269

Chapter 18: Retirement Bond Tent Strategy — 284

Chapter 19: Target Date Portfolios — 292

Chapter 20: Defined Duration Strategy — 300

Chapter 21: Polygamous Portfolios — 322

Chapter 22: Odds And Ends — 332

Chapter 23: Portfolio Management — 348

Acknowledgments — 357
Endnotes — 359
About The Author — 363
Disclaimer — 365

THE GOAL OF THIS BOOK

FINDING the right investment portfolio is like finding true love. You spend time learning about yourself, exploring your options, and figuring out what really fits you. What works for someone else might not work for you – and that's okay. You're unique, and your portfolio should reflect that. It's not about finding the "perfect" portfolio for everyone. It's about finding the one that's perfect for *you*.

In *How I Invest My Money*, Josh Brown, CEO of Ritholtz Wealth Management, offers a valuable piece of advice: "One major life lesson I've learned over the years is to never argue the merits of my own portfolio with anyone else." He's absolutely right. Once you've found your perfect portfolio, the only person you'll regularly need to justify it to is yourself – and maybe your spouse, especially if things go south and a portfolio "divorce" starts to sound necessary.

The goal of this book is to help you find your perfect portfolio and hopefully avoid some costly portfolio "divorces" in the process (and certainly any real ones). At one time or another I've married all the portfolios in this book. I've studied them for decades and discovered their pros and their cons.

This book will:

1. Discuss the essential principles for sound portfolio construction.
2. Analyze specific portfolio strategies with the goal of outlining the benefits and drawbacks as they might relate to you personally.

3. Provide actionable outlines for how these portfolios might be implemented and maintained.

WHAT THIS BOOK IS ABOUT

This book is about how to construct a portfolio that works for you. We begin by outlining the general principles for portfolio construction and the goals that investors should have during this process. We then explore many of the most popular strategies that exist. We tear them open, discussing their strengths and weaknesses and why they may or may not be a good fit for you. Remember, this is all about you. I am here as an independent analyst providing objective critiques of these strategies to help you find the portfolio (or portfolios) you're most compatible with. In the end, you might find that you like one or even many of the portfolios. But the overarching goal is to help you find your perfect portfolio.

WHO IS THIS BOOK FOR?

This book is for anyone and everyone who wants to start constructing a sensible portfolio that suits their needs and wants. Some of the portfolios are complex and some of them are very simple. My goal is to provide a broad review of many differing styles knowing that all of you are different and unique. My hope is that both novices and sophisticated investors can utilize this book to learn about and broaden their understanding of how we can all find a perfect portfolio.

HOW THIS BOOK IS STRUCTURED

This book is broken up into two specific parts. Part 1 deals with background and some principles that I believe are essential for understanding the portfolios discussed in the book. In Part 2, we dive into different portfolio strategies and how they work. If you would prefer to study the portfolios only, I recommend skipping Part 1.

Within Part 2, I've organized the portfolio discussion sequentially, starting with the simplest strategies and progressing to more complex ones. A sophisticated investor might find the early chapters too simplistic. And novice investors might find the later chapters too complex. My goal is to start with the broader basics and build the portfolios progressively so we can see how certain strategies differ from one another and can also be utilized together.

The reader might find that certain chapters aren't pertinent to them. Maybe you don't like gold, bonds, managed futures or other specific assets. There's nothing wrong with that! And you might find that it's useful to bounce around from chapter to chapter. Despite the metaphor within, this book isn't a love story, so you don't have to read it sequentially to understand the conclusions. This is all about you and your personal needs so navigate it how you prefer. Use this book as a reference guide. My goal is for the entire text to be a guide, but you might also find that only specific pieces are useful to you.

My hope is this book will shed some light on how these different approaches can help you find a portfolio you love and cherish, for better, for worse, through sickness and in health, for rich and for poor, but hopefully for rich and for richer.

DATA KEY

This data key will be useful throughout the book when we're discussing how the different portfolios were assessed.

Real returns: Inflation-adjusted annual returns. Inflation is accounted for using the Consumer Price Index (CPI).

Volatility: The standard deviation of returns.

Sharpe ratio: A measure of risk-adjusted returns that quantifies the amount of risk in achieving returns. 0.5–1.0 is considered average. 1.0–1.5 is considered above average and below 0.5 is considered below average.

Sortino ratio: A measure of risk that tries to improve upon the Sharpe ratio by more equally measuring upside and downside risk. 0.5–1.0 is considered average. 1.0–2.0 is considered above average and below 0.5 is considered below average.

Max drawdown: The maximum peak to trough downturn.

Max drawdown (post-1945): Market returns are often broken into two time periods due to the extreme volatility of the Great Depression and World War 2.

Ulcer index: A measure of how deep and how long a drawdown typically is. This ranges from 0–50. 0–5 is considered more stable, 5–10 moderately stable. 10–50 varies from stressful to extreme stress.

Market correlation: The correlation to the broad US stock market.

Where possible I use real-time fund data from existing funds instead of relying on hypothetical backtests. As a result of this you might notice that some of the performance analysis in this book does not go back as far as we'd like. And some of the time periods over which we analyze the portfolios are very different because the theoretical and real-time data differs depending on the assets and funds we analyzed. When I had to choose between more theoretical data versus less actual data, I tended to defer towards using the actual dataset if it went back 15–20+ years at a minimum and captured a high inflation (2021–2024) and large recessionary environment (2008–2011). Some datasets (like emerging market stock returns or bond aggregate data) are constrained by the fact that many of these indices did not exist before 1990.

INTRODUCTION: DOES THE PERFECT PORTFOLIO EXIST?

IN 1999 I was a know-nothing college student studying finance at Georgetown University. The internet was the hot new thing, and I'd just purchased a computer that was the size of a small refrigerator. Despite my ignorance of investing, I had a profound curiosity and a voracious appetite to understand the world of money.

It was during this time that I destroyed my very first investing relationship. Luckily it was only a simulation. I was taking a course on derivatives, and we'd spent a significant amount of time studying some of the most famous fund implosions in investing history, which often included leverage and derivatives. Ironically, having studied the dangers of these strategies, the course included a simulation during the quarter in which I managed to turn $100,000 into $100 by actively day trading soybeans and lean hog futures. I didn't even know what a soybean was at the time, but that didn't stop me from incinerating the value of them within my portfolio as I impatiently day traded with leverage. I'll never forget the note from my professor, in big bold red letters, about the performance: "WOW."

When I stopped day trading futures in 1999, I began obsessively reading Warren Buffett's shareholder letters. I had learned that decimating soybean futures wasn't for me, and I evolved into a "value investor." I was getting wiser but starting from a low bar.

I began pouring my weekly earnings from waiting tables into a stock called Sirius Satellite Radio and a handful of other techie names that appeared, to me, to fit the value investing criteria. Sirius had fallen 75% from its peak and, based on my amateurish analysis, was a good value and had bright prospects. I had never really considered that a stock that is down 75% can fall another 75%. And it did. I was crushed as I watched my beer-drinking money go up in smoke. I can't be sure if it was youth, ignorance, or a bit of both, but I had not learned the art of patience at this point in my life.

In retrospect, I had also failed to understand one of the most important trends in the market – the macro trend. I had no idea at the time, but we weren't just in a bear market at this point in history – we were undergoing a seismic macro market event that was devastating everything in its path. The implosion of the Nasdaq bubble welcomed me into the world of investing like a punch in the face, and as Mike Tyson famously quipped, I did not have a plan to deal with it.

As I dusted myself off from the dot-com bust, I started to find my footing. I had landed a job out of college working at Merrill Lynch and our team was managing hundreds of millions of dollars for retail investors. My boss was a brilliant old-school stock and bond picker, and I had the good fortune of learning from some of our best research analysts in the firm. I was learning fast, but my impatience again got the best of me, and I determined that the high-fee sales commission world wasn't for me. I left the firm, struck out on my own, and lucked into managing an event-driven strategy that focused on trading illiquid stocks and futures contracts in the overnight market. This turned out to be what we now know as the "overnight effect" – the fact that stocks generate much of their excess return when the market is closed. Over a five-year period, I generated 20.75% annual returns (15% net of fees), while the S&P 500 remained flat. I felt like a genius for a brief period, but this strategy also got side-swiped by a macro trend – what we now know as the Great Financial Crisis (GFC). I was fortunate to generate a 15% return in 2008, but as all markets froze in 2008 and 2009 I found myself seeking a more stable and structured process that didn't entail 100-hour weeks and waking up at 3 a.m. to flip stocks.

Although I wasn't even 30 years old at this point, I'd cycled through dozens of investment strategies already. I was like a speed-dating junkie unable to remain committed for more than a few years.

The GFC was formational for me and illustrated the importance of having a more robust, long-term and all-weather style of portfolio. I soaked up everything I could learn about macroeconomics and macro investing, and pivoted again, this time towards more sustainable financial planning-oriented strategies grounded in what I like to think of as a first principles approach to portfolio construction. I wrote a paper in 2011 called "Understanding the Modern Monetary System," which quickly jumped to being one of the most read papers in the SSRN research database for a decade. Like me, investors emerged from the GFC hungry for a more grounded and operationally sound understanding of money and investing.

During this period, I tirelessly studied the top portfolio strategies from the world's best investors, all in pursuit of the perfect portfolio. Over the course of the last 20 years, I've had the good fortune of getting to know some of the greatest investors in the world. And I've helped oversee billions of dollars and helped thousands of investors achieve financial independence putting all these lessons to work. Over this time, I've realized that portfolio management is like dieting – we're all on an endless search for our six pack that too often ends up with us on the sofa with a plateful of chocolate brownies. Good portfolio management is a delicate balance of behavioral control and risk optimization. And like any sustainable diet, it must be customized to your personal needs and wants.

If you're like me, you've tried a million different fad diets and workout regimes. In theory, being healthy is easy – eat right and exercise. But in practice it can be difficult thanks primarily to the existence of snacks and sofas. Dieting is especially troublesome because it's difficult to remain loyal to a single diet. But what if you could find the Holy Grail of dieting: a diet you enjoyed that helped you stay healthy? How much easier would your life be and how much better would you feel?

In 2015 and 2018, researchers published papers about the efficacy of different fad diets.[1] You probably know most of them – I certainly do because I've tried and failed all of them at one point or another.

The interesting conclusion from their research was that there is no Holy Grail of dieting for all people. In fact, what they found was that the only diet that worked was the one you stayed faithful to. In other words, *all the diets* work if you find the one you can stick with.

Portfolio management is not so different. You don't need to find the perfect portfolio for all people at all times. You need to find the portfolio that's perfect for *you* and then you need to remain loyal to it long enough for it to work for you.

There's a perfect portfolio out there waiting for you to find it. You'll have to test the waters and see what works for you. More importantly, your portfolio might have to evolve over time. The financial markets and the economy are constantly evolving and adapting. Your portfolio will have to adapt and evolve too, not only to account for the changes in the world, but also for the changes in your life.

What works for one person is unlikely to work for all people. That is, after all, what makes markets work. People have different goals and different needs. So don't settle for the portfolio that someone else uses (or promotes) just because it works for them. You'll need to search out

INTRODUCTION: DOES THE PERFECT PORTFOLIO EXIST?

and test different portfolios to help you find the one that works best for you. It's out there. You just need to keep looking.

I hope that this book will be a testing ground for you to learn and understand different portfolios so you can begin to narrow down this search for yourself. At best, I hope this book will help you find a portfolio you can fall in love with while avoiding some of the expensive divorces I encountered along the way. At worst, I hope reading this book helps you learn a few useful concepts. I am here to help as best as possible. I have my own preferences and biases in this process so don't treat my word as gospel. Treat this book as an open-ended exploration of different concepts and not a bible of conclusions.

That said, this is probably a good time for me to note that if you have questions or positive feedback please email me at cullenroche@disciplinefunds.com. If you have hate mail please contact the current head of the Federal Reserve at chairperson@federalreserve.gov. They had nothing to do with writing this book, but the Fed Chair is always a logical scapegoat for anything that goes wrong in the world of finance.

Alright, let's get going.

PART 1

THE TEN ESSENTIAL PRINCIPLES FOR PORTFOLIO CONSTRUCTION

BEFORE diving into the analysis of specific portfolios, it's helpful to first outline the core principles that guided their selection.

These 10 principles represent what I consider essential to any sound portfolio construction process. They draw from both behavioral finance and evidence-based investing. Here they are:

1. You are a saver, not an investor.
2. You are your portfolio's worst enemy.
3. Beating the market is hard. Really hard.
4. Diversification is the only free lunch.
5. The Cost Matters Hypothesis.
6. Real, real, returns are all that matter.
7. Risk is uncertainty of lifetime consumption.
8. Asset allocation is a temporal conundrum.
9. Past performance is not indicative of future returns.
10. Set realistic expectations and stay the course.

Let's go through each of these in more detail.

ESSENTIAL PRINCIPLE #1

YOU ARE A SAVER, NOT AN INVESTOR

WHEN I was writing my first book *Pragmatic Capitalism*, I kept running into an odd problem – the word "investing." I was writing a book about economics *and* finance, but this word doesn't have a consistent meaning in these two worlds. I know, what a weirdly essential word to be confused about, right?

In economics, investment means to spend for future production. But in finance the word investment means to allocate capital with the expectation of financial returns.

This inconsistency bothered me because the returns that firms generate are a function of how they spend for future production. If a firm allocates investment spending in an innovation, the return from that innovation is reflected in stock prices. Firms sometimes issue stocks or bonds to *finance* investment spending, but buying stocks and bonds is not the actual act of spending for future production. You generate income from your job, save some portion of that income and then reallocate it to assets on a secondary market like a stock or bond market.*

This distinction is important because most of us are not "investing" when we buy shares of stocks or bonds. In the case of secondary market transactions like most purchases/sales on a stock exchange, we are not financing a firm's investment spending and we certainly aren't spending for future production. We are reallocating our existing savings by buying/selling assets whose returns are largely a function of how the underlying firm *invests* and spends for future production.

The investments that most of us make in life are in ourselves and our skills. We then generate a certain amount of income selling those skills and what we don't spend is leftover as savings. We can allocate some of those savings to stocks or bonds or other assets, but the process of buying those instruments is not investment in the proper economic sense.

I don't like calling portfolios "investment portfolios" because it misconstrues this point. Instead, your investment portfolio should more appropriately be thought of as a "savings portfolio." This is a valuable clarification because "investing" is generally synonymous with an aggressive "get-rich," high-return-on-investment sort of endeavor, whereas saving is often thought of as prudent and boring. You're not a gambler, you're a prudent and thoughtful saver.

I like to think of our personal income statements and balance sheets as part of a "Total Portfolio." We generate income, typically by selling our skills. Some portion of this goes towards the things we consume. And the rest flows into this Total Portfolio as savings. Your savings can be allocated across your investment portfolio and/or your savings portfolio. Your investment portfolio is comprised of the ways you spend for future production, typically by enhancing your skills,

---

* I have to use the language we have and not the language Cullen wants so please excuse me if I use the word "investing" in its more common usage at times in this text.

going to school, or starting a firm. Your savings portfolio is the savings you allocate into assets that help grow and protect the savings you earn from optimizing your total portfolio.

Figure 0.1: The Total Portfolio

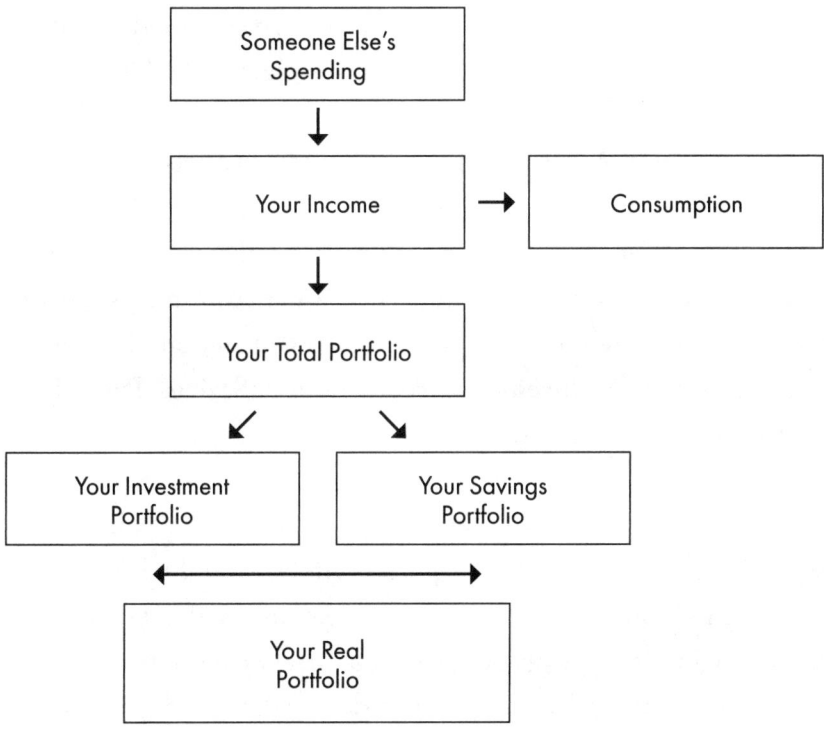

Our Total Portfolios, as depicted in Figure 0.1, are comprised of financial assets and non-financial assets. Financial assets are your liquid, cash-flow-generating instruments to help meet personal financial expenses. This can be broken down as follows:

Savings Portfolio – The financial assets that finance specific future expenses such as retirement spending. This will ideally be comprised of liquid cash-flow-generating financial assets with a high probability of future returns and principal reliability.

Investment Portfolio – This is where you spend for future production. If you are self-employed this would include any spending on your business. If you're employed this could include any spending to enhance your personal skills or side skills.

Non-Financial Assets include your illiquid real assets:

Real Portfolio – The non-financial assets that you own for various reasons (real estate, cars, etc.). These instruments often have elements of both savings and investment and can therefore span both your Investment Portfolio and Savings Portfolio depending on specifics.

The strategies in this book will apply to constructing your Savings Portfolio. They are not get-rich-quick portfolios and if you're looking for a get-rich-quick book then you should throw this book in the garbage right now. The portfolios and approaches in this book are best utilized as planning-based portfolios designed to help you allocate your savings in a prudent and thoughtful manner. That doesn't mean you can't potentially make a lot of money from these portfolios, but it's smart to go into this process looking for a long-term companion and not a one-night stand.

ESSENTIAL PRINCIPLE #2

YOU ARE YOUR PORTFOLIO'S WORST ENEMY

A THOUSAND years ago, a man walked out of his hut to retrieve some water from a nearby river. As he bent over, he noticed a gray wolf staring at him from the opposite side of the water. His immediate instinct was fight-or-flight. Being unarmed and afraid, the man's instinct was to run. And if you've watched as much Discovery Channel as I have, you know running is the worst thing you can do, as it triggers the wolf's instinct to attack.

Just a few lifetimes later modern man is rarely face-to-face with this physical danger, but we encounter similar psychological dangers in our economic lives all the time. And while the technological world has evolved very rapidly, our brains have not. The result is we are not well equipped or evolved to handle the sort of stress that often comes with the financial markets.

Biologist E.O. Wilson once said: "We have Paleolithic emotions, medieval institutions and Godlike technology."

The investment world is a godlike technology that confounds our paleolithic emotions. For example, when we see our account balances falling for reasons we don't understand, our fight-or-flight instinct often kicks in. Like an unarmed person, we typically lack a defense mechanism to control what's happening, so our instinct to flee takes over. This natural response is the behavioral equivalent of selling a volatile asset in favor of a more stable one to eliminate the perceived threat of downside volatility. But when we abandon our asset allocation, we often fall prey to an irrational impulse – realizing a short-term loss at the expense of potential long-term gains.

A better approach is to identify our behavioral flaws before we face these kinds of environments and to build a portfolio that is robust enough to handle them, arming us psychologically to navigate the dangers ahead. We know there is risk in the financial markets and we need to prepare ourselves to be able to combat these threats *before* they happen so we don't succumb to a million-year-old instinct that might not serve us well in the modern world.

Simon Ramo wrote a book in 1999 titled *Extraordinary Tennis for the Ordinary Tennis Player* in which he described how amateur tennis is a "loser's game" that isn't won by making optimal shots, but by limiting the number of errors you make. Asset allocation is very similar in the sense that it's not so much about building the optimal portfolio as it is about avoiding colossal mistakes along the way.

A lot of this book is filled with theories about how to best manage a portfolio. But if you can't control your own emotions these textbook concepts will be irrelevant. This is where the school of behavioral finance has added so much value in recent decades. It takes the

ESSENTIAL PRINCIPLE #2

theoretical underpinnings of finance and puts those theories in perspective by helping us understand how our behavior can impact the implementation of that theory.

After all, the process of portfolio management is similar to driving a car. You can understand every aspect of how a car operates, but if you don't understand human behavior, you can't fully understand how and why the vehicles on the road do certain things.

Ben Graham famously said: "The investor's chief problem, and even his worst enemy, is likely to be himself."

The world of portfolio management is a battleground of good/bad narratives. And fear, unfortunately, is a more powerful emotion than hope. Many of the narratives in the media and on the internet will prey on your fear to sell you certain goods or services. I would encourage you to never let fear or politics influence your financial planning. There's nothing wrong with a hefty dose of skepticism, but an optimistic view with a dollop of critical thinking will serve you much better in the long run than falling victim to persistently pessimistic narratives.

I try to constantly remind myself of something I call the Viktor Frankl life hack. Frankl, the author of *Man's Search for Meaning*, somehow found optimism while imprisoned in the Auschwitz concentration camp during World War 2. He teaches us that our surroundings do not dictate how we feel about those surroundings. Applied to the financial markets, this means the stock market cannot make you scared – you feel fear only if you allow the stock market to scare you. Over the course of my life, I've become virtually immune to market volatility, largely because I no longer allow myself to succumb to stock market fear. I control my reaction to the market; it cannot make me feel a certain way unless I give it that power.

Figure 0.2: The stock market wall of worry

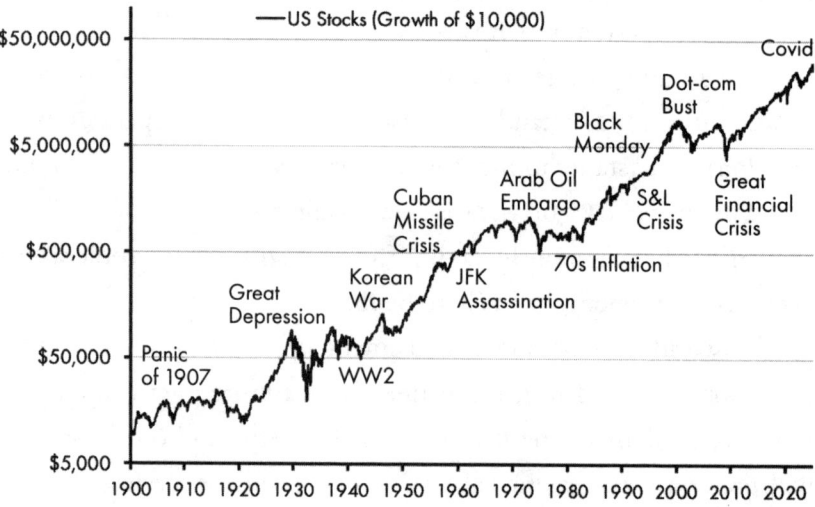

This notion is especially important in inherently volatile markets like the stock market. As shown in Figure 0.2, the market's long-term rise is filled with short-term scares. The stock market is one of the few places where, when everything goes on sale, everyone runs out of the store. That's customers losing their battle with the fight-or-flight instinct. To be the customer who runs into the store when things are frightening, you must first understand your own weaknesses – and then learn to overcome them – so you don't let your animal instincts interfere with good long-term outcomes.

The strategies in this book are selected for their behavioral robustness. Some of them are behavioral hedges, designed to maintain portfolio stability without necessarily outperforming the market.

ESSENTIAL PRINCIPLE #3

BEATING THE MARKET IS HARD. REALLY HARD.

If you walked into a Certified Financial Planner's office, they would never tell you that your financial goal is to "beat the market." They would start with a budget, financial analysis, and estate plan, then help you construct a prudent and holistic strategy to meet your financial goals. This, unfortunately, is not how most investment portfolios are sold to investors.

Investment managers often think in different and even conflicting terms whereby they try to justify their fees by building market-beating portfolios. And while many investors spend their time and money trying to beat the market, for the average person this is irrelevant to their financial goals. Most people don't need to beat the market. They need to optimize their income/skills and then allocate their savings in a manner that gives them a high degree of financial certainty in the future.

Ironically, the history of the investment management business can be summarized as selling the *hope of superior returns* in exchange for *the guarantee of high fees*. Most expensive active managers do not outperform basic index funds after accounting for taxes and fees. As shown in Table 0.1, according to S&P's annual SPIVA report cards, 94% of active managers will underperform their benchmark over a 20+ year period.[2] That's astounding and just goes to show how hard it is to beat the market.

Table 0.1: Fund underperformance rates – US equity categories

	1 Year	5 Years	10 Years	20 Years
All domestic funds	77%	76%	86%	94%

But don't worry, it's okay if you're not outperforming the market. After all, beating the market is not a practical financial goal and trying to do so usually involves taking more risk to generate higher returns. While this approach may be suitable for certain individuals, it often leads to increased volatility of returns and poses greater behavioral challenges.

To emphasize this point it can be useful to discuss William Sharpe's arithmetic of active management:

- Before costs, the return on the average actively managed dollar will equal the return on the average passively managed dollar and;
- After costs, the return on the average actively managed dollar will be less than the return on the average passively managed dollar.[3]

I don't love the distinction between "active" and "passive" investing because we're all ultimately active for various reasons, but that doesn't change the fact that less activity is, on average, superior to more activity, all else equal.

ESSENTIAL PRINCIPLE #3

This is basic math. If the stock market generates an 8% return in a given year, more active investors are likely to incur additional taxes and fees that less active investors can avoid. This means, on average, the less active investors will generate better returns than the more active investors. And this explains why so many active managers don't beat the market in the long run.

Instead of trying to "win," you should formulate a sound financial plan and then apply a strategy that matches that plan and your needs over time. Don't worry if your strategy isn't consistently optimized or beating the market. They say perfect is the enemy of the good and this is nowhere more applicable than portfolio construction. In Chapter 13 we talk to William Bernstein, who teaches us that a "suboptimal portfolio you can stick with is better than an optimal one you can't."

ESSENTIAL PRINCIPLE #4

DIVERSIFICATION IS THE ONLY FREE LUNCH

IN 1952 the godfather of modern finance, Harry Markowitz, wrote a paper called "Portfolio Selection." One of the many useful conclusions from the paper was that diversification is the only free lunch.

What Markowitz meant by that was that an investor can generate better risk-adjusted returns by adding uncorrelated assets to their portfolio. When you diversify through uncorrelated assets with positively skewed long-term returns, you create less variance in your portfolio without necessarily sacrificing returns.

For instance, let's take two stocks that generate the same 6% return over a one-year period, but they generate their returns in almost exact opposite ways. The returns might look something like Figure 0.3.

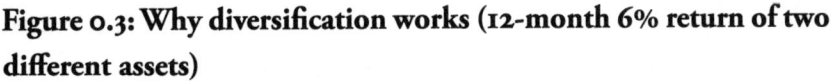

Figure 0.3: Why diversification works (12-month 6% return of two different assets)

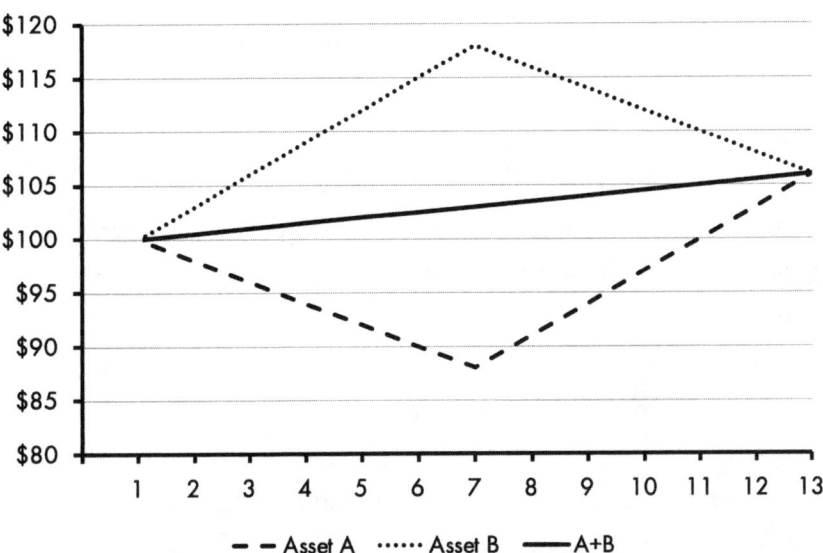

If you held one of these stocks alone, your 6% return ends up being quite bumpy. If, on the other hand, you'd added this basic bit of diversification, your portfolio return would look like a blended profile of these two stocks. In the diversified case you end up generating the same return, but with a much smoother return profile. In other words, you got something for nothing just by adding more diversification to your portfolio.

This is an oversimplified, but powerful, example that highlights the importance of building a portfolio that doesn't have an excessive amount of concentrated asset class risk. Diversification is important in asset allocation because it helps reduce the variance of returns and when done appropriately it can mitigate or eliminate the risk of catastrophic losses that can derail a financial plan.

In 2004, J.P. Morgan began publishing a study titled "The Agony and Ecstasy,"[4] which highlighted the difficulty of picking individual stocks. Get a load of some of the staggering facts they uncovered:

- Since 1980, over 400 companies have been removed from the S&P 500 due to financial distress.
- 40% of all companies that were ever in the Russell 3000 Index experienced a catastrophic decline of over 70%.
- 40% of the time, stocks in the Russell 3000 Index experienced a negative absolute return, meaning you would have been better off owning cash.
- 66% of all stocks in the Russell 3000 Index would have underperformed the index itself.

Picking stocks is hard. Beating the market is hard. Diversification works in large part because picking stocks is so difficult.

But while we say diversification is the only free lunch, it doesn't mean it won't come with behavioral hurdles that will try to steal that lunch. Brian Portnoy, the founder of Shaping Wealth, once said that diversification is learning to hate some part of your portfolio all the time. In other words, if your portfolio is all moving in the same direction all the time then it's probably not well diversified.

A recurring theme in this book is the goal of structuring assets that are generating positive long-run returns that are uncorrelated in the short term. Like the illustration in Figure 0.3, you want Asset A in months 1–12 because you believe it will perform well over all 12 months, but you also have to understand that Asset A is going to drive you nuts during months 1–6. You need to learn to hate some part of your portfolio all the time. And then, right when you start loving Asset A, you'll start hating Asset B. Good portfolio construction is learning to embrace this reality time and time again without constantly divorcing the parts that are driving you mad.

ESSENTIAL PRINCIPLE #4

Okay, but what's the right amount of diversification?

Great question. Most studies find that a portfolio of 25 or more diversified stocks will sufficiently reduce single entity risk. Investing in an index fund like the S&P 500 eliminates single entity risk almost entirely.

But when we study diversification using other instruments the answer gets much murkier. Azra Zaimovic, professor of finance at the University of Sarajevo, and her colleagues find that there is no optimal level of diversification because the portfolio depends not only on so many variable factors, but also on the goals of the person implementing the portfolio. So, we know that diversification is good, but the appropriate level of diversification is deeply personal, and you'll need to assess and find that level for yourself.[5]

This is why an underlying plan is so important. Different instruments will diversify your portfolio in different ways. For example, if you have short-term liquidity needs diversifying solely within the stock market it is unlikely to be able to satisfactorily address the short-term risks associated with those needs. For short-term liquidity needs, you'll need to diversify into cash, money market funds, Treasury bills or other inherently short-term instruments. This is one reason why I like to think about diversification not just across asset classes, but also across time horizons. In Chapter 20 we discuss what I call Defined Duration Investing and how you can introduce the element of time into a diversified asset allocation plan. That is, you shouldn't only diversify specific asset class risk, but you should also be keenly aware of the temporal risks certain assets expose you to. After all, good financial planning optimizes certainty of consumption across time.

Then again, we want to be careful about *diworsification*. This is what happens when someone overcomplicates a portfolio to the point where you get so much diversification that it makes the portfolio worse.

The financial services industry has mastered the art of using complexity to create the illusion of sophistication. When I was a financial advisor at big Wall Street firms we had perfected this process. We would pick 25 stocks for a client, add 10 mutual funds, five closed-end funds and a fancy sounding "alternative" product. In the end we had constructed something that looked a lot like a 60/40 stock/bond portfolio, but the portfolio included so many different products that it was impossible for the client to unwind and even harder for the client to understand. Then we'd send them a statement every month that they couldn't navigate because it was 40 pages packed with 10,000 numbers that looked like someone had dumped into a blender and translated into Mandarin. This. Was. Not. A. Good. Process.

You'll find, especially as you age, that complexity breeds the necessity of simplicity. This is nowhere truer than in your finances. Life will get complex and messy as you age and simplifying your financial management will not only make it more efficient, but it will make you happier.

Because diversification is essential to sound financial planning, in this book I analyzed portfolios and approaches that specifically help you diversify your savings portfolio. At the same time, I've been mindful about the impact of diworsification and understanding that we want a sophisticated portfolio, but not an unnecessarily complex portfolio.

ESSENTIAL PRINCIPLE #5

THE COST MATTERS HYPOTHESIS

JOHN BOGLE was the founder and CEO of Vanguard Group and arguably the most important person in the development of low-cost indexing strategies that have come to revolutionize the world of investing. In 2005 he wrote:

> Gross returns in the financial markets minus the costs of financial intermediation equal the net returns actually delivered to investors.

What Bogle was saying was that the return investors earn is guaranteed to be reduced by the amount of friction investors incur. Bogle was always a harsh critic of high fees in large part because the guarantee of high fees rarely results in the guarantee of higher returns. But he also hated fees because these seemingly small sums add up to large costs in the long run.

Let's quantify some figures here. For instance, if you invested $100,000 in US stocks 30 years ago with a 1% annual fee, you would have $1,632,788. Sounds great, huh? Well, if you had incurred fees of 0.5% per year along the way you'd have $1,897,459. That 0.5% fee sounds small, but it added up to $264,671, or a 14% smaller return. As we see in Figure 0.4, a seemingly small figure compounds to a relatively large difference by the time you might be retiring.

Figure 0.4: The big impact of small fees

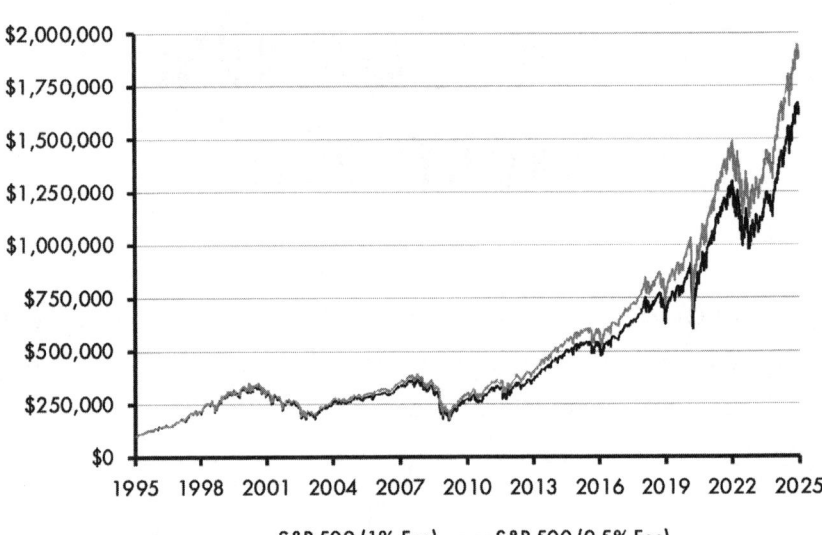

There's an old saying in finance: "Where are the customer's yachts?" The answer is that *your* yacht is sitting in New York harbor in your investment manager's boat slip after they accrued $264,671 in fees while very likely underperforming a highly correlated index.

These fees not only seem like small amounts, but they can oftentimes be hidden because you don't write a check or hand over cash to the manager. Meb Faber of Cambria Investments likes to tell a story that puts this into perspective – imagine you have a $1,000,000 portfolio and your investment manager charges 1% per year. When you meet with them once per year you will go to the ATM before that meeting and withdraw $10,000 and place it in a briefcase. When you leave that meeting you take the briefcase and leave the cash. Now ask yourself how that makes you feel? More importantly, do you pay your doctor that much? Your accountant? Your lawyer? Most likely not.

This doesn't mean fees are never worth it. We will all incur some level of fees and the quality of services provided by financial professionals will vary greatly, but as a rule, a high fee (which I'd define as anything in excess of 0.5%) will have a higher probability of leading to diminishing returns for the client. At the same time, you don't want fees to dictate all your decisions. The lowest-cost option is not necessarily the best option, but avoiding very high costs is one smart way to reduce the potential frictions you'll experience across your lifetime.

I formulated all these portfolios with an emphasis on being able to reduce fees as best as possible.

ESSENTIAL PRINCIPLE #6

REAL, REAL RETURNS ARE ALL THAT MATTER

WHEN we consider fees it's important to remember that investment managers aren't the only ones charging fees on our investments. The government also charges fees in the form of taxes and they can add up to sums that are even more impactful than investment management fees.

Further, there is another fee that you might not see, but is always lurking – inflation. Simply put, inflation is when the price of a broad basket of goods and services increases and as a result $1 of nominal income buys less with time. Your portfolio of assets might rise or fall, but if you earn a return that is equivalent to the rate of inflation, you are not actually better or worse off. You are merely running in place. That's why you should always consider the impact of inflation on your portfolio.

When we consider the risks to our portfolio, we need to balance the risk of principal losses with the risk of purchasing power loss.

ESSENTIAL PRINCIPLE #6

After all, we all want stability of our portfolio with maximum growth. Unfortunately, these two things don't always go hand in hand and, in fact, you usually need to sacrifice short-term stability in exchange for long-term growth. The stock market, for example, can be extremely volatile in the short run, but will generate high real returns in the long run. Something like cash, on the other hand, will be very stable in the short run and provide significant principal stability but will also expose you to higher risk of purchasing power loss in the long run.

To build a portfolio that protects you from principal instability and purchasing power loss you need to balance these risks while always optimizing your returns to account for the dilution that can come from taxes, fees, and inflation.

Most investment data is quoted in nominal terms. In this book I quote the investment returns in real terms to account for the most damaging fee of all – inflation. More importantly, when I analyzed these portfolios, I tried to focus on portfolios that would be good inflation hedges in the long term.

ESSENTIAL PRINCIPLE #7

RISK IS UNCERTAINTY OF LIFETIME CONSUMPTION

RISK has many definitions in finance. It can be standard deviation or volatility, anomalous events, principal loss, or a loss of purchasing power from inflation. In reality, it is all these things to a varying degree at different times, and all of which lead to uncertainty about the future.

I like what Ken French, a Dartmouth College finance professor once said about risk: "Risk is uncertainty of lifetime consumption." In other words, financial risk is not having enough money at certain times in life. This could result from taking too much risk, not taking enough risk, or even taking the wrong types of risk. But in the end what we're all striving for is having enough money to be able to pay for things in the future.

The reason we diversify our assets and use financial instruments like cash, bonds or insurance is because the future is so uncertain. In financial planning you hope for the best and plan for the worst.

A properly constructed portfolio must account for this unpredictability and help you navigate all of life's uncertainty. This is why it's so essential to start with a holistic financial plan that allows you to understand how things like income, expenses, insurance, and asset allocation all work together to help you optimize certainty across your lifetime.

In this context it's important to understand the role of different instruments in a portfolio. For example, cash will provide you with virtually unmatched principal protection over the short term and relatively poor inflation protection over the long term. Stocks, on the other hand, are uncertain in terms of principal protection over the short term, but provide you with a very high level of inflation protection in the long term. As depicted in Figure 0.5, you can think of short-term principal protection and purchasing power protection as relative trade-offs.

Figure 0.5: Scale of purchasing power versus permanent loss protection

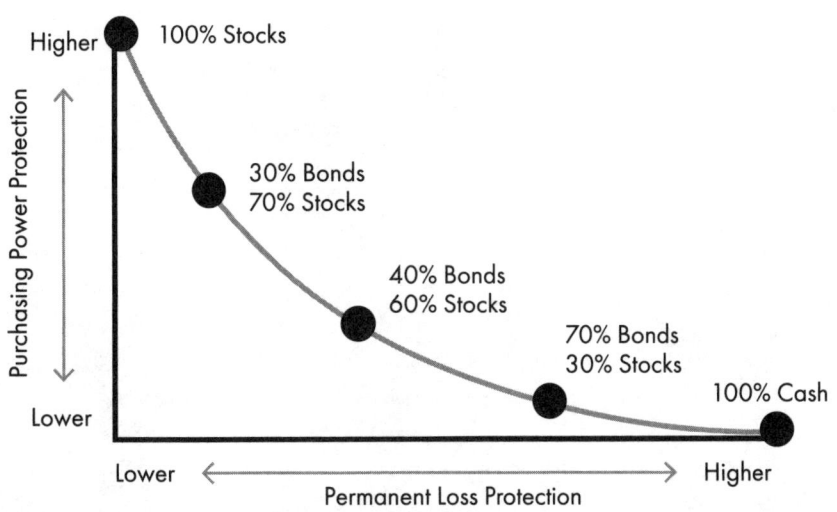

When you blend stocks and bonds, you are creating diversification across both purchasing power protection and principal protection. This helps diversify your portfolio and gives you greater certainty of consumption by reducing the degree to which any particular instrument exposes you to extreme purchasing power or principal risk.

This is the main reason asset class diversification works. It gives you greater certainty of consumption over time by reducing portfolio performance variance.

The portfolios in this book were selected because they can be utilized within a financial plan to help you increase certainty of consumption over time.

ESSENTIAL PRINCIPLE #8

ASSET ALLOCATION IS A TEMPORAL CONUNDRUM

WARREN BUFFETT said:

> The biggest thing about making money is time. You don't have to be particularly smart – you just have to be patient.

I like to say that asset allocation is a "temporal conundrum." In other words, we are all trying to have as much money as possible at specific times in the future to optimize our certainty of outcomes.

The problem is that asset markets generate uncertain returns, and our lives are a sequence of evolving and uncertain needs. The best we can do is try to quantify our future expenses and liabilities and then find certain assets that might help us maximize the certainty of meeting those expenses in the future.

The financial services industry does a terrible job of explaining time horizons to investors. We talk about vague concepts like "stocks for the long run," but rarely quantify these ideas. Worse, Wall Street is structured around quarterly earnings calls and monthly or year-end financial targets. If you turn on financial TV, you might think that the time horizon of the stock market is a single day, week or month. Even professional analysts structure forecasts around months, quarters, and years.

Ironically, the stock market is a very long-term instrument. The average corporation in the S&P 500 has a lifetime of 18 years.[6] It takes decades for corporations to grow and become the entities that we see in our everyday lives. I've quantified the current time horizon of the global stock market at 18 years using a methodology I call "Defined Duration." But even when you look at safer instruments like bonds, the time horizon is longer than you might think. In the case of the total US bond market, the average maturity of bonds is 8.4 years as of 2025.

WONKY SIDE NOTE

I refer to the term "duration" a lot in this book. In traditional bond metrics, duration refers to a bond's sensitivity to interest rates. For example, if rates rise 1% and a bond has a duration of 5, then that bond can be expected to fall by 5%, and vice versa.

I also use the term "defined duration" to mean "point of indifference" in the context of the Chapter 20 portfolio which I call Defined Duration Investing. This refers to the time period over which an investor is indifferent to an instrument's potential real losses.

ESSENTIAL PRINCIPLE #8

Let's reinforce this point with a basic example.

Consider a five-year Treasury note that pays 4%. This instrument is designed to pay you 4% per year over a five-year term. This instrument cannot mathematically earn more than 4% per year over the course of its existence, but as interest rates change it will generate more or less than this in some of those years. If you want to capture the entirety of that 4% average annual return over a five-year period you must be patient enough to allow that instrument to pay out the income it's designed to pay out over five years. You cannot squeeze 5% of blood, on average, from this stone.

The stock market is not really that different. Warren Buffet once wrote:

> I believe… that stocks, in economic substance, are really very similar to bonds. I know that this belief will seem eccentric to many investors. They will immediately observe that the return on a bond (the coupon) is fixed, while the return on an equity investment (the company's earnings) can vary substantially from one year to another. True enough. But anyone who examines the aggregate returns that have been earned by companies during the post-war years will discover something extraordinary: the returns on equity have in fact not varied much at all.[7]

This is important because the stock market is an instrument that, if you hold it for many decades, will generate about 5–6% real returns per year. But there will be years where it's down 50% and in many stock markets even decades of negative or flat returns. This instrument accrues its returns over inherently long periods because the time horizon over which corporations reliably pay out profits is extended. It takes time to generate revenue and profit and grow a firm into a large entity. This process cannot be accelerated no matter how impatiently we flip our assets around on stock exchanges.

To emphasize this point, consider the average time horizon over which you might make money by holding a portfolio of US stocks, shown in Table 0.2.

Table 0.2: Probability of positive returns over rolling periods

Period	Probability of positive return
1 month	41%
3 months	62%
1 year	68%
3 years	77%
5 years	79%
10 years	88%
20 years	99.94%

This data is interesting because it highlights the randomness of the stock market over shorter time periods. At a very minimum you wouldn't want to view the stock market as anything less than a five-year instrument, but to have very high certainty of positive returns you really need to view it more like a 10–20-year instrument.

All of this creates a high behavioral hurdle for investors. We want short-term certainty, but we're allocating our savings into inherently longer-term instruments. Keep that in mind as we discuss these portfolios. Understanding your personal intertemporal conundrum is a key aspect of choosing the portfolio (or portfolios) that can best match your personal needs.

I hope that many of these portfolios will help you better understand how time relates to your portfolio.

ESSENTIAL PRINCIPLE #9

PAST PERFORMANCE IS NOT INDICATIVE OF FUTURE RETURNS

SOME of the analysis in this book relies on using past returns to provide perspective on what the portfolios have done over time. Using past data to forecast future outcomes is called "extrapolative expectations"-based forecasting. In other words, we are extrapolating the past into the future. That's a fine approach for providing a general idea of future risk and return, but good portfolio management always requires a certain degree of outright forecasting.

Some part of this will involve accepting the reality that you'll be wrong at points. As Wall Street legend Barry Ritholtz says: "The simple reality of life is that everyone is wrong on a regular basis. By confronting these inevitable errors, you allow yourself to make corrections before it is too late."[8] Remember, a good portfolio is diversified, and diversification requires learning to hate some part of your portfolio all the time. Even when you're wrong about something you tried to forecast. You'll have to learn to roll with the punches and evolve, even when you're wrong.

The world will change with time and your portfolio will have to keep up. This will not only require a certain degree of prognostication, but it will require a certain degree of activity. And that's fine. I always like to say that there's no such thing as a truly passive investment strategy, but there are smart ways to be active and silly ways to be active. Smart active looks like this: a clear plan, low fees, low turnover, and solid diversification. Bad active? That's high fees, lots of trading, concentrated bets, and no underlying plan.

Unfortunately, almost all the data we have to support portfolio analysis is thin. The US stock market, for example, has only existed for about 100 years. In that time, it has experienced only a few dozen business cycles. And in that short time frame the US market has changed substantially from what was predominantly an emerging market in the 1800s to the largest developed market in human history as of today.

Most global markets can also be viewed within two time horizons differentiated by World War 2, which decimated many European and Pacific economies while catapulting the US into what it is today. And during the post-war era there has been just one legitimate debt deflation (2008/9) and just three legitimate inflation scares (1945–1952, 1970–1980 and 2021–2024). The point is these datasets are all very thin. They need to be treated with a certain degree of rational skepticism.

The key in all of this is to find a portfolio that is rooted in first principles, has an empirical track record, but also one that you believe is likely to perform well in the future regardless of what it has done in the past.

So yes, use all the past evidence you can to support your portfolio construction process. But also remember that the future is very likely to look different from the past. I've chosen portfolios that have significant historical data and sound underlying empirical support, with the hope that these factors can help us better assess future potential performance.

ESSENTIAL PRINCIPLE #10

SET REALISTIC EXPECTATIONS AND STAY THE COURSE

WHEN we allocate our savings it's important to have realistic expectations of future returns that are grounded in historical data, but also a sound understanding of why certain assets generate certain types of returns. Remember, the financial markets are not where you get rich. Your real "investments" in life are made in your own skills and the skills of others. This is where you are most likely to get rich. Your savings portfolio is there to generate growth and stability based on your financial needs and your financial plan. It can certainly make you richer, but it's not the engine of your wealth creation.

Thinking your portfolio will do more than it realistically can is a fast track to frustration and poor results. For example, investors often hear that the stock market returns 10% annually and assume they can hit that target by picking stocks and going all-in on an aggressive allocation. The problem is, those returns are an average over long time horizons – and they ignore the huge impact of fees, taxes, and volatility.

Reality is that the stock market can go through sustained periods of negative or low returns, and the returns you eat are the real, real returns net of inflation, taxes, and fees. As a result, your actual returns from a stock allocation will not only be highly uneven over time, but they will be lower on average than the headline figure we often hear about in the financial media.

Worse, you will read a million articles in your life about how you could have turned $10,000 into $1,000,000 in a few years by picking XYZ stock. Remember the Agony and Ecstasy data – all of these articles are eye-ball-chasing cherry picking. These types of narratives will skew your perspective and warp your expectations. Ignore them.

John Bogle used to always tell investors to "stay the course" and avoid the urge to tinker with your portfolio and succumb to short-term behavioral biases. Having realistic expectations is an important piece of the process to ensure you aren't constantly chasing returns and strategies. The grass will always look greener somewhere else, but rather than trying to live on someone else's lawn you need to spend more time nurturing your own and not abandon it every time it starts to look a little brown.

★★★

Okay, now that we've covered the basic principles, let's start looking at our potential suitors.

PART 2

THE PORTFOLIOS

BEFORE we dive into the portfolios let's briefly discuss why they were selected in the first place.

HOW THE PORTFOLIOS WERE SELECTED

There are millions of different options when selecting a portfolio. I've narrowed it down to 21 strategies and asset allocation options based on specific criteria that have strong empirical investment support and can be used to help investors meet their financial and behavioral needs. I refer to these strategies as "the world's most powerful" because each one has unique attributes that can empower you in your pursuit of financial independence. I hope to help you in picking out your portfolio and, as a father of two daughters, I understand the importance of choosing suitors, so I took great care in selecting your potential portfolios.*

These portfolios can be utilized within a broader approach, but it's important to note that you need a plan and a process before you enter a relationship with any of these strategies. Your asset allocation is just one piece of a broader financial plan and so I would encourage you to construct an overarching plan and goals before you select a strategy (or strategies) that can be applied to match those goals. As a financial advisor who also operates as a portfolio manager, I've often found there to be a conflict between the way portfolio managers think of asset allocation (generally trying to generate the highest returns

---

* Just kidding. Your father does not exist to choose your spouse for you. He exists primarily to carry heavy things, eat your leftovers, break down cardboard boxes that arrive from Amazon, and intimidate potential suitors before your high school prom.

relative to risk) versus the way financial planners try to construct prudent plans that rely on generating *appropriate* returns relative to the financial plan and investor risk profile. Blending these two worlds is often a delicate balancing act.

It's also important to keep in mind that you don't need to only pick one portfolio. Yes, many of these portfolios are one-stop-shop portfolios, but you can also mix and match. Don't worry, your stocks won't mind if you cheat on them a little bit with your bonds or alternatives.

Let's jump in.

1

THE WARREN BUFFETT PORTFOLIO

OUR search for the perfect portfolio begins where my perfect portfolio journey started – with Warren Buffett. When I was 19 years old, I started reading Warren Buffett's annual shareholder letters. I was so enthralled that I went back further in time to read the Buffett Partnership letters, his original hedge fund notes from before the Berkshire Hathaway days. This was the most educational investment reading I ever encountered, and I highly recommend it for anyone who hasn't read the letters.*

While it was educational it also filled my head with delusions of grandeur as I was convinced that I would soon become the next Warren Buffett. My marriage to the Warren Buffett portfolio (the "Buffett Portfolio") did not last long, in large part because I did not understand just how intricate the strategy really was. While it's probably impossible to replicate his results, there are some very valuable lessons from analyzing this brilliant approach and structure.

---

* The letters are compiled here for reference: www.pragcap.com/warren-buffett-partnership-letters.

FUN SIDE NOTE

I became so obsessed with Buffett that I would write him letters on occasion. He didn't always respond, but when he did it was in typewritten form from his secretary. How can you not love that?! On that note – here's a life tip: never be afraid to reach out to total strangers (even famous ones) and ask them for help. You'll be shocked at how often they respond.

★★★

As a novice investor I had the right mix of youthful arrogance and inexperience to perfectly misunderstand the scope and complexity of Warren Buffett's approach to investing. And after reading the annual shareholder letters I was convinced that the approach was simple – you find good companies selling at reasonable prices and then buy and hold them until your net worth explodes.

I soon found out that companies selling at "reasonable prices" are often selling at reasonable prices for the exact reasons that Gene Fama, the father of the Efficient Market Hypothesis claimed – because they're often bad companies that deserve to be selling at those prices. I had fallen into a classic value trap, where you think value is underpriced market inefficiency when it's actually market efficiency pricing securities below intrinsic value because the firm is performing poorly and is expected to continue performing poorly.

I had the unfortunate misunderstanding that low prices were similar to value. I can't even tell you how much time I spent dabbling in penny stocks and low-priced stocks in those early investing years. The price of a stock, of course, has very little to do with its value (in fact, stocks trading below $5 are generally terrible firms that have failed to even meet the basic listing requirements of most exchanges). But these were all things that a much younger Cullen didn't understand.

To compound all of this I also had the unfortunate timing of building up my first savings portfolio into the teeth of the dot-com bubble. Let's just say that my first bear market tested my patience and made it difficult to remain disciplined. But with time I learned that the genius of the Warren Buffett strategy wasn't just good stock picking. It was a brilliant institutional structure and phenomenally disciplined process.

Let's take a closer look.

HOW BUFFETT'S MONEY-MAKING MACHINE WORKS

In 1956, a 26-year-old hedge fund manager named Warren Buffett began buying up shares of a dying windmill company named Dempster Mill. The manager of Buffett Partners, Ltd slowly gobbled up 70% of the business, which was a sizable 20% of the Partnership's total assets. Mr. Buffett believed the business was substantially undervalued and he agreed with the advice of a new partner named Charlie Munger that they should replace the CEO. Munger introduced Buffett to Harry Bottle, who would go on to become CEO of Dempster and play an essential role in its turnaround.

Buffett had turned into what we currently call an "activist" investor by buying a large stake in a firm and then actively altering the management and operations of the firm in the pursuit of profits. The Partnership would ultimately make a 3× gain in Dempster before divesting and rolling much of the profit into a textile firm named Berkshire Hathaway.

The early days of the Buffett Partnership are interesting in large part because they catapulted him into the position to purchase Berkshire through actions that Buffett isn't well known for – concentrated risks and an activist approach wrapped in a high-fee hedge fund structure. Young Warren Buffett sometimes sounds more like Gordon Gekko than Benjamin Graham, his mentor whom he is most often compared to now. But the Berkshire days are when the real magic begins to happen.

In 1955 two companies named Berkshire Fine Spinning and Hathaway Manufacturing joined forces to become a company named Berkshire Hathaway. This made it the largest textile firm in New England, but the merger was a death pact. Berkshire would see its net worth shrink by almost 40% in the ensuing years, but Buffett noticed a curious operation by management – they were buying their own shares. Buffett Partners began accumulating shares at a steep discount of $7.50 versus book value of $20.20. Buffett says this felt like picking up discarded cigarette butts with one puff left. The puff seemed pretty good though and Berkshire's CEO, Seabury Stanton, agreed to repurchase Buffett's shares for $11.50. But when Buffett received a tender offer of just $11.375 he was enraged. Instead of selling, he purchased more, took a controlling interest, and fired Stanton. The problem was that Buffett was now sitting on his own value trap as the textile firm was failing fast.

It was around this time that Buffett decided he needed to stop dating cigarette butts and start looking for companies he could marry. In 1967 he purchased his first insurance company, a firm called National Indemnity Company. Although the old textile firm was failing, Buffett had begun accruing what he famously refers to as "insurance float" – the cash flows from insurance premiums, not yet paid out as claims, that operated like interest-free loans to the operating company.

Buffett would lean into this structure over the coming decades and utilize this leverage in a brilliant manner to scoop up undervalued firms and amass the equivalent of a low-cost, leveraged private equity entity. Combine this with the transition to more long-term and disciplined thinking and Berkshire Hathaway was well on its way to becoming what we all know today.

The secret sauce to the Buffett Portfolio isn't just good stock picking and an extraordinarily patient temperament. The Buffett money-making machine is all about utilizing cash flows from various entities to fuel a broader investment process. Buffett's strategy is a specific infrastructure around a portfolio, not just a portfolio strategy on its own.

Warren Buffett has what I would describe as the two ultimate asset allocation superpowers:

1. The ability to build an investment infrastructure that optimizes for cash flows and margin of safety.
2. The ability to be extremely patient, waiting to insert pieces into this infrastructure in a way that allows them to operate within the efficient confines of that infrastructure.

Let's talk a little bit about both.

In many ways Buffett was a true innovator in the US capital markets. First, the original Buffett Partners hedge fund was unique in its structure as a performance-driven hedge fund. Buffett famously charged performance fees that were aligned only with positive returns. Second, Buffett was an early adopter of the private equity approach to capital allocation. In Chapter 17 we'll discuss the importance of private equity allocations and how the Endowment Portfolios were early movers there, but Buffett was light years ahead of the game in the 1950s.

While Buffett is famous for his public stock market allocations, it was his private market investments that were some of the best return-generators across his lifetime. And perhaps most importantly, it was these private equity investments that ultimately resulted in the specific structure that allowed Buffett to create a cash-flow machine that could be reallocated to the other investments he made.

But what about patience?

You will notice that time is a recurring theme in this book because it's the ultimate form of wealth. Time is the only thing you can't buy more of and when it's gone it's gone forever. Buffett has utilized his time in an extraordinary manner.

First, he started investing when he was incredibly young.

Second, he allowed his investments to compound over time without tinkering too much. In his wonderful book, *The Psychology of Money*, Morgan Housel tells a story about the importance of time and compounding. Warren Buffett started investing when he was 10 years old and had accrued an inflation-adjusted net worth of $9.3 million by the age of 30. He went on to compound his wealth at 22% per year and by the age of 90 he had a net worth of $84.5 billion. $84.2 billion of this was accumulated after the age of 50. Had he started investing with a sum of $25,000 at the age of 30 he would have $11.9 million at the age of 90.[9] (You'll notice discipline, patience, and time will be recurring themes in this book, you can think of them as the main characters in our exploration.)

Julius Caesar once said: "It is easier to find men who will volunteer to die, than to find those who are willing to endure pain with patience."

Consider how many hugely painful downturns, recessions, and bear markets Warren Buffett endured while exercising extraordinary patience.

That patience didn't just compound his wealth over time – it did so efficiently, as he structured his assets within a cash-flow-generating engine that optimized both tax and income efficiency across decades.

CHAPTER 1

BUILDING YOUR OWN BUFFETT PORTFOLIO

As I've noted, the current day Berkshire Hathaway is nothing like the cigarette-butt-seeking Buffett Partners. While Buffett Partners was a sleeker, sexier asset management approach, the Berkshire we've come to know and love is more of a diversified income monster.

Replicating Buffett Partners is probably impossible in today's efficient markets. But replicating the current Warren Buffett strategy is relatively straightforward. I do need to caution readers that, given Buffett's age of 96 and the corresponding age of Berkshire, it might not be the most forward-looking strategy to copy.

I am starting to think that he's Methuselah, the mythical man who lived to be 969 years old, because Buffett appears to be genetically invulnerable to Cherry Coke and cheeseburgers, but I also know that Father Time is undefeated.

There are four general ways in which we might go about building the Buffett Portfolio:

1. Start a hedge fund, buy insurance companies or other entities that allow for embedded leverage, become a master private and public equity investor.
2. Buy Berkshire Hathaway stock.
3. Try to replicate Buffett's stock-picking methods.
4. Buy a 90/10 Stock/T-bill portfolio.

Let's explore each option.

You can certainly try #1, but the likelihood of this working is about the same as me looking like Brad Pitt when I wake up tomorrow morning. So, on to option #2.

Berkshire Hathaway stock (ticker: BRK-A) is the easiest and lowest-cost way to follow the Warren Buffett strategy. Berkshire is now a trillion-dollar company by market cap, its total market weighted value. As of 2025 it's the eighth largest company in the world. Despite being an ultra-diverse, tax efficient, cash-flow machine, Berkshire doesn't pay a dividend or charge you a management fee to own it. Said differently, Berkshire Hathaway is a lot like a zero-fee and tax-efficient index fund.

It's worth noting that Berkshire has gradually evolved to resemble the S&P 500 more closely over time. Most of its huge outperformance came when Berkshire was a very different animal in the 80s and 90s. From the period of 1980 to 2000 Berkshire Hathaway beat the S&P 500 by an astounding 11% per year. That margin shrank to just 1.4% over the last 20 years and is down to just 1% per year in the last 10 years. Its recent correlation can be seen in Figure 1.1 below.

Figure 1.1: Berkshire Hathaway versus the S&P 500

Of course, the Berkshire of tomorrow might not look like the Berkshire of yesterday. While I have no doubt the company is well equipped to navigate Buffett's succession, you also have to consider the risk that the firm is simply too big to generate the returns Buffett is so famous for. In other words, it might be capped by sheer size, but have the downside of deteriorating after Buffett is gone. That's why we're going to jump right into the allocation Buffett himself recommends – buying index funds and owning a slug of cash in the form of T-bills.

And yes, we're skipping right over option #3. Sorry to disappoint, but I hope that one of the big takeaways from this book is that you should not spend an excess amount of time picking individual stocks. The pros are bad at it and I don't think most retail investors should spend a lot of time bothering with it when there are so many diversified fund options.

Buffett himself famously recommended option #4. He says:

> Among the various propositions offered to you, if you invested in a very low-cost index fund where you don't put the money in at one time, but on average over 10 years, you'll do better than 90% of the people who start investing at the same time.... In my view... the best thing to do is to own the S&P 500 index fund... the trick is not to pick the right company. The trick is to essentially buy all the big companies through the S&P 500 and do it consistently and to do it in a very, very low-cost way.

FUN SIDE NOTE

I wasn't always so militantly against stock picking. In fact, from 2005–2010 I ran a small partnership that took advantage of what is now known as the overnight effect – the tendency for stocks to outperform overnight. I spent years buying stocks every day at the close and selling them at the open, or preferably in the pre-market when I could take advantage of illiquidity. Sometimes with an event-driven bet in mind, but oftentimes just due to illiquidity and inefficiencies.

I generated 20.75% per year while the S&P 500 generated 0.5% per year, which, for someone in his 20s, was enough to pay for $2 beers back when I was a poor guy living at the beach in San Diego. The GFC exposed the flaws in such a strategy and after six months of not making one dime in the middle of 2009 I had to pivot out of the stock-picking world, which was too much work and too unscalable given the illiquid markets I relied on. To this day I still can't decide if my performance was sheer luck, fortunate timing, a little bit of smarts, or all of the above.

One of my favorite stories from this period is when I nailed someone on a fat finger trade only to get nailed myself. I had purchased a position in what was then Sears Holdings into earnings and when their earnings report hit the news wires at 3 a.m. Pacific Time a bid came on the board at a 20% premium. I'd been doing this for years at this point and I could pinpoint the good and bad in an earnings report in minutes and I knew this one was a stinker. I had a $100,000 position in the stock and I hit someone's fat fingered bid and went to bed around 4 a.m. thinking I'd just made the easiest $20,000 of my life. But I woke up at 8 a.m. to see an alert that a trade had been "busted," the term for a reversed trade. I now owned $80,000 of Sears Holdings and I'd seen a $40,000 reversal in four hours. I wrote to Nasdaq to inquire about the reversal and never did get an answer, but let's just say that I had to stick to $2 beers for a while after that one. Stock picking was a tough way to make a living....

If an indexing component is one important element of how Buffett recommends we invest then the other essential element of the Buffett strategy is the way he generates cash flows and exercises its optionality.

Buffett holds this optionality position in the form of Treasury bills, super-safe, high interest-bearing bills issued by the US government.

CHAPTER 1

Holding a portfolio of T-bills is like holding a money market fund that you build yourself.

Historically, Buffett has held about 10% of his assets in T-bills. In his 2023 letter, Buffett explained the rationale of holding that 10% T-bill position:

> [Berkshire] also holds a cash and US Treasury bill position far in excess of what conventional wisdom deems necessary. During the 2008 panic, Berkshire generated cash from operations and did not rely in any manner on commercial paper, bank lines or debt markets. We did not predict the time of an economic paralysis, but we were always prepared for one.
>
> Extreme fiscal conservatism is a corporate pledge we make to those who have joined us in ownership of Berkshire. In most years – indeed in most decades – our caution will likely prove to be unneeded behavior – akin to an insurance policy on a fortress-like building thought to be fireproof. But Berkshire does not want to inflict permanent financial damage – quotational shrinkage for extended periods can't be avoided – on Bertie or any of the individuals who have trusted us with their savings.

Buffett thinks of cash like it's an insurance holding. Insurance will be another recurring theme in this book and so remember this point – cash is sometimes the ultimate form of insurance because it gives us principal stability, certainty, and optionality.

Now, if you wanted to implement this it could be as basic as two positions, as seen in Figure 1.2:

- S&P 500 ETF (ticker: VOO): 90%
- T-bills (individual bills or ETF, ticker: BIL): 10%

That's as simple as we're going to get in this book so buckle up from here on out.

Figure 1.2: The Buffett Portfolio

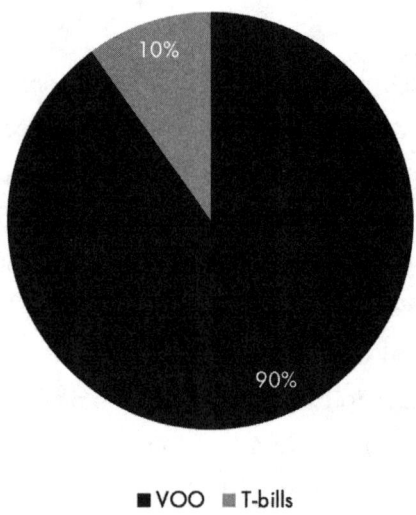

BUFFETT PORTFOLIO ANALYSIS

Let's take a closer look at how the Buffett Portfolio works and see if this is a potential suitor.

In 2013, Frazzini, Kabiller, and Pedersen published a paper titled "Buffett's Alpha."[10] The paper did a deep dive into the drivers of Buffett's returns. They concluded that the Buffett structure was built around:

- The use of structured leverage of 1.6:1
- Buying low-beta, high-quality stocks with a low price-to-book ratio and high quality (profitable, stable, growing, and high payout ratios).

How did this structure perform over the last 100 years? According to Frazzini, et al., if you could have hopped into a time machine and picked a single stock in 1926, the very best performing stock in the next 90 years would have been Berkshire. Incredible.

Regarding point #1, the authors found that Buffett's unique business structure allowed for strategic leverage via cheap financing in the insurance segment of the Buffett Portfolio. He then utilized this leveraged structure to purchase stocks that are high quality and inexpensive. That might not be easily replicated unless you happen to own an insurance company, but we can all think of our existing incomes as the cash-flow machine that fuels our investment portfolios. And then we can structure our entities by feeding specifically efficient structures like 401(k)s, IRAs or LLCs to house the cash flows and investments in a manner similar to Buffett.

Point #2 is more about the specific type of entity Buffett would target. And the S&P 500, while not technically a factor tilt like value or high quality, captures all the factors by definition. No need to overthink what Buffett specifically recommends. Don't worry, we'll do a deep dive into Factor Investing in Chapter 6, which could help you apply certain factors to a Buffett Portfolio if you are interested in implementing the strategy similarly to point #2.

You aren't going to repeat Buffett's performance buying a 90/10 stock/T-bill portfolio, but you'll still do very well with time. So, let's look at the metrics of a 90/10 stock/T-bill portfolio.

With this portfolio you can expect high real returns with a high level of volatility. A 90/10 portfolio would have generated 6.30% real returns per year with volatility of 15.67%. There is the outside chance of very large drawdowns at times and the Ulcer Index, at 19, is consistent with a portfolio that will cause you higher levels of stress at times.

Figure 1.3: 90/10 stocks/T-bills real returns

Table 1.1: Portfolio analysis (1900–present)

	Buffett Portfolio	US Stocks
Real Returns	6.30%	6.65%
Volatility	15.67%	17.70%
Sharpe Ratio	0.44	0.44
Sortino Ratio	0.62	0.62
Max Drawdown	−74.00%	−79.20%
Max Drawdown (Post-1945)	−53.00%	−58.20%
Ulcer Index	19.12	21.84
Market Correlation	0.90	1.00

Figure 1.4 provides perspective on how the drawdowns would have looked. As you can see, this one's pretty volatile at times. None of this is terribly surprising considering the high allocation to stocks.

Figure 1.4: 90/10 stocks/T-bills drawdowns (%)

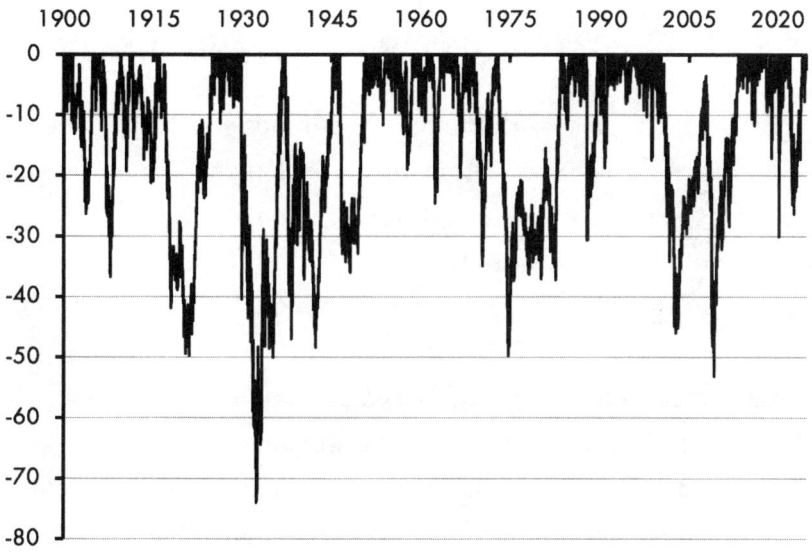

In terms of implementing and maintaining such a strategy, you'd want to be hands-on with your cash and dollar cost average regularly into the 90% stock component. You might also benefit from the optionality of investing larger sums during market downturns – for example, trying to be systematically more aggressive whenever the stock market declines 20% from a previous high. Although Buffett is not a big market timer, he is notoriously greedy when others are fearful.

If you are the aggressive and adventurous type you could try adding a bit of leverage to the portfolio through something like a leveraged S&P 500 ETF. This would better replicate the leverage Berkshire has embedded in it, but this also accelerates the fee and risk profile.

If you wanted to replicate something more akin to the Buffett Partners approach, you might consider some private equity allocations. We'll discuss this in more detail in Chapter 17, the Endowment Portfolio. It might be worth revisiting the Buffett Portfolio after you digest some of the later chapters to see how you can customize your own Buffett Portfolio.

BUFFETT PORTFOLIO PROS, CONS, AND LESSONS

All of this looks great with the benefit of hindsight, but let's look at both sides of the coin here. After all, are we looking at a suitor who's a suave 25-year-old or is this portfolio more reflective of the actual 90+-year-old who made it so famous?

First, let's get the bad news out of the way:

1. The Buffett Portfolio is roughly a 90/10 stock/T-bill allocation. This is a volatile portfolio that will test your patience.
2. It's hard to replicate the low-cost insurance leverage within Berkshire. Replicator portfolios are likely to incur higher financing costs. Any leverage utilized will exacerbate the behavioral risks of the already risky 90/10 allocation.
3. The Berkshire of tomorrow is unlikely to look like the Berkshire of yesterday. After 50+ years of outstanding returns we have to consider that Berkshire is now so big that it will not grow at the same rate that it could when it was a smaller stock. If you're choosing to own BRK you have to assess this risk.
4. Owning the S&P 500 isn't going to replicate Buffett's actual returns and could leave you feeling dissatisfied with the results when compared to Buffett's historical track record.
5. Because this is a stock/bond-only portfolio with a heavy tilt on stocks, it will encounter periods where the portfolio isn't significantly diversified across relative asset classes, especially considering it holds no alternative assets.

CHAPTER 1

And now the good news:

1. Portfolio structure can have a big multiplier effect across tax and operational efficiency, especially when combined with an efficient, income-generating machine.
2. This portfolio is super lean, tax and fee efficient, and can be replicated and maintained within a very clear process.
3. A relatively simple factor-based methodology (such as value investing) is effective when adhered to over the long run and after reading Chapter 6 you might revisit the Buffett strategy to consider how the S&P 500 could be tilted to certain factors more consistent with a Buffett stock-picking approach and Frazzini's research.
4. This is a reliable long-term return generator given the broad diversification.
5. The T-bill component not only gives you optionality but could serve as a decent behavioral buffer at times when the 90% stock piece is very volatile.

In short, lots of good and some bad.
But who is this portfolio good for?

SUITORS FOR THE BUFFETT PORTFOLIO

The Buffett Portfolio, no matter how you implement it, looks like a good potential suitor, but we do have to be careful about extrapolating past returns into the future. This is especially pertinent given the key man risk in this specific entity if you choose to use the pure Berkshire option.

Further, it's worth noting that one of Buffett's main strengths is that he doesn't need a lot of money. Buffett lives in the same house he bought in 1958. He doesn't live extravagantly and so his liabilities are extremely low relative to his income and assets. This is crucial because it allows him to be extremely aggressive without needing consistent cash flow to fund his short-term expenses. This is another Buffett superpower – he doesn't need much and that gives him an extra amount of behavioral bandwidth in his portfolio.

No matter how you might implement the Buffett Portfolio, you have to be someone who has the same general attributes that made Buffett so successful. You have to be disciplined, patient, and behaviorally robust.

FINAL THOUGHTS

There are numerous useful lessons from understanding Warren Buffett's approach:

1. **Cash flow fills your moat**. Optimize your cash flows to feed your portfolio. Your portfolio should have what Warren Buffett refers to as a moat – a margin of safety around it that makes it invulnerable. But the way you fill that moat is by constantly replenishing it with new cash contributions to the plan.
2. **Infrastructure is your foundation**. Use your available infrastructures to optimize for taxes and fees. While Buffett leverages a corporate insurance structure, the rest of us can optimize via the use of tax-deferred accounts, corporations, trusts, and other account types to optimize for taxes and cash flows.
3. **Patience and discipline**. Create a plan that adheres to long-term principles while also taking advantage of some short-term volatility.

Wait a minute now. We went all the way to 90% stocks with the Buffett Portfolio. Why not just go all-in and implement a 100% Stock Portfolio? If that's what you're thinking, then keep going. That's our next suitor.

2

WHY NOT 100% STOCKS?

OVER the course of your life, you will consistently encounter bull and bear markets. Bear markets are the price of admission to benefit from bull markets. Stocks need to go down at times in the short run to be able to sustainably go up in the long run. And while we often focus on the dangers of bear markets, bull markets can be equally perilous as they will test your patience and tempt you to alter your asset allocation.

As bull markets rage upward, you could be tempted to ask yourself: "Why diversify at all, why not move to 100% stocks?" Of course, when the bear market comes (and it always does eventually), the opposite question will be posed: "Why invest in stocks at all, why not remain mostly bonds and cash?" Don't worry – we'll answer that question in the next chapter.

This sort of all-in and all-out mentality is commonplace across the market cycle, but remember that you're a saver and not a gambler. You should never move all-in or all-out with your portfolio as that leaves you undiversified and subject to the biases of your own worst enemy (that's right, you). This rollercoaster ride of emotions, as depicted in Figure 2.1, is something you will need to get used to. We all go through it.

Figure 2.1: The stock market emotion roller coaster

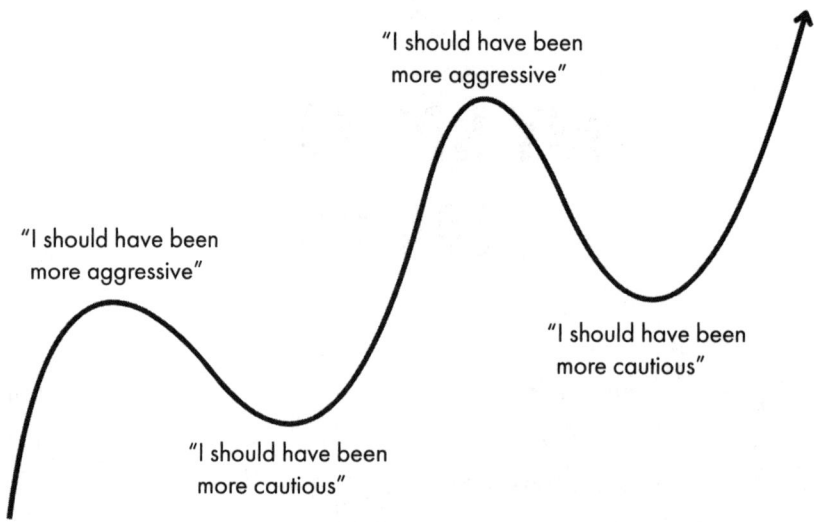

That said, it could be perfectly appropriate for certain segments of your portfolio to be very aggressive, even up to 100% stocks, not too dissimilar to the way Buffett manages Berkshire. This would be especially true in inherently long-term parts of your portfolio, for example, a 25-year-old allocating to a Roth IRA they won't touch for 30+ years.

The 100% Stock Portfolio is an important strategy to touch on because it helps formulate the building blocks for many of the later portfolios we'll discuss, and I also hope it gives you some perspective on what we're trying to achieve when we allocate assets from a financial planning perspective.

Let's get into it.

CHAPTER 2

WHY DOES 100% STOCKS WORK?

As we discussed earlier, corporations are best thought of as long-term entities. Buffett can be extremely patient with Berkshire's portfolio because he has always understood that the stock market is, as Ben Graham famously said, a "voting machine in the short run and a weighing machine in the long run."

That's another way of saying that markets can be inefficient in the short run, but are more efficient in the long run. I always like to point out that the stock market is a system that preys on the behaviorally weak to the benefit of the behaviorally robust. The behaviorally robust understand that the stock market is an inherently long-term instrument because its underlying entities are long term by nature.

By the time a corporation qualifies to be included in one of the prominent indices, it has likely been around for many decades as it takes time to reach the multi-billion-dollar valuation required to qualify for listing. For example, as of 2025 the minimum requirement for being included in the S&P 500 is a market capitalization (total market value) of $20.5 billion. These are very large companies that have grown into behemoths over long periods of time.

When you buy a diversified pool of these entities you are hitching your wagon to the long-term trend in corporate earnings. And what have corporate profits done in the long run? Well, they generally go up over the long term because capitalism, despite some of its faults, is very good at incentivizing people to innovate, produce, and maximize profits. Figure 2.2 shows the upward trend in pre-tax corporate profits from 1940 to 2025.

In a sense, when you buy stocks, you are betting on an increase in human production and innovation. That flows to corporations as profits and will be reflected in corporate stocks as higher market values.

Figure 2.2: Pre-tax corporate profits ($bn)

The stock market tends to be a good nominal and real return generator because corporations are inherent inflation hedgers. That is, corporations buy commodities at cost, build goods and services, and then sell them at a mark-up.

This is especially powerful when viewed through the lens of something like an index fund. For example, a FTSE All-World index fund is a diversified pool of over 4,000 of the best corporations in the world. These are mature, profit-generating companies that you can own a small slice of. And the diversified index structure is important because the ownership of something like an index fund is a systematic way of keeping your wagon perpetually hitched to the best corporations in the world.

This is because an index fund works by systematically rebalancing its portfolio, shedding so-called losers and replacing them with winners. For instance, if XYZ Corp falls to $1 billion in market capitalization, it may no longer qualify for inclusion within the index. The Index

Committee will review alternatives and replace this entity with a newer firm that now meets the criteria. In this sense you are buying a systematic fund that maintains exposure to a dynamic set of the market's strongest companies.

In some ways this is similar to momentum investing in that you're consistently allocating to firms that meet minimum (and rising) standards over time. This isn't technically the momentum factor strategy (which we'll discuss more in Chapter 6) or the Trend Following strategy (which we'll discuss in Chapter 15), but it applies a similar concept using underlying corporate fundamentals.

Further, when indexing strategies like this are done at scale they can benefit from extremely low costs. This is one of the true superpowers of index funds. Although there might be a lot of activity going on under the surface of the index fund, the scale at which they operate makes them very efficient.

But all this long-term efficiency comes at a short-term cost as the stock market can be extremely volatile in the short run. The stock market is a lot like a dramatic movie – certain tough scenes may feel tense or painful, but it typically has a happy ending in the long run.

Figure 2.3 puts some of this short-term emotion in perspective. These drawdowns show the maximum loss from a previous high. As you can see, some of these drawdowns have been excruciatingly painful and it's not uncommon to experience regular 20% or 30% downturns in stocks.

Figure 2.3: US stock market drawdowns (%)

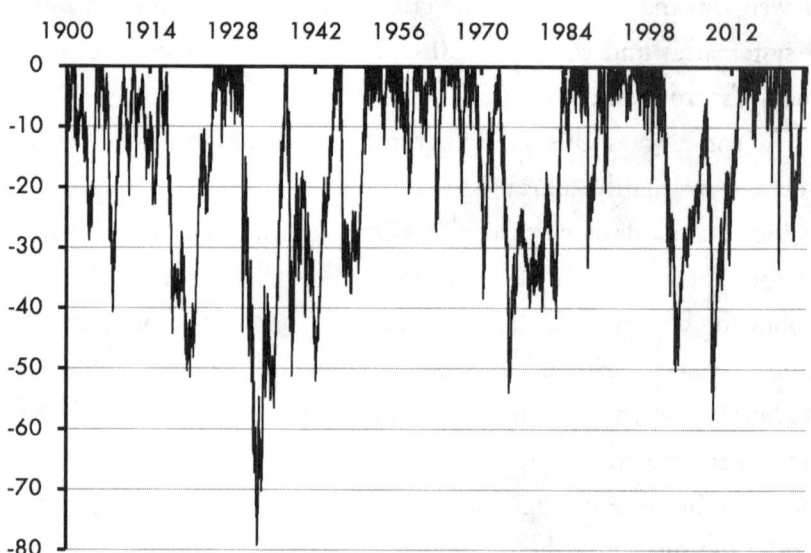

In short, stocks "work" because they generally track corporate profits and earnings over time. And because these cash flows are uncertain, they will tend to earn a premium above the risk-free rate and inflation. This short-term uncertainty is reflected in greater short-term volatility that is rewarded by long-term appreciation.

BUILDING YOUR OWN 100% STOCK PORTFOLIO

Okay, so all that risk sounds good to you, you're a patient person and you think a 100% Stock Portfolio might be a good fit for your portfolio, or a portion of your portfolio.

But what's the best way to build that portfolio?

If you enjoy stock picking you need to choose a methodology for picking stocks. In the prior chapter I emphasized that most investors shouldn't waste time picking stocks and, as Buffett stated, should stick to picking diversified, low-cost index funds. As we learned in Part 1, beating the market is hard and usually not worth the effort and added cost.

Okay, maybe I've convinced you not to pick stocks, but how do you pick your index funds? There are many ways to skin that cat.

The simplest portfolio to own is something like Vanguard Total World (ticker: VT) or MSCI All World Stock Index (ticker: ACWI). These are diversified, low-cost vehicles that give you access to thousands of stocks allocated on a global market cap basis.

Investing in global stocks, as opposed to only domestic stocks from your own country, can be advantageous for the following reasons:

1. It boosts overall diversification.
2. It reduces domestic economic and market risk.
3. It reduces currency risk by diversifying into companies with foreign currencies.

Owning one fund might be suboptimal for reasons we'll discuss throughout this book. So, you could choose to disaggregate the global stock market using the following three allocations:

1. Vanguard Total US Stock Market ETF (ticker: VTI)
2. Vanguard Total International Stock Index (ticker: VXUS)
3. Vanguard Emerging Markets Stock Index (ticker: VWO)

You can then choose to allocate this in the same proportions as something like VT or ACWI and rebalance annually. If you just prefer to own domestic stocks then stick to owning funds that are similar to your home country's total market index.

Easy peasy. No need to overthink all of this just yet. And don't worry, we're going to overthink all of this later with many strategies that are much more intricate versions of a 100% Stock Portfolio, but we're just getting warmed up here.

Let's dig into the data and learn more about what it really means to be 100% stocks.

100% STOCK PORTFOLIO ANALYSIS

The 100% Stock Portfolio is a maximally aggressive portfolio that will capture high real returns with high volatility. Since 1900, the US stock market has generated 6.65% real returns per year with numerous 30% downturns, average annual volatility of 17.70%, and an Ulcer Index of 21.84.

Figure 2.4: US stock market total real returns

Table 2.1: Portfolio analysis (1900–2025)

	US Stocks
Real Returns	6.65%
Volatility	17.70%
Sharpe Ratio	0.44
Sortino Ratio	0.62
Max Drawdown	−79.20%
Max Drawdown (Post-1945)	−58.20%
Ulcer Index	21.84
Market Correlation	1.00

With this portfolio you'll have to get used to a high level of stress as the Ulcer Index of 21.84 is close to the most ulcer-inducing allocation you can experience. And while the Great Depression downturn of −79.2% is unlikely to be repeated in the future, we do know that real drawdowns of 50%+ are possible as it's happened twice in the post-war era.

Let's look more closely at the pros and cons here.

100% STOCK PORTFOLIO PROS, CONS, AND LESSONS

In 2023 Anarkulova, Cederburg, and O'Doherty published a paper that was highly critical of strategies that help glide path investors into retirement with hefty bond allocations (we will discuss these strategies in-depth in Chapters 18 and 19).[11]

The authors argued that investors should consider maintaining a constant 100% equity allocation diversified equally across 50% domestic stocks and 50% foreign stocks. The broader thinking is that stocks outperform diversifiers like bonds and alternatives by such large margins in the long run that investors should be able to stomach the inevitable short-term drawdowns that come with such a portfolio.

Cliff Asness of AQR did not like this paper and he pulls zero punches.[12] In fact, my favorite thing about Cliff is that he sometimes (rightly) kicks people in the shins for making outrageous claims:

> It should be obvious that higher expected return assets do generate higher realized returns. The fact that stocks beat bonds in the long run is not only not-earth-shattering, but what every finance 101 textbook teaches.

This is fundamental, but important, and you'll notice that Asness specifically mentions the time horizon. The fact that something is *likely* to generate superior returns *in the long run* does not mean it's guaranteed to *always* generate better returns. While the long-run returns of stocks are very likely to beat the long-run returns of bonds and alternatives, we really have no idea what stocks will do in the short term. We can't even be 100% certain they'll beat bonds in the long term, even though we have a high level of confidence that they will.

Here's Cliff again, responding to the paper:

> In particular, this… new paper makes one statement that is just an indefensible whopper. They state, 'Given the sheer magnitude of US retirement savings, we estimate that Americans could realize trillions of dollars in welfare gains by adopting the all-equity strategy.' This is very poor economic reasoning.

Cliff goes on to debunk the "cash on the sidelines" myth. That's the persistent narrative that a large amount of uninvested cash is just waiting to pour into the market. The problem with this narrative is that all assets are always held by someone (including cash). So, when someone sells their cash to move into stocks, the person on the other side of the trade is selling stocks and moving into cash. There is no "sideline" here. The assets are always in play, always held by someone. It is mathematically impossible for 100% of US equity investors to own a 100% equity portfolio.

Cliff killed this paper, but I am a pretty good shin kicker as well so let me add some other critiques to consider.

The 100% Stock Portfolio ignores the fact that lower return–generating assets can be perfectly reasonable parts of a long-term financial plan. I would make this especially clear in the case of something like insurance. Insurance sometimes gets a bad reputation in finance, but insurance is a logical part of most portfolios. Berkshire Hathaway could not underwrite billions in insurance otherwise. That's because the asset holder views insurance as a necessary part of their financial plan.

For example, a simple 20-year term life insurance policy is perfectly prudent financial planning for a household with dependents and one working parent. One theme you'll notice in this book is that I think of many alternative asset classes as being similar to insurance and there's nothing wrong with owning insurance in a portfolio, even if it's a low or negative expected real return instrument.

We also need to be careful about assuming the past will look like the future. It's no coincidence that papers like this tend to come out after large stock bull markets and especially after one of the most unique runs in US stock market history. The stock market can and does go through long and excruciating downturns that would make a 100% Stock Portfolio untenable.

It would be remiss of me, as a financial advisor to many retirees, not to highlight that a 100% Stock Portfolio is especially vulnerable to what we call sequence-of-return risk. This is the risk that you begin withdrawing from your portfolio during an unlucky stretch of poor returns early in retirement – which can permanently impair your nest egg even if long-term averages look fine. In other words, it's not just your *average* return that matters; it's the *order* in which those returns occur that can make or break your retirement plan.

For instance, imagine the 100% equity investor who retires in 2007. They then begin drawing down their portfolio to fund retirement needs and then, BAM, 2008 hits. This investor undergoes one of the most traumatic 50%+ downturns in stock market history. If they had a 4% withdrawal rate on a portfolio of $1,000,000 that falls to $500,000, this investor is instantly put to the ultimate behavioral test as their sequence-of-returns risk is through the roof. They are now drawing 8% of their portfolio per year, in order to maintain their previous level of spending, and they are exposed to a perilous financial future.

There are numerous other examples of stock market environments where prolonged or deep bear markets would have destroyed someone's financial plans. And while this is not necessarily a significant risk, it is a devastating situation for the small percentage of people unlucky enough to encounter it. And given the ease of eliminating this risk (through simple asset class diversification) it is imprudent not to consider doing so.

All that said, it's not all bad. While a 100% Stock Portfolio probably doesn't make a lot of sense for your entire portfolio, there are many pros to a large equity allocation or even segments of your portfolio that are 100% stocks, including:

- Higher expected returns. As we've noted already, stocks should outperform most other assets classes in the long run because they give you the purest claim on corporate cash flows.

- Superior inflation hedging. Stocks are a wonderful long-term inflation hedge because their underlying corporations are inherent inflation hedgers.
- Reduction of single entity risk. When implemented in a diversified equity allocation you can significantly reduce exposure to single entity risk.

SUITORS FOR THE 100% STOCK PORTFOLIO

So, there it is. The 100% Stock Portfolio. What did you think? Is it right for you?

Still not sure?

Let me outline for whom or where this portfolio might be right.

1. Ultra-aggressive investors with a high income. I like to think of your income as a bond. For example, if you have a salary of $100,000 per year you can think of that as a $1,000,000 bond that yields 10% per year. Your income is a de facto bond allocation that allows you to take more risk across other assets. As a result of this it might be perfectly fine for this investor to have a very aggressive stock allocation.
2. Someone with a very long time horizon. If you can afford to have a very long time horizon (perhaps your age, income or unique circumstances allow for this), then you can afford to be very aggressive knowing that the stock market is likely to go up in the long run and that you can ignore any large downturns in the short term. As I will discuss in detail in Chapter 20, I like to think of stocks as being similar to a 20-year bond that will generate average annual 5–6% real returns if you hold them for multiple decades.
3. Investors with a very high risk tolerance. This asset allocation will inevitably test your patience and your behavior. Given that it will

consistently fall more than 20%+ you need to have a high tolerance for risk, uncertainty, and volatility.
4. Investors who want to target a certain asset location. You can think of different accounts as different asset allocations with different time horizons. For example, if you are a 20-year-old with an income and a Traditional IRA, you will most likely first touch that money at some point in 40+ years. You can afford to think of that retirement account as a totally different animal and different time horizon inside your broader asset allocation. The 100% Stock Portfolio allocation could be perfectly appropriate if it's located within that IRA account.

FINAL THOUGHTS

One hundred percent is a lot. It's a lot of returns, a lot of risk, a lot of drawdowns, a lot of emotions. And what if the 100% Stock Portfolio is too much for you? Well, the polar opposite is 100% cash. And while we're now at risk of swinging the pendulum too far in the opposite direction, your cash portfolio could end up being the most important part of your entire financial plan.

The 100% cash portfolio, while boring, is also a surprisingly confusing portfolio that's oftentimes the most mismanaged part of a person's financial plan. So, let's look at this very boring and very important part of our portfolios in more detail.

3

T-BILL AND CHILL (OR WHY NOT 100% CASH?)

ONE of my favorite movie scenes of all time is when John Goodman berates Mark Wahlberg in *The Gambler* because he's not saving any of the money he's been winning. Goodman says:

> You get two-and-half million dollars and any a**hole in the world knows what to do.
>
> You get a house with a 25-year roof, an indestructible economy sh$tbox car and you put the rest into the system at 3–5% and you pay your taxes. That's your base. Get me?
>
> That's your fortress of f***ing solitude. That puts you, for the rest of your life, at a level of 'F*** You… Someone wants you to do something? F*** You. Boss pisses you off? F*** You.
>
> Own your house. Have a couple of bucks in the bank. Don't drink. That's all I have to say to anybody.

Holy cow. If he had told people never to forget leg day he'd have given us all the advice anyone ever needs in life. I kid, but not about the leg day. Never. Skip. Leg. Day.

In all seriousness, the interesting part of this advice is putting the money "in the system" at 3–5%. He's implicitly referring to cash and safe government bonds. He's promoting what I like to call the "T-Bill and Chill" strategy, although I would avoid throwing around F-bombs because that is not very chill.

Of course, getting the $2.5 million is the hard part (and $2.5 million ain't what it used to be), but putting the $2.5 million to work in the system is easier than you might think. And you don't need $2.5 million to make your cash work better for you.

So, let's dig into it.

★★★

I have a secret that Wall Street doesn't want you to know – the fees on cash management are egregiously high, arguably the most egregious fees in finance. And most of you probably don't notice them because they're largely invisible.

"Cash" is one of the more misleading terms in finance. It's dirty in much the same way that the word "money" is dirty in economics. It has so many different meanings to so many different people in so many different contexts.

For instance, when you hear the word "cash" you probably think about physical dollars. Ah, but you'd be wrong. That's *one* form of cash. Deposits are cash equivalents. So are Treasury bills. So are Banker's Acceptance Notes. So is Commercial Paper. So are Money Market Funds. There are lots of different instruments that are "cash equivalents" and while many of us think of them as convertible and similar, the reality is that the cash equivalents can be quite different.

We spend a lot of time in financial circles obsessing over the high fees of investment management and financial advice. But the biggest fees of them all are often the seemingly small fees you don't see. For example, as I am writing this a three-month T-bill yields the equivalent of 4% per year. At the same time, the most prominent "high-yield" savings account (HYSA) in the USA offers 3.25%. This might sound like a good deal on your cash savings. But when you look under the hood it's very likely that this financial firm is buying T-bills earning 4% and then giving clients a cut of that action at 3.25%. That 0.75% skim might sound modest, but it amounts to nearly a 19% reduction in your gross return – a massive implicit fee on a risk-free asset you could have purchased yourself.

Even worse, there are often commissions and worse tax treatment on this instrument. While the bank is likely getting favorable state tax treatment on the T-bill (bills are exempt from state and local taxes), you get the privilege of paying state and federal taxes on the savings account. This could be more favorable for foreign holders of US Treasury bills, as the US government will exempt taxes on T-bills for most foreigners. After all is said and done (or not said at all), you're likely paying the equivalent of a 1%+ fee and giving up a full 25% of your gross return on an instrument that is risk-free. For the bank, that's one of the best risk-adjusted returns they'll earn. For you, it's a seemingly invisible fee that is significantly more expensive than most other fees you'll pay in finance (and yes, I know that Whole Life Insurance policies are a thing).

WHY DOES T-BILL AND CHILL WORK?

In 2017 Hendrik Bessembinder wrote a paper called "Do Stocks Outperform Treasury Bills?"[13] He concluded:

> Four out of every seven common stocks that have appeared in the CRSP database since 1926 have lifetime buy-and-hold returns less than one-month Treasuries. When stated in terms of lifetime dollar wealth creation, the best-performing 4% of listed companies explain the net gain for the entire US stock market since 1926, as other stocks collectively matched Treasury bills. These results highlight the important role of positive skewness in the distribution of individual stock returns, attributable both to skewness in monthly returns and to the effects of compounding. The results help to explain why poorly diversified active strategies most often underperform market averages.

Woah. We've already discussed how hard it is to pick stocks, but this really puts things in perspective. It doesn't mean we shouldn't own stocks, but it highlights that cash isn't just a 0% nominal or negative real return-generating instrument. When used properly, cash is an important insurance-like instrument that gives you nominal principal stability, optionality, and even some inflation protection.

I especially like this conversation in the context of inflation and currency debasement. If you spend enough time debating inflation on the internet (not recommended) you'll inevitably run into the idea that the US dollar has lost 90%+ of its value. And it's true. If you had taken a single physical dollar in 1900, left it under your mattress, never earned any income, and never invested that dollar, your purchasing power would be 98% lower today. If, on the other hand, you'd invested that dollar in a portfolio of T-bills earning interest you'd have the equivalent of $1.36 in today's dollars. You would have retained your purchasing power when compared to inflation.

So, T-bills give you some level of inflation protection, and you get a very high degree of principal stability. Not bad.

T-Bill and Chill is starting to sound pretty good, huh?

CHAPTER 3

Let's get into the details and talk about how you can build your own optimized cash management account.

BUILDING YOUR OWN T-BILL AND CHILL PORTFOLIO

There are many great options for cash that go beyond leaving money in the bank or getting lured in by the suboptimal returns advertised by certificates of deposit (CDs) and HYSAs. I am generally critical of "high-yield" savings accounts and CDs because of their hidden costs through lock ups, surrender fees, worse relative returns, and taxes, but nothing is worse than leaving large amounts of excess cash sitting in the bank earning 0%. While we all need a little cash on hand to pay bills and whatnot, it's always smart to be hands-on with your cash. Especially excess cash in a brokerage account or retirement account.

Personally, I think a lot of investors get this backwards. While stocks are long-term assets, cash is an inherently short-term instrument. It needs to be managed more proactively because of this. Meanwhile, most of us talk about stocks as the asset we try to be more "active" with. In reality, stocks are the asset that should be mostly left alone while cash is the one that benefits from more active management.

My personal preference for managing cash is to take a hands-on approach with Treasury Bills by building T-bill ladders. An individual T-bill can be purchased in one-, two-, three-, four-, six- or 12-month maturities at any brokerage firm in $1,000 increments. The "laddering" of it refers to the strategy of buying specific rungs sequentially across time to mimic a ladder. In other words, you might buy a three-, six- and nine-month T-bill and roll each new bill into a new nine-month bill as you "climb the ladder" and the bills mature every three months.

A T-bill is a little different from a standard bond in that you purchase it at a discount and it matures at par. For example, if you buy a three-month T-bill with a 5.4% annual yield and a face value of $100, you would pay $98.65 today (roughly one-quarter of the stated annual yield) and the T-bill's value would gradually increase until it reached $100 at maturity in three months. Most money market mutual funds function the same way, but have less favorable tax treatment or higher fees.

RANDOM SIDE NOTE

One instrument that will come up on occasion in this book is a Total Bond Market fund, which is a common recommendation for a one-stop-shop for bond allocation. I find these funds troublesome at times because they're what we call "constant maturity" funds. In the case of the actual Total Bond Market ETF, we're talking about an eight-year instrument on average. This means that you own an income-generating instrument that is being used to give you near-term income and principal stability, but it cannot achieve the latter because it doesn't ever mature.

The beauty of disaggregating your bond holdings (or holding something like individual T-bills) is that you have a more tangible principal stabilizer. You could build your own constant maturity Treasury ladder with an average maturity of eight years, but because you own each rung of the ladder in a disaggregated component, you have a tangibly liquid component in your short-term bills and notes. I've found that this creates a more behaviorally robust portfolio for investors who need principal certainty from their bonds/cash because it gives you the ability to predict, with near certainty, how much money you'll have at certain points in the future.

If you purchase the individual T-bills in a brokerage account you can typically auto-roll them or roll them manually. You can build simple ladders by diversifying your T-bills out over different maturities.

For instance, if you had $100,000 in cash needs over the coming 12 months you might ladder this out over a four-rung ladder of $25,000 increments in T-bills of three-, six-, nine- and 12-months' duration. When the first three months is up your three-month bill matures to cash, your six-month is now a three-month, your nine-month is now a six-month and your 12-month is now a nine-month bill. At this point you can either disburse cash as needed or roll the maturing rung into T-bills of the duration of your choice (in this case we'd buy a new 12-month bill to maintain our sequential rungs on the ladder). And then the same thing after six months, nine and 12 months, as depicted in Figure 3.1. It's easier than it sounds and many brokerage firms will allow you to automate the rollover process.

Figure 3.1: How a bond ladder works

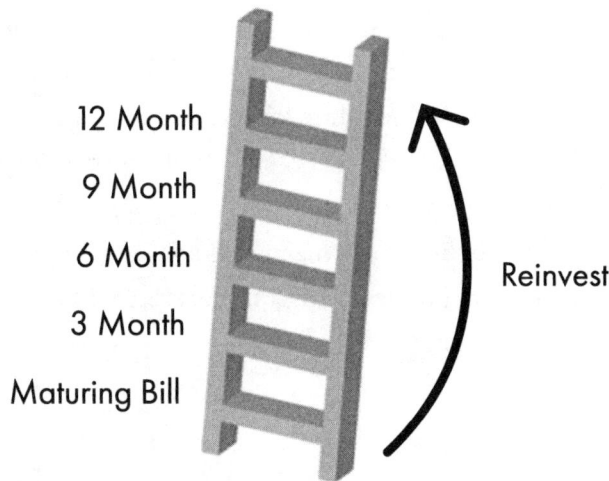

If that sounds too daunting or like more work than you'd prefer then there are plenty of good alternatives that are near equivalents, such as:

1. SPDR 1-3 Month T-Bill ETF (ticker: BIL).
2. Vanguard Government Money Market Fund (or similar low-cost government money market funds).
3. iShares and Bullet Shares also offer ETFs with specific maturities and customizable bond ladders.
4. Alpha Architect 1-3 Month Box ETF (ticker: BOXX).

The first two options are low-cost ways of owning T-bills through a fund. You don't need to do anything except pay a small expense ratio.

The third option is an ETF-based way of owning something that has the same general features of the individual bonds. These are fine in my view and some people swear by them, but if you're going to buy the ETF in a structured ladder, I don't see why you wouldn't just buy the individual bonds from a broker.

That last one is a little more complex: a synthetic T-bill ETF that builds a box spread using options to replicate T-bill returns. It's a clever tax loophole that allows the investor to turn T-bill income (which is often taxed as ordinary income) into long-term capital gains. So, if you hold that fund for 12+ months you can avoid the distributions from a T-bill and instead incur realized gains as capital gains, which gives you an added tax benefit compared to actual T-bills. Again, maybe more complex than you want to deal with, but these are all fine options for optimizing your cash holdings.

CHAPTER 3

T-BILL AND CHILL, PROS, CONS, AND LESSONS

The T-Bill and Chill strategy is a wonderful cash management strategy, but it ain't all sunshine and rainbows. Let's consider some of the cons:

1. While you'll likely be keeping up with inflation using this strategy, you will be lucky if you consistently *beat* inflation.
2. In a low or zero interest rate environment like the one we experienced in 2010–2020, you will almost certainly lose purchasing power using this strategy.
3. You still have significant currency risk using this strategy. T-bills are nominally risk-free, but any form of government-issued bonds or bills will get demolished in a hyperinflation.

What about the good news?

1. You have a nominally safe and very liquid instrument that can be liquidated and transferred almost instantaneously to meet short-term spending needs.
2. The taxes, fees, and income are very favorable compared to bank deposits, high-yield savings accounts, and CDs. This is especially magnified if you're in a high-tax US state.
3. You can structure a T-bill portfolio in a time-based ladder that gives you near certainty in managing your cash-flow needs over time.

T-BILL AND CHILL ANALYSIS

These cash equivalents are the definition of nominally risk-free instruments so there's not a whole lot to analyze here. We're just talking about cash equivalents after all and in the case of T-bills you're looking at an instrument whose performance is roughly similar to the rate of inflation on average and has virtually zero volatility when structured properly.

SUITORS FOR THE T-BILL AND CHILL PORTFOLIO

The T-Bill and Chill Portfolio is best utilized for a portion of your portfolio that needs to remain highly liquid for withdrawals, emergency needs, etc. Since it will barely retain purchasing power over time, you'll need some diversification elsewhere to boost your purchasing power protection.

So, this portfolio is best used for very short-term cash-flow needs or in cases where an investor wants to maintain a very behaviorally conservative portfolio for specific purposes.

FINAL THOUGHTS

Speaking of greater purchasing power protection – we need some diversification in these portfolios, huh? So, let's talk about the most famous diversified portfolio of all time – the 60/40 stock/bond portfolio. Believe me, it's a lot more interesting than you might think, so read on.

4

THE GOLD STANDARD OF PORTFOLIOS – THE 60/40 STOCK/BOND PORTFOLIO

THE 60/40 stock/bond allocation (the "60/40 Portfolio") has become one of the most popular portfolios in the world. It is a common benchmark thanks to its consistently strong performance and broad diversification.

But how did this portfolio come to be so widely utilized? Weirdly, no one knows the exact origin story of the most famous asset allocation strategy in the world, but my research shows that the 60/40 Portfolio grew from the ashes of one of the most impactful events in financial market history – the Great Depression.

One of the most important factors that will influence your investment strategy is the environment in which you're born. Consider an investor who was born in 1910 and was just entering the workforce and starting to earn and save when the Great Depression occurred. When they were 30 years old and in their prime working years, they probably got shipped off to fight in World War 2. From the age of 20 to 35 all this investor knew was a world of horrific turmoil. Little did they know that they had the Korean War, Vietnam War, and Cold War to look forward to as well, before retiring into the inflation trauma of the 1970s. You can only imagine how risk-averse this might make someone.

The Great Depression and the stock market crash of 1929 scarred stock market investors for a long time. No one was writing about 100% stock allocations in the years after the Depression. But following World War 2, optimism soared and the US economy prospered. Corporate America didn't miss out on the ride and this era formed the bedrock for the industries that many of us now think of as staples of American innovation and production.

When Harry Markowitz wrote his famous 1952 research (as discussed in Part 1), he showed that a portfolio of diversified stocks could help generate superior risk-adjusted returns. He expanded on this work in his 1959 book, *Portfolio Selection: Efficient Diversification of Investments*, in which he showed that other asset classes, like bonds, could expand the benefits of diversification. Markowitz consistently stated throughout his life that he was a proponent of a 50/50 stock/bond portfolio (as well as factor tilts, which we'll discuss in Chapter 6). Not because it was necessarily optimal, but because it appeared good enough. He wrote:

> ... I should have computed the historical covariances of the asset classes and drawn an efficient frontier. Instead, I visualized my grief if the stock market went way up and I wasn't in it – or if it went way down and I was completely in it. My intention was to minimize my future regret. So I split my contributions 50/50 between bonds and stocks.[14]

CHAPTER 4

Ben Graham, arguably the most influential investor of this era, also discussed how a balanced 50/50 allocation to stocks/bonds would be appropriate for a more defensive investor.[15]

It's not hard to imagine why an investor living through this era would come to such a conclusion – a large stock allocation, such as the previously discussed 100% Stock Portfolio, would have appeared reckless to most investors following the experience of the Depression.

Figure 4.1 provides a look at what happened to a $1,000,000 portfolio during this brutal period. Imagine watching your account balance tick down month after month, eventually falling over 80% over the course of three years.

Figure 4.1: Great Depression US stock drawdown

But as time went on research increasingly showed that a reasonably sized stock allocation could blend well with increased bond exposure to create a balanced style of returns.

Interestingly, this concept was already in practice by a mutual fund called the Wellington Fund, which was formed in 1928 by an accountant named Walter Morgan. Morgan was scarred by his own experience investing in high-risk stocks and preferred a more conservative approach to asset allocation which involved a large bond component. Morgan couldn't have chosen a much worse launch date for the fund, but it performed well in relative terms thanks to its conservative emphasis, and it attracted assets and attention quickly despite the stock market crash.

In 1944, as the investment management business grew in popularity, the Weissenburger Investment Company began publishing an investment yearbook to track common funds and their benchmarks. The Wellington Fund was a perennially strong performer and averaged an asset position of roughly 60/40 stocks/bonds for the period 1944–1966. As a result of this strong performance the Wellington Fund became its own sort of benchmark over time and this "balanced" methodology became increasingly popular.

In 1949 a young man named John Bogle was working on his thesis at Princeton University. The thesis was a 130-page review of the mutual fund industry and Bogle had some controversial ideas for how the industry could be reshaped, including his claims that the industry "could be maximized by reducing sales charges and management fees." This was what would famously become Bogle's Cost Matters Hypothesis and it was arguably the most important insight of Bogle's career. His alternative perspective on the industry caught the eye of Walter Morgan, himself a 1920 Princeton graduate. Morgan read Bogle's thesis and eventually hired him to work at Wellington.

After years of success under Bogle and Morgan's leadership, the Wellington Fund struggled in the 1970s as interest rates rose and the fund drifted from its traditionally conservative strategy, reaching an all-time high stock allocation of 77% in 1971, just before the market peaked. In Chapter 12 we'll discuss Bogle and the Countercyclical Rebalancing Portfolio and why this sort of allocation drift can be dangerous.

While US stocks generated -1.58% annual returns in the 1970s, bonds fared no better, with US government bonds earning -1.12% annually over the decade. The story had come full circle: after the Great Depression led many to believe stock investing was dead, the inflationary 1970s brought a similar obituary for bond investing. The Wellington Fund eventually settled back into its more traditionally balanced mix of around 60% stocks and 40% bonds. From there, the 60/40 Portfolio had one of the greatest 40-year runs of all time, proving that balanced investing was not only far from dead, but more alive than ever. Wellington and other balanced funds boomed in popularity and the rest is history.

The exact background of the 60/40 Portfolio is lost in time, but it grew in popularity thanks in large part to Walter Morgan, John Bogle, and the formation of the first "balanced" fund. It garnered even greater credibility as Markowitz and Graham advocated for 50/50 stock/bond portfolios and it became cemented as the gold standard of balanced portfolios after Wellington generated decades of stable returns using an approximately 60/40 allocation. The industry not only had theoretical underpinnings for diversification, but also had the historical and empirical evidence that such a strategy could thrive in good times and bad.

WHY DOES 60/40 STOCKS/BONDS WORK?

The 60/40 Portfolio allocates 60% to corporate stocks and balances it with 40% in corporate and/or government bonds. The reason this works is essentially the same reason 100% stocks works – corporations tend to generate profits over time.

At an operational level corporations fund their spending in three primary ways:

1. Organic cash flows and revenue.
2. Selling equity (stock).
3. Selling bonds (fixed income).

Both stocks and bonds are claims on the corporation that give the asset owner a certain right to income and/or profits. Stocks tend to increase in value in the long run because corporate profits tend to rise in the long run. And corporate bonds tend to rise in the long run because the average corporation pays out fixed income to lenders with a moderately low level of default risk. Governments functionally leverage their private sector income and so government bond issuance is viable to the extent that the government is taxing a prosperous underlying private sector.

So, think of it like this – a firm that finances its investment spending by issuing 10-year bonds at 5% will pay its bondholders 5% annual income. Bonds are typically safer than stocks because they pay a fixed amount over a specific term and are awarded a higher claim in the capital structure by contractual design.

Meanwhile, let's say this firm is growing profits by 10% per year and its stock returns roughly track that growth. An investor who evenly owns both the stock and bond can expect to earn a blended return of 7.5% annually. They are essentially combining a slice of higher risk and higher reward equity with the stability of a 5% fixed income bond. By doing so, they reduce the volatility of the stock portion and still offer a potentially higher return than investing solely in the safer bond instrument.

In the case of the 60/40 Portfolio, this "works" because you're diversifying across two cash-flow-generating instruments that have very different degrees of safety across time. And many people prefer this type of asset allocation because you're taking a more "balanced" approach to getting stock market exposure.

Just like Walter Morgan envisioned, you're taking some stock market risk, but not enough to destroy your financial life in an environment like 1929–1932. Or, similarly, you're getting some bond exposure, but not enough to ruin you financially in a period of high inflation like the 1970s. The name "balanced" is truly appropriate in this sense.

This type of structure works beautifully in mutual fund or index fund form because the fund can build a very large and diversified portfolio that takes advantage of its scale to reduce taxes and fees. Further, because the fund systematically rebalances to a 60/40 allocation it is inherently risk-managed to maintain a relatively static level of exposure across both the stock and bond markets.

The background is more interesting than you might have assumed, right?

Now let's talk about how to build this thing.

BUILDING YOUR OWN 60/40 PORTFOLIO

A 60 and a 40. This one's going to be easy to build, huh?

Yes, and no. Here are some ideas:

1. The easiest way to build the 60/40 Portfolio is to buy it within one fund like Vanguard Balanced Index (ticker: VBINX). This is a purely US 60/40 allocation, so it ignores a great big chunk of the global market cap. If you wanted to buy the global 60/40 Portfolio you could buy something like iShares Core Growth (ticker: AOR) which approximates global 60/40.
2. Another way to do this is to disaggregate the holdings however you please. For example, you could replicate VBINX by buying VTI

(Vanguard Total Stock Index) and BND (Vanguard Total US Bond Market). This is a little more work since you'll have to manually rebalance back to 60/40 every year, but it has the advantage of giving you more liquidity (you can tap the 40% bonds as needed) and you could potentially harvest losses for tax purposes in a taxable account. And if you really wanted liquidity, you could break out the 40% bonds into another slice where, for example, you took 30% BND and purchased a more liquid 10% allocation in T-bills or a short-term bond fund such as SPDR T-Bill ETF (ticker: BIL). This has the added advantage of giving you a more liquid holding in case you might need it. Think, 60/30 plus 10% of T-Bill and Chill.

So yeah, that is pretty simple after all.

Now let's look under the hood to get some perspective on why this portfolio is so popular.

60/40 PORTFOLIO ANALYSIS

What you'll notice with this portfolio is that it is true to its name – it creates much better balance when compared to a pure stock or bond portfolio. I couldn't simulate a broad bond index much further back than 1960 before the data starts to look a bit unreliable, but we have 60+ years to assess.

This portfolio does roughly what we'd expect. It beats bonds, but underperforms stocks. While stocks generated 6.28% per year, the 60/40 Portfolio does 5.00%.

Figure 4.2: US 60/40 stocks/bonds

Table 4.1: Portfolio analysis (1962–2025)

	US 60/40	100% US Stocks
Real Returns	5.00%	6.28%
Volatility	9.95%	16.52%
Sharpe Ratio	0.47	0.41
Sortino Ratio	0.66	0.58
Max Drawdown	−39.50%	−58.21
Ulcer Index	12.13	19.11
Market Correlation	0.58	1.00

Importantly the volatility is 9.95% compared to 16.52% for stocks and the Ulcer Index is 12.13 over this period compared to 19.11 for stocks. The max drawdown is -39.50% compared to -58.21% for stocks, so this portfolio is less volatile, but still has a decent amount of downside exposure.

Figure 4.3: US 60/40 max drawdowns (%)

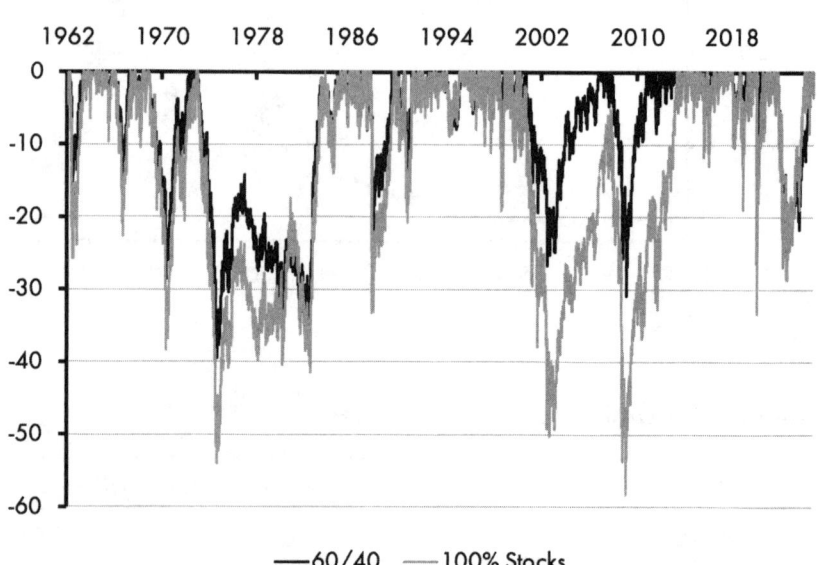

60/40 PORTFOLIO PROS, CONS, AND LESSONS

Well, this portfolio seems like a no-brainer, huh? But don't put the book down just yet. It's not all good news. First, the cons:

1. The 60/40 Portfolio is a homogeneous mix of time horizons. When you blend stocks with bonds what you're really doing is diversifying across time horizons and assets. You're taking inherently long-term assets and mixing them with shorter-term instruments. This is great,

but it may create homogeneous portfolio risk if your portfolio holds short-term assets that you cannot liquidate without also liquidating your long-term positions. In other words, if you own a diversified 60/40 mutual fund and you need liquidity from it, you cannot only sell the short-term bonds in the 40% piece because your redemption results in selling a bit of the entire portfolio. That's not ideal and so disaggregating the portfolio is important if you need liquidity.

2. The 60/40 Portfolio isn't as "balanced" as it might look on the surface. A 60/40 Portfolio is diversified across asset classes, but the more volatile (larger) allocation skews the risk in the portfolio. We often refer to the 60/40 Portfolio as a "balanced" portfolio, but the risks are not equally distributed between the assets. In fact, the stock market has a standard deviation of 18% on average, while the bond market has a standard deviation of just 6%. When you consider where your volatility comes from in this portfolio you are getting 75%+ of the portfolio's volatility from its 60% slice. For instance, in a year like 2008 the 60/40 Portfolio falls 30% because its volatility is driven primarily by the stock allocation even though bonds were positive that year! In that sort of extreme environment 100% of the negative volatility comes from the 60% slice.

3. The 60/40 Portfolio might not provide you with enough diversification in certain environments. There will be many times when stocks and bonds become highly correlated. If both asset classes happen to rise and fall in tandem, you'll need something else to give you more stability. This was especially important in the 1970s and then again in the post-Covid inflation years when bonds did not do a great job of hedging negative stock market volatility. Figure 4.4 shows the historical correlation of the two assets; as you can see, it is not static!

4. A purely domestic 60/40 Portfolio could expose you to a lot of domestic economic and currency risk. This is one reason to consider a global 60/40 Portfolio or adding more global diversification around a domestic 60/40 Portfolio.

Figure 4.4: Stock/bond correlation (three-year rolling)

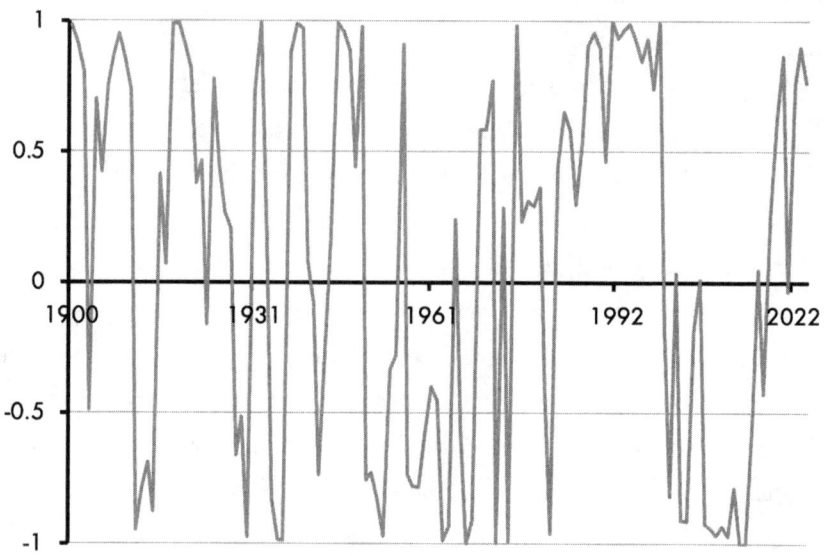

Let's not be too negative though. Now the pros:

1. The 60/40 Portfolio is highly diversified, yet simple.
2. The 60/40 Portfolio is low-cost, tax efficient, and can be purchased using just one fund or split up across a handful of funds.
3. A diversified multi-asset holding like this is a fantastic core holding in a portfolio. When it's surrounded by planning-based satellites (insurance holdings, cash/liquidity holdings, and growth tilts) there's not a whole lot else someone needs.

4. Using my Defined Duration methodology a 60/40 Portfolio is roughly a 12-year instrument so it's not short like cash or T-bills, but also not super long like stocks. It's a good inbetweener if you're thinking about this across specific time horizons.

SUITORS FOR THE 60/40 PORTFOLIO

This portfolio is great for anyone who values balance in their positioning. They want to own stocks, but don't want the full volatility of the stock market. I like to think of the 60/40 Portfolio as a Goldilocks portfolio.* It's not too hot and not too cold.

You also have to remember that this might not be suitable as your entire portfolio in case you need liquidity or want other more aggressive holdings on the satellites of your portfolio. So, in theory this portfolio could be a great core holding for almost anyone, but it may need to be complemented depending on your needs.

FINAL THOUGHTS

The 60/40 Portfolio has earned its great reputation. But it's not a relevant benchmark for most of us because it deviates quite a bit from the broader market.

Speaking of benchmarks – if we wanted to construct the benchmark that is most relevant in the world of investing it wouldn't be the 60/40 Portfolio. It would be the portfolio that reflects the outstanding market value of all stocks and bonds.

This portfolio is behind Door #5 so keep reading because it's arguably the most important portfolio in the entire world.

---

* We won't talk about how Goldilocks dies in the earliest versions of this story.

5

THE GLOBAL FINANCIAL ASSET PORTFOLIO

DURING the GFC I remember reading the prospectus for a new ETF designed to replicate hedge fund strategies. The fund described itself as a "passive" investment fund that was benchmarked to a certain hedge fund index.

What the heck?

This hedge fund ETF made something clear to me – anyone can create an index of their preferred strategy and then start an ETF that tracks that index. The fund is technically "passive" in that it does not actively change its holdings in a discretionary manner, but simply tracks the index, even if that index is a custom index that is super active under the surface.

The idea of "passive investing" took on a different and murky meaning for me from that moment, and I realized that the term wasn't as black and white as I'd always thought. After all, in what world could a hedge fund strategy charging high fees be considered "passive" in the way we've all come to understand the term? Surely it couldn't just mean inactive. And it couldn't even mean indexed.

So what did it mean?

The context in which we discuss the term "active" relies heavily on the specific benchmark we're using. As I'll discuss later, benchmarks are used and abused all over the place. For the purposes of tackling the active versus passive debate, I needed to first identify the most relevant index. After all, we call the S&P 500 a benchmark, but it's certainly not a passive one because it's only 500 stocks out of thousands in the world. It very actively deviates from the broader market. And it deviates massively from something like the 60/40 Portfolio which can be comprised of thousands of stocks and bonds.

As I did more research it occurred to me that at the aggregate level, there is only one portfolio that represents the market value of all outstanding financial assets – the Global Financial Asset Portfolio (GFAP). No one really owns this portfolio in its perfect form because it's impossible to replicate exactly and there are many rational reasons to deviate from it. But this portfolio is as close as we'll ever get to "the market portfolio" or a truly "passive" asset allocation since it reflects the actual outstanding value of global stocks and bonds without discretionary or active deviations.

NOT SO FUN SIDE STORY

I was once on the phone with my counsel and an SEC examiner discussing a potential fund launch, when I found myself in a semantic debate about active versus passive investing in which I tried to convince the SEC examiner that his distinction between the two didn't make much sense. My counsel interrupted me after a 10-minute rant and said, "Cullen, I charge by the hour so could you give me more detail about your views on passive investing – I have all day." What a funny guy. I promptly shut up, but then spent the next few years on my own less expensive quest to pin down the controversial subject of active and passive investing.

At a broad level, there's really no such thing as purely passive investing. There are only degrees of active decision-making – some of them potentially harmful, like high-fee day trading, and others quite beneficial, like low-cost indexing. But this search to pin down a semantic (though important) word led me to the GFAP, which is a much more interesting allocation than you might think.

The simplest version of the GFAP takes the two largest asset classes (stocks and bonds are the largest financial asset classes by a large margin) and breaks them down by their outstanding market capitalization – the market value of all outstanding stocks and bonds in the world. If you wanted to own the one true passive "market portfolio" or what efficient market theorists might call the "efficient market portfolio" you would want to own this asset mix because it reflects the value of what "the market" holds in aggregate.*

WHY THE GLOBAL FINANCIAL ASSET PORTFOLIO WORKS

The Global Financial Asset Portfolio is comprised of global stocks and bonds in accordance with their current market capitalization. An investor in this portfolio is buying all publicly available stocks and bonds that have been issued.

The reason this portfolio works from an operational level is because it is *the* market portfolio. It is the ultimate benchmark portfolio and the portfolio that every passive investor would buy if they were trying to be truly agnostic to any market tilt.

Although the GFAP is a deviation from something like the 60/40

---

* The Efficient Market Hypothesis is the idea that financial markets are "informationally efficient," meaning asset prices already reflect all publicly available information. As a result, "beating the market" through stock picking or market timing is extremely difficult. Under this premise, the best investment strategy is to just own the market through low-cost index funds (or the GFAP).

Portfolio, it works in the long run for much the same reason – stocks and bonds tend to generate positive returns over the long term because the underlying entities tend to grow, innovate, and pay out income over time. One could also argue that this portfolio is efficient in that it would require fewer transaction costs compared to other more active deviations because it more closely tracks what the markets do over time.

The GFAP sounds simple, but when you peel back the layers of this onion you find something increasingly controversial and complex.

Let's get into it.

BUILDING YOUR OWN GFAP

Building the GFAP is not quite as easy as you might think and I spent years going down different rabbit holes over this one. In fact, there's even controversy over what should be included in the GFAP.

An index fund provider must construct an index that is investable and can be publicly replicated. There's a big problem there – all issued assets aren't necessarily investable. For example, China has dual share classes in its stock market where much of the market cap of Chinese stocks ends up not being investable for foreign investors. More recently, central banks have become large purchasers of government bonds and stocks. As a result, you might argue that these assets aren't "investable" as they've been taken out of the public markets.

How does an index fund provider replicate these asset allocations when the actual assets are not always available to be purchased? Or if a central bank or government removes assets from the private sector, how do we account for the actual outstanding assets held in the economy? This has created a debate in academic circles about whether to synthetically replicate these allocations or stick to a strict investable methodology.

Interestingly, index funds like the Vanguard Total World Stock

Index adhere to a pure investable methodology (also referred to as a free float methodology). This is noteworthy because the investable universe of stocks can differ significantly from the total actual outstanding market capitalization of these instruments.

For instance, based on the investable universe, the global stock market is approximately 65% US stocks and 35% foreign stocks. But when you consider the total outstanding market capitalization, those figures flip to approximately 43% US and 57% foreign (see Figure 5.1). This is no small difference, especially when you consider the portfolio from the perspective of a US-based investor who already has concentrated domestic economic risk.

Figure 5.1: Full market cap versus free float investable market cap

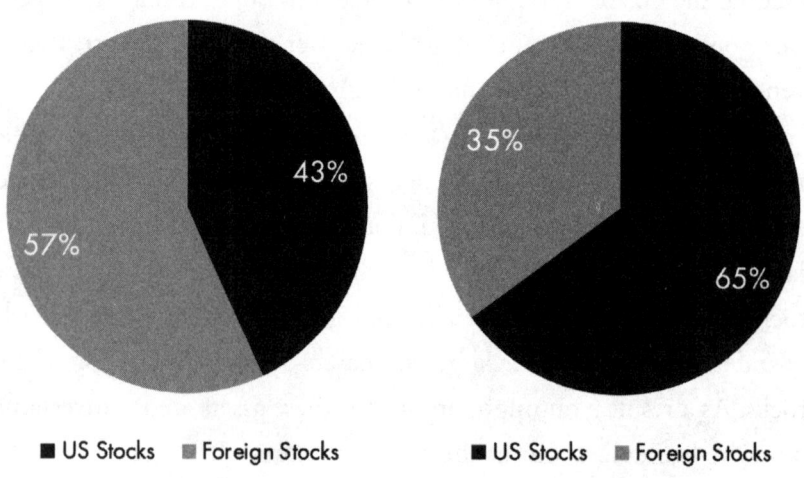

The most comprehensive research on this topic comes from Elroy Dimson and Paul Marsh. I spoke with Dimson and he didn't express a strong opinion about what was the better approach to implement, although he mentioned he uses the investable universe for the sake of practical implementation. But he also highlighted a fact that I found staggering.

If you utilized a full cap weighting instead of the free float investable universe, emerging markets would DOUBLE in size. This is because less than 50% of the market cap of China, India, and Russia is investable. Incredible. It might make you wonder if we're all massively underweight emerging market stocks just because of a somewhat subjective definition of global market cap weighting.

In any case, I find the free float versus full cap distinction interesting for several reasons:

- Someone living in the US who already has significant domestic economic bias might be exposed to even more home bias than they think by owning the investable market cap.
- Does it make sense to be overweight the largest economy in the world when the future empires of the world are likely to look very different as China, India, and other emerging markets converge with the West?
- The domestic US investor has significant dollar exposure, which is exacerbated in a US-heavy asset allocation.

But it gets more interesting.
What about the bonds?
This gets even messier because so much of the global bond market is now owned by central banks following decades of quantitative easing (central banks buying assets to stimulate the economy). How do we treat that? Should we care? Or do we just swap the bonds with the "monetized" cash holdings? And then there are all the asset-backed securities available for purchase like commodity funds and other alternatives. This. Is. Getting. Complex.

I prefer to keep it simple with stocks and bonds and then measure the allocations in their true full, outstanding market capitalization since that reflects assets that have been issued, regardless of whether they're "investable" or not. I don't believe we should ignore certain assets just because they're not readily tradeable. After all, they were issued for some economic purpose and serve a real-world financial need. It's not as if they don't exist so, where we can synthetically replicate that allocation, my view is that we should. If the goal here is to own the world's outstanding financial assets, then our portfolio should reflect what has actually been issued. Large index providers, by contrast, rely on the investable universe because they need to build indices that can be tracked and replicated in practice.

But since this is my book, let's go with full market cap since that's the value of the assets that actually exist in the real world. This data is publicly available and easy to replicate using the SIFMA Capital Markets Fact Book that is issued annually and updated quarterly.[16] The World Federation of Exchanges also issues the stock market data publicly, but you'll have to calculate the relative sizes on your own.[17]

As of 2025, the full cap global stock and bond markets can be broken down as follows:

- Total stock market capitalization: $115 trillion.
- Total bond market capitalization: $141 trillion.
- That's 45% stocks and 55% bonds.

Within each stock and bond sleeve the US versus foreign breakdown looks like this:

- US stocks: 43%
- Foreign stocks: 57%
- US bonds: 39%
- Foreign bonds: 61%

Owning this portfolio is easy. If you wanted a clean four-fund allocation, you'd own something like this:

- Vanguard Total Domestic US Stocks (ticker: VTI): 19%
- Vanguard Foreign Ex-USA (ticker: VXUS): 26%
- Vanguard Total Domestic Bonds (ticker: BND): 21%
- Vanguard Total Foreign Bonds (ticker: BNDX): 34%

This is illustrated in Figure 5.2.

Figure 5.2: The GFAP

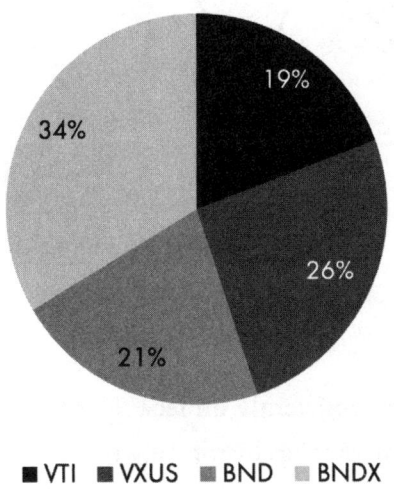

There it is. That's your super simple four-fund GFAP. Update it every year and you have a nice clean total market portfolio.

GFAP PORTFOLIO ANALYSIS

One of the interesting things you'll notice about this portfolio is that it's adaptive. Its allocation changes dramatically over time, in large part because the stock market booms and busts and drives big changes in relative values. Figure 5.3 shows the historical allocation of this portfolio since 1990.

Figure 5.3: GFAP stock/bond weights over time

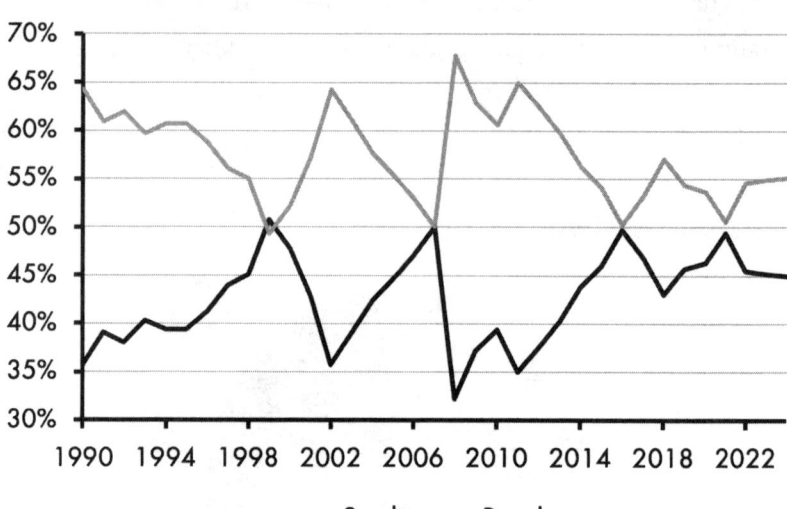

This portfolio is consistently underweight stocks relative to bonds because the bond market has historically been larger, primarily driven by new bond issuance. I focused on the period from 1990 to present because that's when we began to see reliable real-time data and more accurate tracking of foreign market performance.

During this period, the GFAP would have generated 4.05% real returns with 8.31% volatility, compared to a global 60/40 Portfolio, which generated 4.34% with 9.53% volatility.

Figure 5.4: GFAP historical total real returns

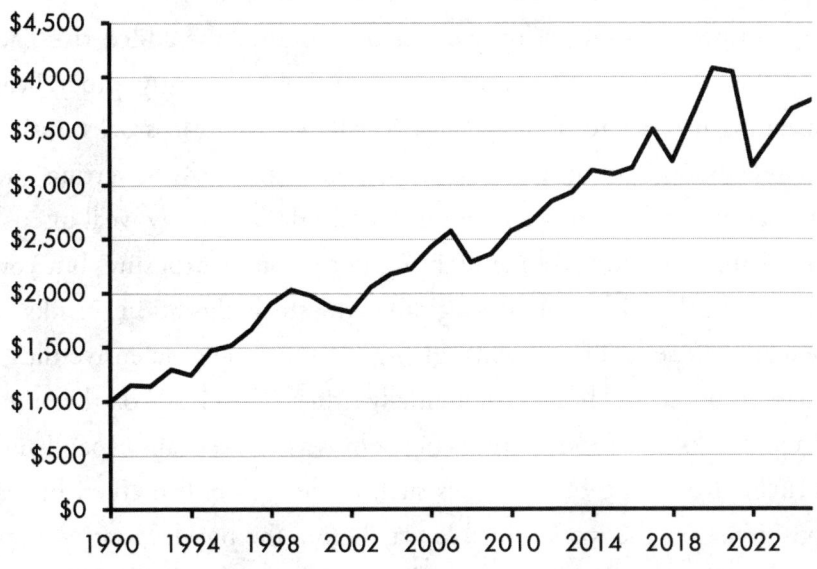

Table 5.1: Portfolio analysis

	GFAP Portfolio	Global 60/40
Real Returns	4.05%	4.34%
Volatility	8.31%	9.53%
Sharpe Ratio	0.45	0.47
Sortino Ratio	0.55	0.66
Max Drawdown	-27.62%	-33.42%
Ulcer Index	12.13	8.91
Market Correlation	0.52	0.47

An interesting fact about the GFAP is if you invert the allocations performance actually improves, even in risk-adjusted terms. In other words, if you swapped the stock and bond weights, using the stock percentage as the bond allocation and vice versa, returns increased to 5.20% per year with only a modest increase in risk.

I suspect this outperformance is due to both the added risk and a reduction in procyclicality. The GFAP is inherently procyclical, meaning it tends to become most heavily weighted in stocks during market booms – right before major downturns. By inverting the allocations and creating a countercyclical mix (a strategy we'll discuss in Chapter 12), you still maintain significant stock exposure, but you are taking that risk more strategically. The stock allocation shrinks as valuations rise and risk builds, giving the portfolio a defensive tilt as markets boom and become potentially riskier. The GFAP, on the other hand, tracks the stocks market's big booms as market caps expand and benefits from long bull markets such as the 90's bull market, but is positioned in the worst possible way before the big devastating bear markets like the dot-com bust and the GFC. Interesting, huh?

GFAP PROS, CONS, AND LESSONS

Let's talk about the good and the bad. As always, here's the bad news first:

1. The GFAP is difficult to define and can be measured in different ways depending on subjective preference.
2. The GFAP isn't a "beat the market" strategy as it is, by definition, designed to track the market. This might be a pro, but depending on the reader it could be viewed as too boring or too conservative given its consistently large bond allocation.
3. Owning foreign bonds is questionable in my view. Foreign bonds are generally much more volatile than US government bonds because many foreign governments and their economies are more unstable. This means that foreign bonds can often behave like

stocks in disguise, especially during periods of turmoil when the goal of bonds is stability. Then again, if the point is to take what the market gives us, then this is something we'd accept as truly passive.
4. The GFAP is comprised of only stocks and bonds, so it can experience periods of turbulence when those two asset classes become highly correlated. It also includes only financial assets, meaning it excludes a range of alternatives that could offer additional diversification.
5. Some might argue this isn't a truly "efficient market" portfolio because it includes instruments like government bonds – assets that don't always reflect private market forces, but rather what governments choose to issue (or impose). That's a fair critique, though it quickly leads us into a deeper debate about what we even mean by "free market." Who wants to argue with me about this on the internet? I'll remind you that I don't sleep much.
6. It's interesting that inverting the GFAP generates better returns. It might make one wonder whether this is such an "efficient" portfolio, after all.

And what about the good news?

1. The GFAP is incredibly clean, simple, diverse, low-fee, and tax efficient.
2. The GFAP offers a simple global asset allocation that closely reflects the market portfolio of outstanding financial assets.
3. This most closely represents a pure passive or efficient market portfolio, ideal for investors who want a neutral approach that simply mirrors the market's own asset weights without making allocation calls.

SUITORS FOR THE GFAP PORTFOLIO

The GFAP is a great option for investors who want a low-maintenance portfolio that holds something close to the efficient market portfolio. With a cash or T-bill component it can serve as your entire investment strategy. But remember that this approach is never going to knock your socks off. It's designed to take what the market gives us, not to beat it.

This approach is best suited for someone who values global diversification and strongly believes in the efficient market hypothesis – someone who sees little reason to deviate from the total market portfolio.

FINAL THOUGHTS

If the Global Financial Asset Portfolio is the ultimate efficient market portfolio, then it would only be appropriate to consider something more active, right?

When Gene Fama developed the Efficient Market Hypothesis, he had to confront the reality that certain components of the market appeared to consistently outperform. After all, how could an inverted GFAP outperform the GFAP if markets were truly "efficient"? To explain this, Fama concluded that there are specific "factors" that drive excess returns. Those factors are behind Door #6.

6

THE FACTOR INVESTING PORTFOLIO

THE GFC had a profound impact on how I view financial markets. I'd been taught that markets were efficient and rational. But in those terrifying days of 2008 and 2009, there was clearly nothing efficient or rational about what was going on. It made me wonder what the point of an "efficient market hypothesis" was other than being a cute textbook concept.

I was and am an ardent capitalist, but was confronted with the difficult economics of the biggest financial panic we'd seen in 100 years. I became convinced that the government needed to step in to help this unusually inefficient environment. While an efficient market would have corrected itself, I viewed this as a scenario where some level of discretionary government intervention in the free market made sense.

The economics of the GFC were fascinating – the private sector was suffering from what economist Richard Koo had famously coined as a "balance sheet recession."[18] This meant that the private sector had become overly indebted during the housing boom and would need to pay down debts and reduce balance sheets to become healthy again.

This is very different from a more traditional recession that is caused by a slowdown in income. The balance sheet recession was important to diagnose because these unusual recessions can turn into prolonged deflationary downturns like the Great Depression or the Japanese deflation in the 1990s.

These extreme deflations can cause a positive feedback loop as people get increasingly convinced that future prices will be lower. In these rare environments, the deflation in balance sheets becomes self-fulfilling. This puts the economy at risk of entering a deep behaviorally driven downturn. So, in my view, some active and discretionary government intervention made sense given how unusual the environment was.

At the same time, I was grappling with the idea that capitalism needs a certain amount of what economist Joseph Schumpeter famously referred to as "creative destruction" – the process by which superior companies are ultimately formed through good companies destroying weaker ones.[19] While some level of government intervention can be rational and even necessary (such as setting rules and regulations) you also don't want to overdo government intervention and create the wrong incentive structure for the private sector to compete and destroy parts of itself in the process of becoming more robust.

While I was largely convinced that low-cost passive indexing strategies were the best way for most investors to allocate assets, I also understood that there was no such thing as a truly passive portfolio. Active discretion was beneficial at times. Or, as we've previously noted, most investors have a practical need to deviate from the GFAP. None of us are passive because none of us operate in a perfectly efficient manner.

More importantly, I knew that the process of creative destruction *requires* discretionary intervention. Entrepreneurs are active investors who intervene to challenge the market's status quo. They are the people who shape the future market capitalization of the financial assets we own. They are far from passive; they are actively disruptive. They are the creators who destroy existing paradigms in order to build better ones.

It's become increasingly clear with time that free markets are superior to a command economy (those in which a government or central authority makes all major resource decisions), but you can believe markets are inefficient while also believing that an authoritarian economy is bad. Arguing that the market is efficient struck me as being similar to saying that the economy is efficient, and therefore discretionary intervention never made sense. But discretionary intervention is sometimes a feature, not a bug, of modern-day capitalist economies. We don't know what the right level of discretionary intervention is (or even the optimal form), but we know that it's sensible to a certain degree.

So, if we believe that the GFAP might not be as "efficient" as the textbooks would tell us, then how would we tilt our portfolio to take advantage of these inefficiencies?

This is the problem factor investing can help us answer. It argues that there are fundamental factors that explain a certain degree of inefficiency and outperformance.

This story begins long before the GFC. In 1964, William Sharpe (of Sharpe ratio fame) created an asset pricing model referred to as the Capital Asset Pricing Model (CAPM). CAPM assumed that risk was the primary factor driving returns and that more risk resulted in higher returns. But as time passed it became increasingly clear that the story was more complex than that, and other factors contributed to returns.

In 1992, two economics professors named Gene Fama and Ken French demonstrated that CAPM was incomplete at best and they proved that there were consistent anomalies in the CAPM. They called their asset pricing model the Three Factor Model and it revealed that size and value explained notable market anomalies. Fama and French would eventually add more factors and over the years other researchers have added their own hundreds and even thousands of factors.

In this section we'll focus on what I would refer to as the "big five" factors:

1. Size
2. Value
3. Momentum
4. Quality
5. Low volatility

Let's go!

WHY FACTOR INVESTING WORKS

So far, we've focused largely on the way in which we can own "the market" portfolio and mostly plain vanilla index funds or ETFs. This is a fine approach and you're likely to do well adhering to that strategy.

But what if you want to try to do better than the market? Are there empirically supported methods that might help you do that in a systematic manner? According to Factor Investing these anomalies could help you outperform.

Let's dig into each one.

The size factor

This one seems rather intuitive. If you're a small firm, then you can be nimbler and more aggressive as you try to grow into a big firm. And if you're a big firm then you've already gone through your high-growth phase and now you're more likely to operate like a big, clunky, inefficient bureaucracy. Or so the theory goes….

The evidence to support this view was once more compelling, but in recent decades, the case for small-cap outperformance has weakened. In fact, over the past 10+ years – especially in the US – it's been the largest firms that have delivered the strongest returns.

Cliff Asness is the factor investing guru and his view is that there actually is no size effect.[20] Or rather, researchers have confused a size effect for other factors. For instance, Cliff shows us that small stocks tend to have higher volatility. They don't generate better risk-adjusted returns per se. They just take more risk. That's your standard CAPM theory. But he has also shown that size is often confused with quality. Many small firms that outperform are not performing because they're smaller, but because they're higher quality.

I think Cliff has this one right. If you buy small-cap stocks, you're likely hitching your wagon to something that will carry higher risk going forward and if you find one that outperforms on a risk-adjusted basis it's likely that it's just a higher quality firm. And there's nothing wrong with that. We don't need to quibble about Sharpe ratios and risk-adjusted returns. What we care about, after all, are real returns across specific time horizons – and if you're willing to take on more risk in pursuit of higher returns over appropriate time horizons that's a perfectly reasonable choice.

Size might not be the best place to go searching for alpha (risk-adjusted excess returns), but it might be a fine place to ty to earn higher returns by taking more risk.

The value factor

This is another one that seems intuitive. We want to buy things trading at a discount. Nobody likes to pay full price for stuff. Who wouldn't love to buy a $1 bill for $0.80?

But "value" is in the eye of the beholder. While a large, mature, dividend-paying firm like the Dutch East India Company was considered beautiful over 300 years ago, today's most admired companies are lean, tech-savvy, and often shun dividends.

Additionally, "value" is relative. When you invest in a firm that appears to be trading at a good value, you might just be investing in a company with low-growth prospects or declining quality.

Like size, the value factor has not been especially kind to investors over the last 20 years. We'll touch on this more in the chapters ahead, but metrics like the price to book and the Cyclically Adjusted Price Earnings ratio (CAPE) have been poor predictors of short-term market performance.

This doesn't mean value doesn't work. It could certainly make a big comeback and factors have a tendency to come in and out of favor. Buffett was famously overweight value in the late 1990s when many investors declared his style dead. And we all know how that played out.

But my general view is that buying value most likely means you're buying something that is a little lower risk than the market because value is often larger, safer entities that sell at lower multiples because they're not especially high-risk entities (this of course can be wrong in the case of a "value trap"). So, the performance of value in recent decades doesn't surprise me all that much because value is lower risk and so, probably, lower return.

Cliff Asness would say the value factor is very much alive, but that you can't time it. I guess time will tell, but the fact is that value, like size, has not been a good alpha-generator for quite some time.

The momentum factor

Momentum is the idea that stocks that have performed well recently tend to keep performing well – at least for a while – and those that have performed poorly often continue to lag. In other words, recent winners tend to stay winners, and recent losers tend to stay losers, over short- to medium-term time frames. This pattern has shown up consistently in market data going back more than 220 years and is known as the momentum premium.[21]

Momentum works by measuring the cross-sectional performance of an asset relative to other, similar assets. When an asset outperforms or underperforms its peers, it's said to exhibit a certain degree of momentum. For instance, if Google (Alphabet) is outperforming Apple over a specific period (typically measured over 12 months) it can be said to have positive relative momentum.

Some people criticize momentum as being a technical analysis-based trading strategy that has no sound theoretical underpinning, but this ignores the fact that there's a huge amount of long-term evidence supporting this factor and momentum in price is likely to be reflected by momentum in fundamentals. In other words, firms that are performing well in the market likely have fundamental, real-world financial or operational momentum as well. You're not just trading a trend-line on a chart. Further, theorists argue that there's a behavioral element to momentum where prices tend to overshoot because investors often exhibit herd behavior.

One reason I've come to embrace the momentum factor is because I view it as quantifiable and systematic. The momentum factor doesn't rely on predicting underlying balance sheet or income statement characteristics (even though that might explain why it works) and instead can be implemented based on pure price trends. Yes, it's a "trading" strategy to some degree, but in the world of alpha-seeking, a pure systematic approach strikes me as a reasonable way to pursue market outperformance when compared to much more subjective underlying trends. We'll talk about this in much greater detail in Chapter 15, Trend Following.

The quality factor

You'll be shocked to learn that this one is exactly what it sounds like – owning high-quality firms. Then again, the definition of "quality" depends on how you choose to measure it. The typical definition of high quality relies on metrics such as gross margins, return on equity, return on invested capital, earnings variability, etc.

This factor is less well-supported than some of the others because it's relatively new. But Asness is again to the rescue here and shows us that when you combine quality with something like value, the story is more compelling as quality firms selling at a reasonable price tend to also exhibit outperformance.

This doesn't surprise me. Momentum in high-quality firms should be evident not just in their stock prices, but also in their fundamentals such as earnings and balance sheet trends. And in certain market regimes, combining quality with value can outperform pure momentum. That's essentially what Buffett owned heading into the Nasdaq bubble in the late 1990s. By owning high-quality value, he was well positioned for a shift in the cycle in which low-quality and high-momentum names (like every tech name in the early 2000s) were likely to underperform.

The low volatility factor

The volatility factor dealt the death blow to CAPM when researchers discovered that lower volatility stocks often displayed better risk-adjusted returns than their high volatility counterparts in the long run. You didn't get more return for more risk necessarily. In fact, you could get more return with *less* risk.

However, real-world applications have been less useful than the historical data led us to believe. Some researchers argue that this isn't really its own factor, but due largely to the size factor or sector biases.

I don't have a strong opinion, but I am skeptical of the idea that low volatility is a causal factor in leading to higher returns. So far, the real-world evidence appears to bear this out.

★★★

Okay, so those are our factors. You can probably guess how I would recommend mixing and matching them, but we'll dive deeper into some different uses here so you can decide what you like.

It's worth noting that one thing I am starting to do here is combining factors rather than highlighting their importance in solitude. For instance, value and momentum tend to be less correlated over time. This is one reason why many factor advocates argue that a portfolio of value plus momentum is the optimal way to tilt to factors. Combining factors could enhance a factor portfolio.

This, strangely, is also a compelling reason for market-cap-weighted indexing – if many factors are uncorrelated over time, then why not just try to own them all inside one clean total market package?

BUILDING YOUR OWN FACTOR INVESTING PORTFOLIO

Factor investing has become so popular over the last 50 years that there is no shortage of factor funds to choose from and for the sake of simplicity I am going to focus on the biggest and most liquid ones with a real-time track record.

Size factor

The size factor can be implemented in numerous ways. One of the more well-known factor firms is Dimensional Fund Advisors (DFA), which was founded utilizing the empirical data that Fama and French created. Fama and French both serve on DFA's Board of Directors.

One of the oldest factor funds is the US Small Cap Portfolio from DFA (ticker: DFSTX). You can also own small caps via a Vanguard fund like Vanguard Small Cap ETF (ticker: VB).

Value factor

As the most popular factor, there's an abundance of value funds in existence. One of the oldest value factor funds is the DFA US Large Cap Value Portfolio (ticker: DFLVX). More recently iShares has created the US Value Factor ETF (ticker: VLUE) and Vanguard operates the Vanguard Value ETF (ticker: VTV).

Momentum factor

The momentum factor is newer and so it can be a bit harder to find real-time historical data based on real-world fund applications. So, we're rather limited by what's been in existence in the last 20 years.

AQR operates one of the older momentum funds (ticker: AMOMX) and iShares operates the US Momentum Factor ETF (ticker: MTUM).

CHAPTER 6

High quality and low volatility factor

High quality and low volatility are also a bit newer and harder to find in the wild. iShares operates the US Quality Factor ETF (ticker: QUAL) as well as the iShares US Minimum Volatility Factor ETF (ticker: USMV).

★★★

That's a pretty good start. There are countless other options, but these will give us a good starting point to analyze and dig into. This is one section where I leaned heavily on shorter time horizons due to actual fund availability, as opposed to using historical factor data, which doesn't always reflect real-world performance of factors.

FACTOR INVESTING PORTFOLIO ANALYSIS

Size factor

The size factor has been a mixed performer in large part due to the outsized performance of large cap tech. While small caps outperformed from 2004 to 2015, they lagged the market from 2015 through 2025.

As seen in Figure 6.1, over this 20-year period the total US stock market generated 7.29% returns annually with 19.15% volatility, while small caps generated 6.35% returns with 22.80% volatility.

Figure 6.1: Small cap factor performance

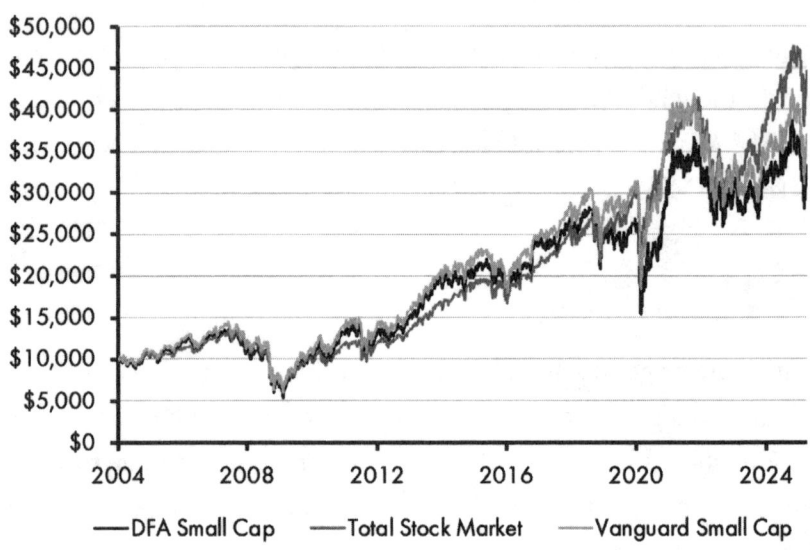

— DFA Small Cap —— Total Stock Market —— Vanguard Small Cap

Table 6.1: Portfolio analysis

	Small Caps	US Stocks
Real Returns	6.35%	7.29%
Volatility	22.80%	19.15%
Sharpe Ratio	0.43	0.51
Sortino Ratio	0.60	0.75
Max Drawdown	-60.46%	-55.90%
Ulcer Index	15.14	14.15
Market Correlation	1.10	1.00

Smalls caps have also generated less favorable risk-adjusted returns over the same period as large cap growth has dominated US stock market returns in the last decade. Figure 6.2 shows that the drawdowns in small caps and the broader market have been relatively similar across time.

Figure 6.2: Small cap factor drawdowns (%)

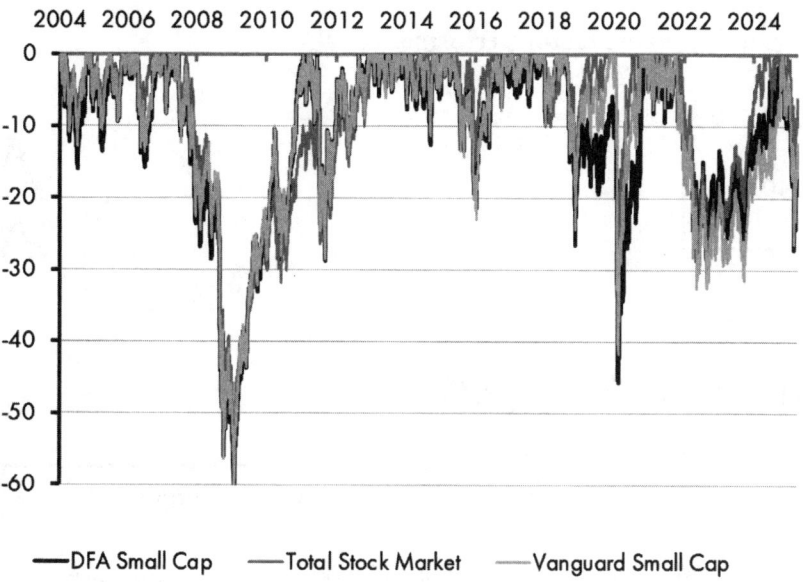

These figures are largely inconclusive in my view, and I think Cliff Asness is correct that if there is a small cap premium it's mostly due to sheer risk across time. Which, again, is perfectly fine. There's nothing wrong with taking more risk to generate more return; however, you probably aren't going to get consistent alpha from the small cap factor.

Value factor

The value factor has exhibited similar characteristics to the size factor over time in that value has underperformed the broader stock market over the last 20 years, but exhibited stronger performance in the

2004–2014 period. Over the entire 20-year period value has generated 6.08% annual returns while the total market generated 7.29% returns with similar volatility. Figure 6.3 shows the extreme deviation in performance in the last five to 10 years.

Figure 6.3: Value factor performance

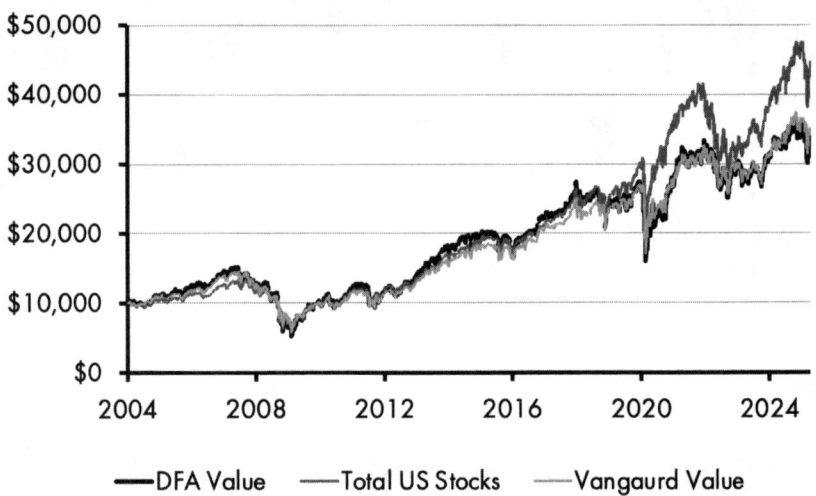

Table 6.2: Portfolio analysis

	Value	US Stocks
Real Returns	6.08%	7.29%
Volatility	19.04%	19.15%
Sharpe Ratio	0.46	0.51
Sortino Ratio	0.64	0.72
Max Drawdown	−60.15%	−55.90%
Ulcer Index	15.95	14.06
Market Correlation	0.94	1.00

The story doesn't improve when we look at risk-adjusted returns and drawdowns. Value investing generated lower risk-adjusted returns with similar volatility to the broader market over this period. It also exhibited larger drawdowns and a high Ulcer Index as seen in Figure 6.4.

Figure 6.4: Value factor drawdowns (%)

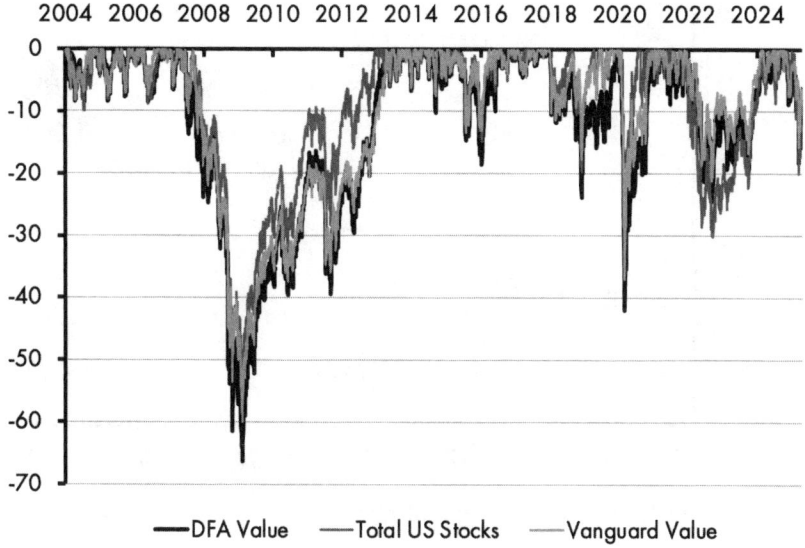

Value has been even less conclusive than size in recent decades. It's hard to say whether value has stopped working or whether it's in a cyclical rut. The evidence from the 2010–2025 period hasn't been kind to value in any case though.

Momentum factor

This is where things get a lot more interesting in my view. The momentum factor has a shorter real-time track record, but the period since 2015 is one of the more telling periods for factors because the US market performance has been so disproportionate due to large cap tech performance. Despite this, the momentum factor has tracked or outperformed the broader market over the entire period. As we see in Figure 6.5, the momentum factor has held up nicely in a market that has been very difficult for most active strategies.

Figure 6.5: Momentum factor performance

Table 6.3: Portfolio analysis

	Momentum	US Stocks
Real Returns	11.41%	10.68%
Volatility	19.75%	17.17%
Sharpe Ratio	0.70	0.70
Sortino Ratio	0.98	0.98
Max Drawdown	-36.46%	-34.54%
Ulcer Index	13.29	9.10
Market Correlation	1.02	1.00

The story is slightly more ambiguous on a risk-adjusted basis as momentum had slightly larger drawdowns and more elevated volatility of 19.75%, versus 17.17% for the broader market, as seen in Figure 6.6. The Ulcer Index is also notably higher, but the US market has been so strong over this period that anything that's come close is worth keeping an eye on.

Figure 6.6: Momentum factor drawdowns

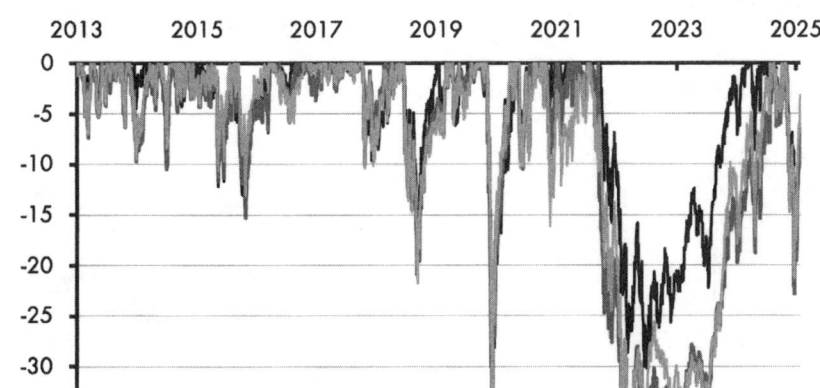

This is a more compelling factor as the outperformance over such an unusual period tells me that the momentum factor is capable of capturing a greater portion of the best-performing parts of the market, perhaps due to the more dynamic nature of the factor. In other words, momentum never constrains itself to a particular underlying set of fundamental features and can instead operate more like a multi-factor instrument.

High quality and low volatility factor

The quality factor has been another interesting one given recent performance. We again have a relatively short performance period, but the quality factor has held up well over the last 10+ years with 9.85% returns versus the total market return of 9.60%, as seen in Figure 6.7.

The factor produced volatility and risk-adjusted returns similar to those of the broader market, with a comparable Ulcer Index over the same period.

Figure 6.7: Quality factor performance

Table 6.4: Portfolio analysis

	Quality	US Stocks
Real Returns	9.85%	9.60%
Volatility	17.54%	17.72%
Sharpe Ratio	0.69	0.67
Sortino Ratio	0.98	0.93
Max Drawdown	−33.69%	−34.64%
Ulcer Index	9.18	9.20
Market Correlation	1.02	1.00

Drawdowns look very similar across this period, as seen in Figure 6.8, and like the momentum factor this one appears to capture most of and potentially more return than the total market on both a nominal and risk-adjusted basis.

Figure 6.8: Quality factor drawdowns (%)

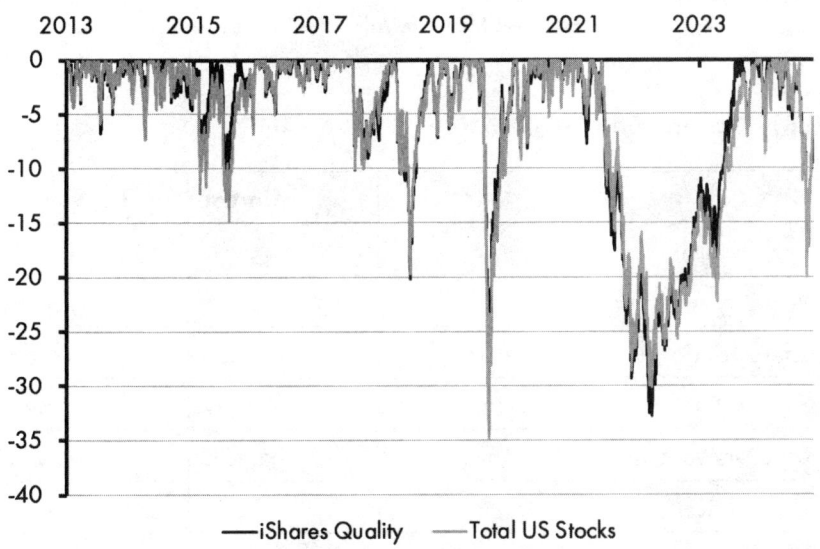

Similar to the quality factor, the minimum volatility factor is intriguing, but the early real-time evidence of the application does not bode especially well. Since its inception in 2011, the minimum volatility ETF has been trounced by the broader market with annual returns of 9.26% versus 11.13%, as seen in Table 6.5.

Figure 6.9: Minimum volatility factor performance

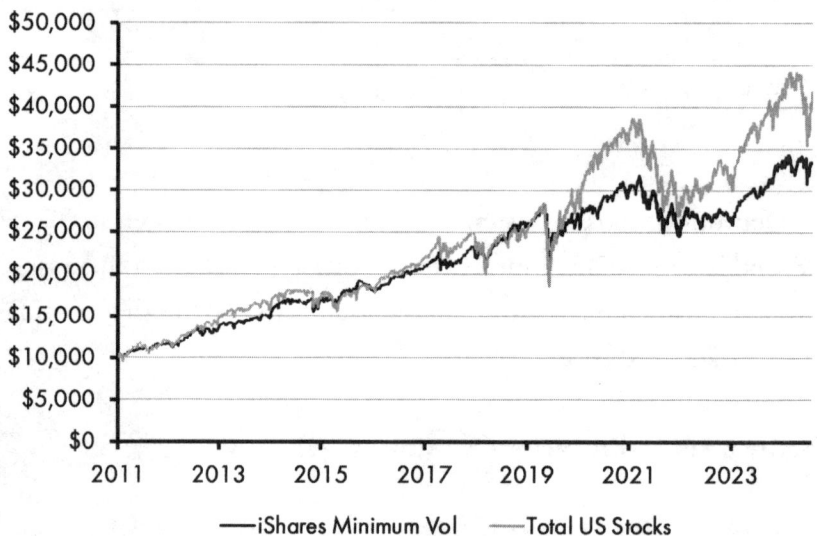

Table 6.5: Portfolio analysis

	Min Vol	US Stocks
Real Returns	9.26%	11.13%
Volatility	13.74%	17.40%
Sharpe Ratio	0.80	0.76
Sortino Ratio	1.12	1.07
Max Drawdown	-32.70%	-34.64%
Ulcer Index	6.82	8.70
Market Correlation	0.73	1.00

However, the data looks much more favorable on a risk-adjusted basis. Since 2011 the minimum volatility fund was true to its name and generated volatility of just 13.74% versus the broader market's volatility of 17.40%. As a result, its risk-adjusted returns are more comparable, with a Sharpe ratio of 0.80 versus 0.76.

You also have smaller and shorter drawdowns with the minimum volatility factor, as well as the lowest market correlation of all the factors, as seen in Figure 6.10. So, despite its poor headline performance the story is more attractive on a risk-adjusted and uncorrelated asset class basis.

Figure 6.10: Minimum volatility factor drawdowns (%)

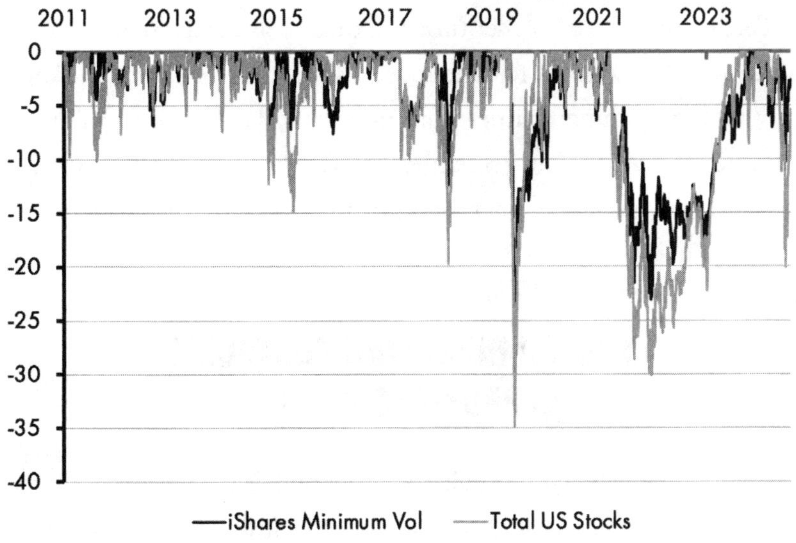

Combining factors

When it comes to mixing and matching the factors, things get more complex and we have to start doing some forecasting.

Based on sheer performance, the quality and momentum factors are head and shoulders above the rest. The risk-adjusted returns of a momentum plus quality portfolio are slightly superior as well.

But what if Asness is right and value, one of the most empirically supported factors, is just temporarily out of favor? In that case you might want to tilt to value with the hope that it will come back into favor in the years ahead. This is often the argument for combining value with momentum. In fact, combining value, momentum, and quality performed in-line with the broader market, but gave you superior optionality over time as the holdings are disaggregated.

How would I combine them?

As you can guess, I don't love the entire factor farm, but I do appreciate the rigorous research behind it. And as a chicken owner, I can confirm: some farm animals are definitely better than others.

Personally, I'd use momentum and quality as a satellite in a broader allocation. If I wanted to take more risk, I'd tilt toward size. And if I wanted something a little more defensive, I'd lean into value and minimum volatility. But remember, don't take my word as gospel.

Speaking of which, let's be unbiased and get into some pros and cons here.

FACTOR INVESTING PORTFOLIO PROS AND CONS

This approach has a mountain of academic evidence to support it and some of the biggest names in finance utilize it. So, it's hard to argue against.

But the factor story is still murky and I've struggled to get fully behind it throughout my career. That said, there are interesting and low-cost ways to mix and match certain factors even if all of them can't be relied upon all the time.

You know the drill by now. First the bad news:

CHAPTER 6

1. Factor strategies rely on historical data and implicitly assume that past performance will continue. But as we've seen – with the value factor struggling over the past 20 years and the size factor underperforming more recently – that assumption doesn't always hold.
2. I've argued before that factor investing is really just another form of stock picking – except instead of selecting individual companies, you're selecting factors based on the assumption that they'll continue to exhibit certain performance characteristics in the future. While it's true that some stocks have historically displayed traits like value, momentum, or quality, that doesn't guarantee those factors will persist or behave the same way going forward. And it certainly doesn't mean the factors you choose today will reliably deliver outperformance in the future.
3. There's reasonable evidence that you would be better off owning all the factors inside a total market ETF rather than trying to pick and time the best factors and risk owning the worst-performing factors.
4. These are inherently stock-only portfolios so you will need other diversifiers as a factor portfolio is not a diversified asset allocation on its own.

And now the good news:

1. As far as deviations from the GFAP go, these are all low friction. Factor investors like to refer to it as "tilting," so you're generally making small shifts hoping to generate a small premium in the process. These can all be implemented in a low-cost and tax-efficient manner and you're not at risk of getting chewed up by insanely high fees in the process of trying to beat the market.

2. There's a lot of empirical evidence to support these approaches even if some of them have come under question in the last five to 10 years.
3. I find the momentum and quality factors especially intriguing. The momentum factor is the one factor that I would refer to as individually dynamic in that any of the particular style factors could end up having momentum. It doesn't constrain you to a specific style, but instead just looks at the pure price movement. As far as active management goes, this strikes me as an eminently sensible way to be more active in something like a very aggressive stock portfolio. The fact that it has fundamental and behavioral underpinnings also makes it more compelling.
4. I don't think there's anything wrong with low-cost factor tilting, even if you don't end up beating the market. It is perfectly fine to tilt to something like size or value, especially if you know it might mean you're taking more risk in the pursuit of generating a higher return.
5. The factor story is more convincing when we mix and match the factors. For example, mixing momentum with value or quality is a way to generate potentially superior risk-adjusted returns.
6. You can also apply factor investing through a behavioral lens using risk profiling. For example, we know that factors like small cap growth and momentum tend to exhibit a little more volatility on average when compared to quality, low volatility, and value factors. In a behavioral framework, a more conservative investor might tilt toward the lower-volatility factors, while a more aggressive investor might lean into the higher-volatility ones.

CHAPTER 6

SUITORS FOR FACTOR INVESTING PORTFOLIOS

Anyone who owns stocks should study and understand factor investing. But it's best suited for the investor who wants to try to earn a bit of a premium and understands the potential risks there.

In short, this can be applied to any portfolio that holds stocks, even an indexing strategy. But it's particularly appropriate for investors willing to make modest tilts in pursuit of higher returns, with the understanding that these tilts may not always produce the market beating returns the academic research claims to find.

As I mentioned in Chapter 1, this might be an appealing approach for someone using the Buffett Portfolio as you could use that 90% component to tilt to certain factors that Buffett likes such as value and quality.

FINAL THOUGHTS

Factor investing gives you a little taste of potentially beating the market. But what if you wanted to try to beat the market by a lot? Or invest in what the market is likely to become? Yes, that's very active, and yes, that's potentially very attractive

Behind Door #7 is the Forward Cap Portfolio. This one's different from the more well-established portfolios we've already covered so keep reading unless you hate interesting stuff.

7

THE FORWARD CAP PORTFOLIO

I HAVE a confession. I lied about having been married to all these portfolios at some point. I know, I am a bad person. This portfolio is not one I have married, but it's like the person I secretly dream about marrying despite being married to another (sorry, honey).*

This is a portfolio I've been thinking about for years, and I'm presenting it publicly here for the first time. While it's still somewhat theoretical and untested, I believe it's a compelling concept – grounded in solid macroeconomic principles and built on a simple, practical framework. Best of all, it can be applied using the core principles we've already discussed.

So, here it is… The Forward Cap Portfolio.

If the GFAP is the efficient market portfolio, or the portfolio that "takes what the market gives us," then the Forward Cap Portfolio could be thought of as the portfolio that tries to "skate to where the puck is going."

---

* This footnote exists only to test whether my wife actually reads this far into the book. I have 2:1 odds she does not. Wish me luck with this bet.

The GFAP is based on the current market cap of existing stocks and bonds, while the Forward Cap Portfolio is an estimate, based on macroeconomic trends, of what future market capitalization might look like. In other words, it's like trying to guess what the *future* efficient market portfolio will look like.

I came up with this concept because this process is essentially what all entrepreneurs try to do when they invent new goods and services. Entrepreneurs do not merely accept what the economy gives them, exist within the status quo, and wait to ride the coattails of other innovators. Entrepreneurs push the envelope to develop goods and services and try to predict ways to create new markets and skate to where consumer demand is going.

The Forward Cap Portfolio does the same thing by trying to predict what the future capitalization of the capital markets will look like in the years ahead.

Let's pull back the curtain on this sucker and see how it works.

WHY THE FORWARD CAP PORTFOLIO WORKS

I have no idea whether this portfolio works or not! We are making reasonable guesstimates about what the future might look like and the backtested data isn't especially reliable because it's not based on my actual estimates at the time.

Further, some people might scream that this is "active" management. Yeah, you bet your ass it is. This portfolio just so happens to strike me as a reasonable way to be active even if we can't backtest the portfolio and analyze it the same way that we might be able to do with other market-cap-weighted portfolios.

In short, I don't know if this portfolio will work, and it shouldn't be used in isolation. Since it's a pure stock portfolio, it needs to be paired with other assets to create a more complete allocation. I would never assume it's sufficient as a standalone investment strategy. But it's certainly useful as a component of a broader portfolio, especially in the context of a more speculative stock growth component. Then again, maybe I am not giving it enough credit. As you will see in the portfolio rationale and outline, it's a diverse and sensible portfolio that could be appropriate as a large equity holding or even an entire equity portfolio.

Alright, enough yapping from me. Let's dig into this one.

BUILDING YOUR OWN FORWARD CAP PORTFOLIO

The Forward Cap Portfolio is relatively straightforward to construct. We are choosing the future expected market cap allocations from macroeconomic mega trends, with the portfolio rebalanced annually to maintain those target allocations. Rebalancing is important because the portfolio has some aggressive components that could heavily skew it over time if they're allowed to grow unbalanced.

How does this portfolio work?

I identified five major macro trends that I believe will have the greatest influence on the future composition – or "Forward Cap" – of financial markets. In theory, you could build this using many different trends, but I chose these five because they're, in my view, the most significant and the most clearly supported by long-term empirical data.

Importantly, the portfolio does not try to own every sector or country, but instead tries to own the ones that will grow into the largest and most influential pieces of the global economy over the next 30+ years. The portfolio does not try to forecast the future stock-to-bond allocation, but instead focuses on the future market cap of equities.

How did I pick the trends that most influenced the asset allocation?

I used long-term trend analysis to build an expectations-based approach for estimating the future market caps of key areas of the

CHAPTER 7

global economy. These are not small trends. They are five of the most dominant mega trends shaping the world today. Here they are:

1. **Mega Trend #1: Technology is eating the world.** Silicon Valley Venture Capitalist Marc Andreessen once said: "Technology is eating the world." The pace of technological innovation is only gaining momentum as time goes on. Before you know it, every company in the world will be some version of a technology firm or heavily influenced by technology firms. We are still very, very early in the growth phase of technological advancement.
2. **Mega Trend #2: Human beings are eating the world.** Humans are consuming more than ever before. Even with slowing population growth, the quantity of consumption per person is increasing. This will gain momentum as emerging markets, with their gigantic populations, evolve to more developed markets and their citizens' wealth increases. This means two things: we will need an ever-increasing industrial footprint to meet the growing supply needs of this consumption, and we will see more discretionary consumer spending.
3. **Mega Trend #3: Emerging markets are eating the world.** The US dollar is the world's reserve currency today, but there's a clear deceleration in the relative weighting of the dollar's reserve currency status. We don't know what country will emerge as the future reserve currency, but it's safe to assume that the dollar's dominance will wane, even if it's not replaced any time soon. As this process unfolds the most likely reserve currencies will come from emerging markets where population growth will converge with technology growth to help them grow rapidly into dominant global economies. Emerging markets are likely to become developing markets that overtake older more developed economies like Europe and the US.

4. **Mega Trend #4: Healthcare is eating the eaters.** This boom in global wealth is coinciding with the worrisome trend of an increasingly unhealthy population. We are eating more calories per person and also eating more unhealthy food, in part because we can afford to. Capitalism has done an incredible job bringing people out of poverty and increasing the wealth of the global economy, but it oftentimes creates this massive low-cost food supply with no regard for the quality of that food supply.

Figure 7.1: Percentage of people living in extreme poverty

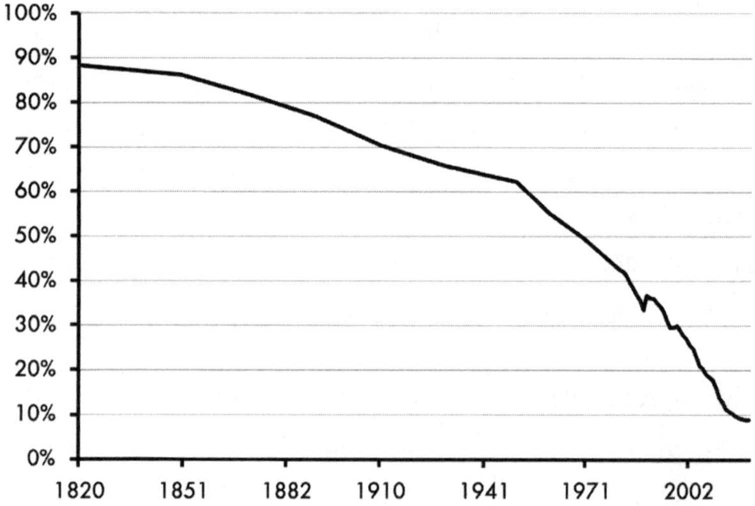

Our living standards have improved dramatically over the last 200 years, but as some problems subside others emerge. While the world is far wealthier in aggregate, this decline in poverty hasn't been a free lunch. In fact, our vast wealth has resulted in eating too much lunch. Quite literally.

Obesity rates and chronic illnesses are on the rise, driven by increased calorie consumption and declining nutritional quality.

This trend has been building for decades and may very well continue to worsen. As a result, the demand for healthcare and biotechnology is likely to grow. A wealthier global population means more people can afford quality care, but at the same time, worsening health conditions will increase the number of people who *need* it.

5. **Mega Trend #5: Decentralization is eating centralization.** An interesting paradox about globalization is that as it makes the world more interconnected, it gives decentralized entities greater power. As global networks expand, individuals and small organizations can more easily access resources and scale their operations without relying on traditional, centrally located infrastructures. This means that entrepreneurship and decentralization is likely to boom over time. We're already seeing it through the rising number of new businesses being started every year as well as the boom in personal brands. In order to succeed in the future people will become increasingly reliant on these personal brands, digital reach, and entrepreneurial growth as opposed to the old model of relying on large centralized firms to earn an income.

★ ★ ★

Now that we've established the five mega trends let's talk about how we can use these trends to build a portfolio.

Technology is eating the world

For this tech mega trend, I took e-commerce sales as a percentage of retail sales to determine the rate at which technology is consuming the world. In 1999 this dataset was 0% and has since grown to 15% (see Figure 7.2).

Figure 7.2: E-commerce as a percentage of retail sales

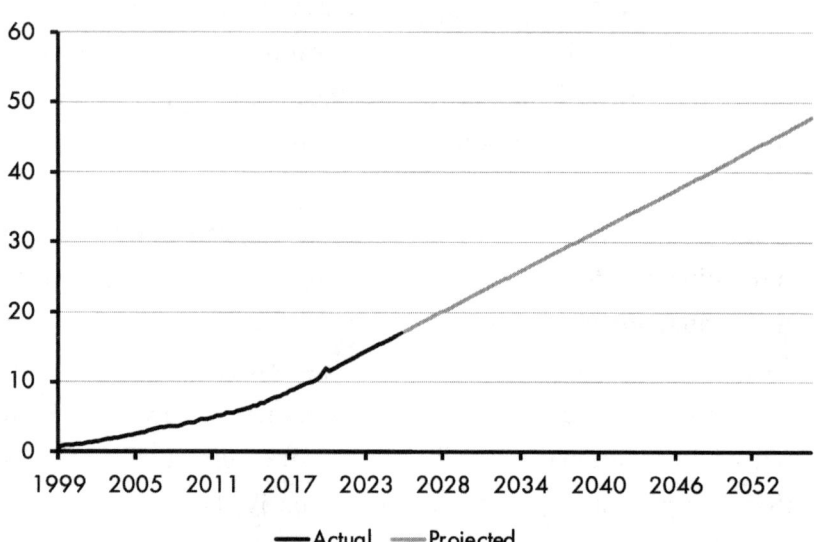

Using an extrapolative expectations projection over 30 years we can assume that this figure could be as large as 45% in 2056. Currently, technology makes up about 28% of the All World Index – so while the market recognizes tech's influence, it likely underrepresents its long-term trajectory.

That's why we're setting our technology allocation closer to 40% or more, which is more in line with where we believe the world is headed. Yes, that's a big number. But this is, without question, the most dominant and transformative trend shaping the global economy today and likely for decades to come.

While technology has been dominated by US firms in the last 20 years, we can reasonably expect this to broaden over the globe, especially as emerging markets grow and adopt the same technological needs as the developed world. To reflect this, we can apply a roughly 50/50 market-cap-weighted split for this component, allocated as follows:

- 20% Vanguard Information Technology (ticker: VGT)
- 20% iShares Global Tech ETF (ticker: IXN)

WONKY MACRO SIDE NOTE

This trend has the potential to be impactful in ways that many are underestimating at present. For example, I can see a world in the next 30+ years where robotics and AI have transformed our entire economy. This is a world where robots are mass producing goods in such vast quantities that the supply overwhelms demand, leading to persistent disinflation or low inflation. The potential slowing or lowering of prices could even lead to the return of what we knew as ZIRP (zero interest rate policy) to combat sluggish price growth. Wages will slow, turnover in employment will increase and governments may respond with ever-increasing spending expansions and stimulative policies. Many of the other macro trends outlined in this book will either be shaped by this technological shift or work to amplify it.

Human beings are eating the world

As the population grows and global wealth booms, societies are likely to become more consumption-oriented. With emerging markets continuing to adopt capitalism and consumer-driven economic models, rising incomes in these regions will fuel demand for non-essential goods and services. The primary beneficiaries of this trend will be consumer discretionary companies.

In the developed world personal consumption makes up 68% of GDP. But in the major emerging markets it comprises just 47%. I expect these figures to converge on one another as the emerging market economies become wealthier with time. If this were to happen, we could see a 40%+ change in the current weighting of emerging market consumption.

Interestingly, to capitalize on this trend, we won't just focus on emerging market or domestic consumer discretionary stocks. Instead, we want a global consumption basket. Developed-market consumers help drive growth and wealth convergence in the emerging world by buying the goods that fuel emerging market output through international trade – making this a truly symbiotic relationship.

Since consumer discretionary is about a 10% weighting at present, we're going to re-weight our Forward Cap Portfolio at 14% and split it up over a domestic and foreign consumer discretionary allocation:

- 7% Vanguard Consumer Discretionary ETF (ticker: VCR)
- 7% iShares Foreign Consumer Discretionary ETF (ticker: RXI)

Emerging markets are eating the world

As globalization becomes a more dominant trend in the coming years, countries will become increasingly dependent on one another to achieve economic success. This is likely to result in a diversification of reliable reserve currencies. In the last 50 years we've begun to see the slow decline of reserve market share for the US dollar. That can best be seen in the total US dollar foreign exchange reserves held by foreign central banks, as shown in Figure 7.3.

As the dollar loses its relative importance in the global economy, the beneficiaries are likely to be the emerging economies of Asia. While there's no clear alternative to the dollar today, it's not unreasonable to expect that this could change over time.

Figure 7.3: USD foreign exchange reserves (%)

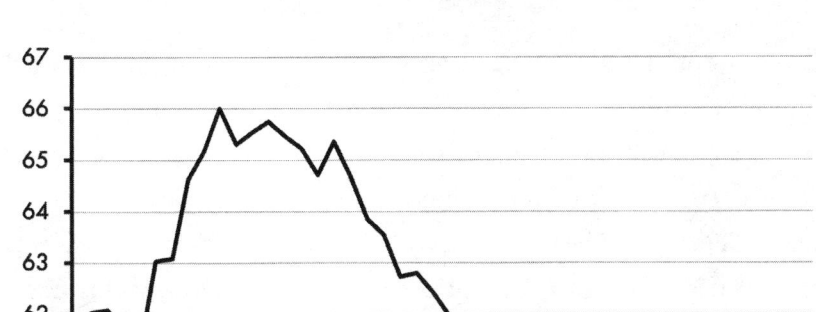

To benefit from this trend, we want to own emerging markets with the expectation that the development into a reserve currency will most benefit firms that develop within emerging markets like China and India. If the US continues to lose reserve currency share at the current trajectory it could decline to 50% with time. That shift would likely result in one or more emerging economies gaining 5–10% of the global reserve market share.

China and India are just 5% of the emerging market weight in the FTSE All World Index. A 10% increase in reserve currency share would likely lead to a similar increase in that region's market cap weighting, as greater reserve status tends to drive capital flows, financial development, and equity market growth. Therefore, we're going to apply a 15% weight to our emerging market holding:

- 15% Vanguard Emerging Market ETF (ticker: VWO)

Healthcare is eating the eaters

Healthcare is one of the fastest-growing components of the Personal Consumption Expenditures (PCE) Index. As global wealth increases, more people can afford better care while at the same time longer lifespans coupled with increasingly unhealthy lifestyles are driving greater demand for healthcare services. Figure 7.4 shows the upward trend in healthcare as a share of personal consumption. If this trend continues it's not unreasonable to estimate that healthcare will increase by 40% over the next 30 years. That implies a sector weighting of 14% versus the current weight of 10%.

Figure 7.4: Healthcare as a percentage of personal consumption

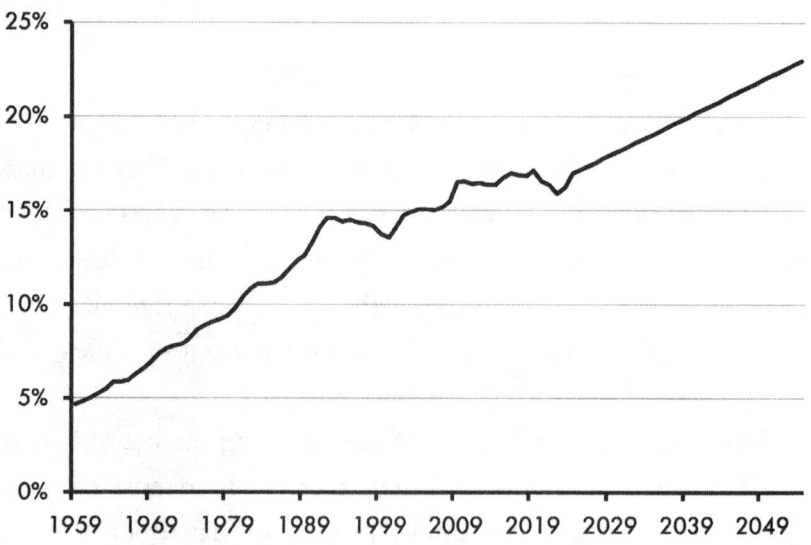

To take advantage of this trend we don't only want to own the plain vanilla healthcare index, but we're going to want to also own the firms that are pushing the innovation curve in healthcare – biotechnology firms. To achieve our 14% weighting here we'll split up the biotech and healthcare exposure evenly as follows:

- 7% Vanguard Healthcare ETF (ticker: VHT)
- 7% iShares Biotechnology ETF (ticker: IBB)

Decentralization is eating centralization

The world is becoming increasingly decentralized, driven by globalization and technology that make us more interconnected while simultaneously empowering smaller, more agile entities.

To reflect this shift, we don't want to limit our exposure to the mega cap firms of the world. Instead, we want to tap into the smaller and faster growing firms that will become tomorrow's giants. Ideally, this would be done using non-public venture capital firms, but we want this allocation to be easily accessible to more investors, so we'll achieve this using publicly listed small cap stocks. Small caps are under-owned in total market-cap-weighted portfolios and represent just 9% of the total market. To reflect this decentralization theme, we're roughly doubling that figure to 17% to round out our Forward Cap Portfolio using a small cap growth ETF:

- 17% Vanguard Small Cap Growth (ticker: VBK)

If you want to add an extra spicy element here, consider a small Bitcoin or blockchain ETF. But be very careful. While Bitcoin or Blockchain funds are decentralized, they're also highly volatile so you'd want to maintain a small allocation and a consistently rebalanced position so it doesn't create excessive portfolio skew.

In summary, Figure 7.5 shows what our Forward Cap Portfolio looks like.

Figure 7.5: The Forward Cap Portfolio

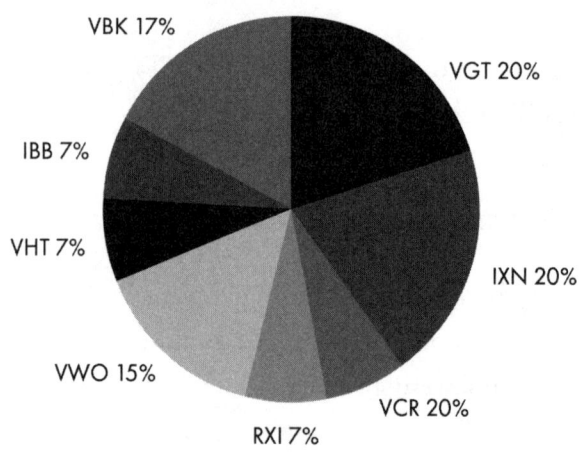

The Forward Cap Portfolio analysis

Backtests are always dangerous so it goes without saying that this backtest is not indicative of future returns. At the same time, this is also a pretty interesting perspective. Had I been smart enough to put this portfolio together 20 years ago, it would have trounced both global and US stocks (see Figure 7.6). Also, I am writing this *after* constructing the underlying rationale. In other words, I am not fitting the allocations to optimize the data relative to benchmarks. I constructed the model from the underlying empirical evidence and then applied it.*

---

* Yeah, yeah, of course I kind of knew what happened here, but if you'd held a gun to my head and asked me to guess the returns I would have never guessed it performed better than the US market and global stocks by this degree.

Figure 7.6: Forward Cap Portfolio performance

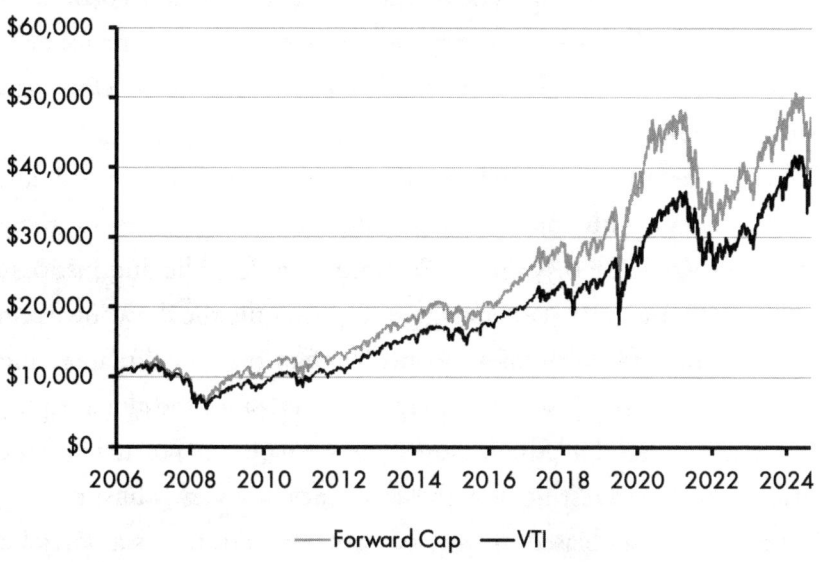

Table 7.1: Portfolio analysis

	Forward Cap Portfolio	US Stocks
Real Returns	8.75%	7.67%
Volatility	21.39%	20.07%
Sharpe Ratio	0.55	0.52
Sortino Ratio	0.76	0.73
Max Drawdown	-55.10%	-56.04%
Ulcer Index	14.68	14.95
Market Correlation	1.03	1.00

The Forward Cap Portfolio would have generated 8.75% annual returns with volatility of 21.39%, compared to the US average market return of 7.67% and volatility of 20.07%. So, we're getting more return and more risk, but the risk-adjusted returns of the Forward

Cap are superior. But what's especially interesting here is that the US market is the wrong benchmark. The Forward Cap Portfolio is a global allocation, which, in my view, makes this performance even more surprising since global stocks have been trounced by US stocks over this period.

Over this 20-year period the global stock market returned just 5.12% annually with volatility of 20.55%. The Sharpe ratios on these portfolios would be 0.55 for the Forward Cap Portfolio and just 0.40 for the global market. Perhaps more importantly, the drawdowns on the Forward Cap Portfolio were smaller than the global market and the Ulcer Index was just 14.68 compared to 17.39 for the global equity market. Frankly, I don't think those figures can be extrapolated into the future, but it's interesting nonetheless as these are very robust metrics.

I am obviously biased in various ways here, but this is a portfolio that I find extremely compelling for a multitude of reasons.

But let's check our biases at the door – I am, after all, here to objectively present all the portfolios.

THE FORWARD CAP PORTFOLIO PROS AND CONS

Let's talk about the pros and the cons here. Bad news first, of course:

1. This portfolio is inherently aggressive. It will test your behavioral biases at times.
2. This portfolio is "active" in nature, built on sensible guesstimates about an unknown future.
3. The portfolio doesn't capture the market cap of the entire world and is designed only to capture large mega trends. This could result in potentially significant deviations from a portfolio like the GFAP.
4. The portfolio is limited to equities; you will need some other diversifiers to manage any cash-flow needs or reduce portfolio instability.

5. The strategy is essentially a sector-style bet. If the selected sectors or countries underperform, you won't benefit from the same level of diversification that a broader index fund would provide.

What about the good news?

1. I created this portfolio and that means it must be good, right? RIGHT?
2. Despite being just five mega trends, the Forward Cap Portfolio is extremely diverse for an all-stock portfolio. It holds over 7,000+ stocks and is diversified across large swaths of the global economy.
3. The portfolio can be implemented in a very simple and low-cost manner that only requires rebalancing once a year.

SUITORS FOR THE FORWARD CAP PORTFOLIO

The Forward Cap Portfolio is best utilized by someone who wants to try to beat the market and is willing to undergo periods of significant volatility in the process of trying to achieve high long-term returns. You need a long time horizon and a high level of patience to let it work. You also need to believe that the person who created it is somewhat talented.[*]

The point is, it's a full gas, no brakes type of asset allocation, so if you like a smooth and comfortable ride this is not the portfolio for you. If, on the other hand, you're looking for a wild ride and a potentially very exciting time, then this portfolio is for you.

---

[*] This is currently undergoing significant debate with most of the pushback coming from my wife, who claims I am a bad driver and even worse listener. In my defense I would argue that I have mastered the art of selective listening. And I haven't had a moving violation in over 20 years so the driving claim is just BS.

FINAL THOUGHTS

Well, that was an interesting one, huh? I'm not sure if it's something you should go all-in on, but you might use it for a piece of your portfolio. One drawback of this portfolio is that it isn't designed to weather all market environments. Given its aggressive, future-oriented outlook, it's safe to say this portfolio will put your emotions to the test at times.

The Forward Cap Portfolio tries to beat the market by taking relatively unbalanced risk in specific sectors and economies. But what if you wanted to try to beat the market *and* maintain a more balanced allocation? And no, we're not talking about 60/40 style "balance." We're talking about true balance. True… parity, you might say. Yep, Risk Parity is up next.

8

THE RISK PARITY PORTFOLIO

IN August of 1971 Richard Nixon changed the fiat monetary system forever when he removed the US from the gold standard (an event referred to as the "Nixon Shock"). On that hot summer day, a young clerk at the New York Stock Exchange excitedly waited for the market to open expecting a market crash.

But the exact opposite happened and stocks surged 3.8%. This was the moment that the young man, named Ray Dalio, recognized the extreme unpredictability of the financial system as well as the need to develop an understanding of what he would famously call "the economic machine."[22]

Dalio went on to start Bridgewater Associates, the largest hedge fund in the world. And the strategy he became famous for developing was called the Risk Parity strategy.

FUN SIDE NOTE

Speaking of the "economic machine" – I would recommend that you seek out Dalio's popular YouTube video called "Understanding the Economic Machine." It's only 30 minutes long and does a very nice job of explaining the monetary system at a high level. If you want a nice complement to that video, you might consider reading a paper called "Understanding the Modern Monetary System" by a gentleman named Cullen Roche. It might be the greatest paper ever written, but that's just my independent and obviously unbiased opinion. Sorry for that commercial break. Now back to the chapter at hand…

WHY THE RISK PARITY PORTFOLIO WORKS

Risk Parity is a smart approach to portfolio construction that focuses on where the actual risks lie within your asset allocation.

As we mentioned in Chapter 4, the risks in a portfolio like the 60/40 Portfolio aren't proportional to its allocation. The 40% invested in bonds typically carries much less volatility and principal risk than the 60% invested in stocks. That means, while it may look balanced on paper, the portfolio behaves more like an 85/15 allocation in terms of risk – with stocks driving most of the volatility.

Risk Parity aims to balance a portfolio by equalizing the amount of risk each asset class contributes – not just the dollar amount invested. While a traditional 60/40 Portfolio ends up with most of its risk concentrated in equities, Risk Parity strategies adjust for this imbalance, often by increasing exposure to lower-risk assets like bonds (sometimes using leverage) so that each piece of the portfolio plays a more equal role in driving overall volatility. The result is a more

CHAPTER 8

diversified risk exposure, with the goal of producing steadier returns and better risk-adjusted performance over time. Looking at many of the various asset classes based on expected returns and risk, we can reasonably formulate an understanding of their relationships, as shown in Figure 8.1.

Figure 8.1: Traditional expected return versus expected risk

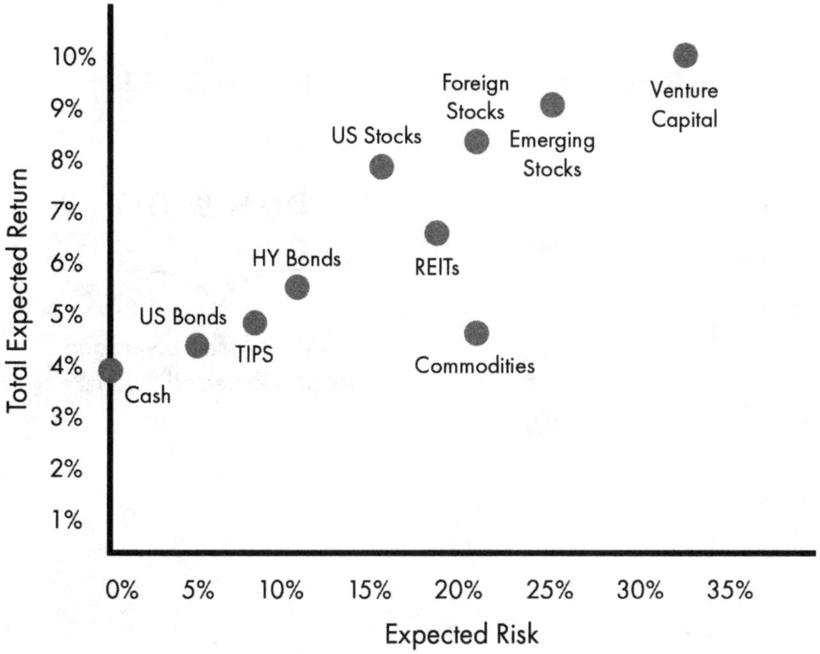

[Scatter plot of Total Expected Return (y-axis, 1%–10%) versus Expected Risk (x-axis, 0%–35%) showing asset classes: Cash (~0%, 4%), US Bonds (~5%, 5%), TIPS (~7%, 4.5%), HY Bonds (~10%, 5.5%), US Stocks (~15%, 8%), REITs (~18%, 6.5%), Commodities (~20%, 4.5%), Foreign Stocks (~20%, 9%), Emerging Stocks (~25%, 8.5%), Venture Capital (~33%, 10%).]

If we want to create parity across the risks in a portfolio holding these assets then we need to somehow balance the risk exposures – either by owning smaller relative amounts of the high-risk assets, or leveraging the amount of the lower-risk assets.

For instance, if stocks have a standard deviation of 15 and bonds have a standard deviation of 5, then you could create risk parity by leveraging the bonds in your portfolio to create equal exposures to risk inside of both asset classes. The goal is to leverage the risks with the hope that you're creating more balanced expected returns, thereby resulting in superior risk-adjusted returns relative to something like the 60/40 Portfolio. As we can see in Figure 8.2, Risk Parity attempts to equalize the risks across different asset classes with the goal of creating a more diversified and uncorrelated set of return streams that achieve higher expected returns with a level of risk that is more consistent with a diversified portfolio like 60/40 stocks/bonds.

Figure 8.2: Risk Parity-targeted return with optimal risk

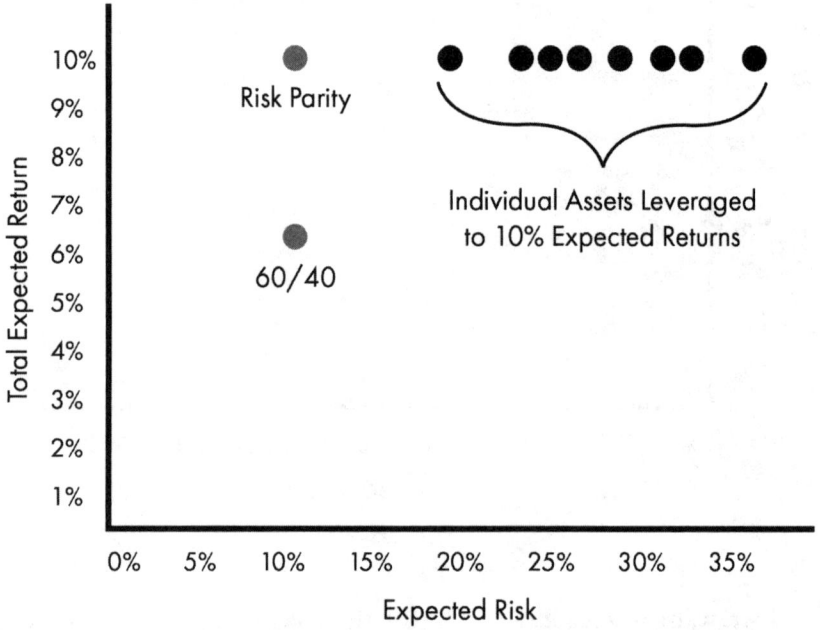

Further, Risk Parity argues that the stock and bond markets are not sufficiently diversified to weather all environments, especially recessions and inflations. Therefore, even though a Risk Parity Portfolio might underperform during periods like large stock market booms, it could outperform in outlier environments like high inflations and recessions, therefore helping to capture most of the expansionary upsides while also reducing the volatility of the most uncertain types of environments.

This "works" for the right investor who seeks broader diversification than a 60/40 Portfolio and one who has the patience to undergo periods of FOMO (fear of missing out) where stocks are surging relative to alternative assets like commodities, which often undergo long periods of negative or poor relative performance.

In my view these kinds of diverse strategies work because while they're likely to generate lower expected returns, they will also generate lower volatility due to broader risk distribution. This means you're unlikely to get better nominal returns, but the added diversification gives you the potential for much better risk-adjusted returns.

BUILDING YOUR OWN RISK PARITY PORTFOLIO

Building your own Risk Parity Portfolio is not easy. Dalio has stated that you would want at least 15 different uncorrelated "return drivers" to create a sufficiently diversified portfolio for this strategy.[23]

Building a Risk Parity Portfolio requires evaluating expected risks and returns, and deciding whether or how to use leverage to construct a balanced portfolio. As you might imagine, this can quickly become a complex task. This is especially magnified by the fact that borrowing costs can vary and eat into the cost of the portfolio.

To give you a simple example of how we might balance the risks in a portfolio using 15 uncorrelated assets, we might take the following instruments with the following standard deviations:

- US stocks (ticker: VTI): 18%
- Foreign stocks (ticker: VXUS): 18%

- Gold (ticker: IAU): 18%
- Silver (ticker: SLV): 31%
- Bitcoin (ticker: IBIT): 87%
- Long US Treasury bonds (ticker: VGLT): 15%
- Foreign bonds (ticker: BNDX): 5%
- High-yield bonds (ticker: HYG): 11%
- REITs (ticker: VNQ): 30%
- TIPS (ticker: TIP): 6%
- Managed futures (ticker: CTA): 13%
- Minimum vol stocks (ticker: USMV): 15%
- Currency carry (ticker: CCRV): 19%
- Out of the money tail risk (ticker: CAOS): 4%
- Commodities (ticker: PDBC): 18%

If we weight these in a portfolio to balance the risks we'd implement the following weightings:

- US stocks: 4.38%
- Foreign stocks: 4.38%
- Gold: 4.38%
- Silver: 2.54%
- Bitcoin: 0.91%
- Long US Treasury bonds: 5.25%
- Foreign bonds: 15.75%
- High-yield bonds: 7.16%
- REITs: 2.63%
- TIPS: 13.13%
- Managed futures: 6.06%
- Minimum vol stocks: 5.25%
- Commodity carry: 4.14%
- Out of the money tail risk: 19.69%
- Commodities: 4.38%

Without using leverage, that gets us to a parity of holdings based on the risk exposures of each asset in the portfolio, as shown in Figure 8.3.

Figure 8.3: Unlevered Risk Parity

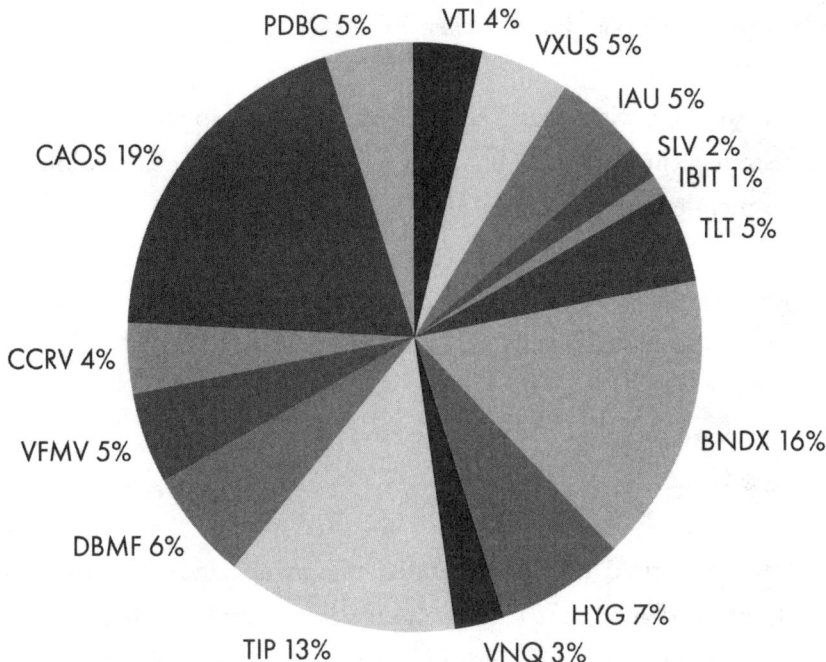

Now, even though I've oversimplified this approach, this is still pretty complex. Implementing leverage, most efficiently through futures, will make this even trickier and may be an unrealistic approach for most investors trying to do it themselves.

Because of this, it's usually easier and more efficient to rely on outside fund managers for this kind of strategy. Of course, if you know Ray Dalio then you should just reach out to him about this. Tell him I'd like to talk to him while you're at it. He's not currently accepting my phone calls.

Here are some existing funds that implement Risk Parity strategies in a single wrapper:

- SPDR Bridgewater All Weather ETF (ticker: ALLW)
- RPAR Risk Parity ETF (ticker: RPAR)
- AQR Multi-Asset Fund (ticker: AQRIX)

It's worth noting that Dalio mentioned a simplified version of this strategy in a popular book several years ago. The allocation he recommended was as follows:

- 30% US stocks
- 40% Long-term Treasury bonds
- 15% Intermediate-term Treasury bonds
- 7.5% Commodities
- 7.5% Gold

I was surprised he recommended this as an alternative to Risk Parity given that it's not true to the methodology he's referred to in the past. After all, there's no real parity in this portfolio, especially when you consider that long-term T-bonds are a very high-volatility instrument that oftentimes undergo significant periods of negative real drawdowns.

There certainly hasn't been parity in Dalio's simplified portfolio so I'd defer towards the AQR fund and the actual Bridgewater ETF when considering a pure play on this strategy. Therefore, I will ignore Dalio's simplified portfolio for the sake of this analysis and instead focus on other real-time versions of the strategy that more fully reflect the actual approach.

CHAPTER 8

RISK PARITY PORTFOLIO ANALYSIS

The Bridgewater ETF is very new and hard to analyze because of its infancy, but that's obviously the most logical way to approach this. That said, the other publicly available versions of the Risk Parity Portfolio haven't performed all that well in their relatively short histories. But let's peel back the onion because this one deserves a fair shake.

Over the last 15 years, the AQR Multi-Asset fund has generated annual returns of 3.27% compared to 6.93% for the global stock market, as seen in Table 8.1. Of course, we're comparing a multi-asset fund to a stock fund so this isn't an apples-to-apples comparison. But it is interesting that the risk-adjusted returns are similar across time. While the AQR fund generated a Sharpe ratio of 0.58, the global stock market generated a Sharpe ratio of 0.56. And the AQR fund had just a 31% market correlation over this period.

When compared to a global 60/40 Portfolio, the Risk Parity strategy generates 3.27% versus 4.37% annual returns, with volatility of 9.02% versus 10.40%.

Figure 8.4: Risk Parity performance

Table 8.1: Portfolio analysis

	RP	Global 60/40
Real Returns	3.27%	4.37%
Volatility	9.02%	10.40%
Sharpe Ratio	0.55	0.59
Sortino Ratio	0.75	0.82
Max Drawdown	−24.11%	−23.73%
Ulcer Index	8.97	7.00
Market Correlation	0.31	0.55

The data in Figure 8.5 also shows smaller drawdowns, comparable risk-adjusted returns, and a significantly lower market correlation for the Risk Parity Portfolio compared to the global 60/40 Portfolio.

Figure 8.5: Risk Parity drawdowns (%)

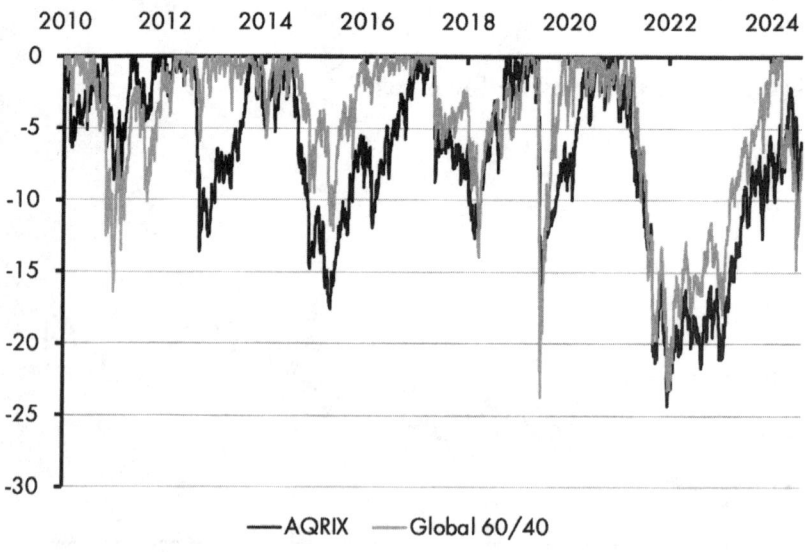

This data is more interesting under the surface than it might appear at first glance. While the performance hasn't been outstanding, there is a reasonable argument that the Risk Parity strategy creates a unique diversifier in a portfolio that could complement other more aggressive holdings like strictly equities.

Let's get into the pros and cons.

RISK PARITY PORTFOLIO PROS, CONS, AND LESSONS

As usual, let's get the good news and bad news out of the way. First the bad news:

1. It could be difficult to create your own Risk Parity strategy. This means you might have to rely on higher-fee ETFs or funds to replicate this approach.
2. The strategy is likely to experience periods of "diworsification" because it holds so many uncorrelated assets, which can lead to significant return drag – especially when the portfolio leans heavily on non-cash-flow-generating assets like commodities. Without a sophisticated process for assessing risk and return, these portfolios often become so diversified that they produce more stable, but ultimately lower, returns. Real-world evidence seems to support this outcome. Further, the portfolio requires significant turnover and trading. Many instruments in the portfolio could incur high taxes, fees, and leverage costs as a result.
3. If you use a fund structure, you're ultimately relying on the manager's estimates to navigate returns and assess the relative risk of each asset class. If they adjust those risk assumptions based on expected market conditions, the strategy introduces a significant layer of forecasting risk.

4. Leverage creates its own unique risks and embedded costs that can magnify any forecasting errors within the particular Risk Parity methodology.
5. There's a strong argument to be made that these funds are excessively expensive compared to alternative options and that their extra costs don't outweigh the potential benefits. For example, the new Bridgewater ETF costs 0.85%, which is quite high for a diversified ETF.

What about the good news?

1. The Risk Parity Portfolio is extremely diverse and easy to maintain in a single fund structure. Given its very low correlation to the broader stock market it could serve as its own diversifier.
2. This portfolio gives you the potential for superior risk-adjusted returns.
3. The focus on Risk Parity typically results in lower average volatility, and has the potential for smaller drawdowns and more stable returns over time.

SUITORS FOR THE RISK PARITY PORTFOLIO

I'd argue that the Risk Parity Portfolio is best used as a slice of a broader diversified portfolio. It's unlikely to outperform stocks over the long run, but it might outperform a traditional 60/40 mix – so it could make sense as a replacement for that portion of your allocation.

This strategy is better suited for investors who either have the expertise to build it themselves or trust someone else to do it well. I would say it's for the more experienced and adventurous investor who understands the challenges involved and believes those trade-offs are worth it compared to something simpler, like a 60/40 Portfolio.

CHAPTER 8

FINAL THOUGHTS

A portfolio designed to achieve true balance makes a lot of sense. But maintaining asset class parity requires predicting risks and returns, which means the portfolio has to be actively managed – and that involves a fair amount of guesswork.

But what if you could take a similar all-weather approach but implement it with a simpler, more permanent strategy you could set and forget? If you were clever you might call it the Permanent Portfolio. And you guessed it – it's up next.

9

THE PERMANENT PORTFOLIO

RAY DALIO wasn't the only investor whose views were transformed by the Nixon Shock. Around this time, an investment advisor named Harry Browne began advocating for broad diversification beyond equities and fixed income to combat what he believed would be a period of widespread currency devaluation due to reckless government intervention in the economy.

While Dalio concluded that he needed more balance across his portfolios, Browne advocated for a portfolio that was "fail safe."

Harry Browne was a Libertarian and was one of the party's most vocal advocates for many decades. During this time, he used his financial expertise and skepticism of government to advocate for "fail-safe investing." Browne's theory was that investors needed broad diversification to protect them from all types of potential economic outcomes.

While Risk Parity tries to create balance across the risks inherent in the specific instruments you hold, the fail-safe approach focuses on balancing risk across economic environments. Browne's general thinking was that the economy cycles through four consistent types of environments, expansion, recession, inflation, and deflation, as seen in Figure 9.1:

Figure 9.1: The four quadrants of the economic cycle

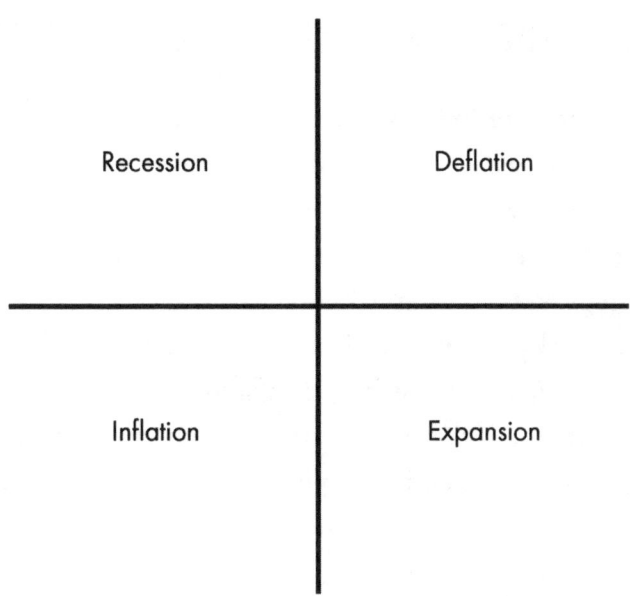

Browne argued that you can protect against these environments using four simple instruments that provide permanent protection if held for the long run:

1. Stocks protect you in an expansion.
2. Cash protects you in a recession.
3. Gold protects you in an inflation.
4. US government bonds protect you in a deflation.

This portfolio has some similarities to the Dalio methodology, but it's far simpler under the hood. You don't need to measure the expected volatility of assets or rebalance them based on volatility contribution and environment. You just need to hold four equal slices of four assets across all time horizons. But does this work and why?

Let's dig deeper.

WHY THE PERMANENT PORTFOLIO WORKS

The Permanent Portfolio is a clever concept that allocates assets to specific buckets to help insulate you from specific economic environments. The reason the portfolio works is because the economy is consistently turbulent. Expansion, recession, inflation, and deflation are recurring conditions throughout history.

A more in-depth analysis of economic cycles reveals something interesting though. Expansion and inflation are far more common than recession and deflation, but recession and deflation have significant asymmetric impacts on our financial lives. In other words, while economic expansion and inflation are the norm, recession and deflation have acute and devasting consequences when they do occur.

You might think of recession or deflation protection as being similar to insurance. You don't buy life insurance because you expect to die tomorrow. You buy life insurance because death, while unlikely at any given time, would have devastating financial consequences for those who depend on you. Similarly, protecting your portfolio from rare but harmful economic shocks is about preparing for the unexpected, not predicting it.

Figure 9.2, which shows the year-over-year percentage change in GDP, illustrates that while the economy tends to grow steadily over the long term (as evidenced by mostly positive figures in the chart) short-term growth rates can be quite volatile.

Figure 9.2: Real GDP (YoY%)

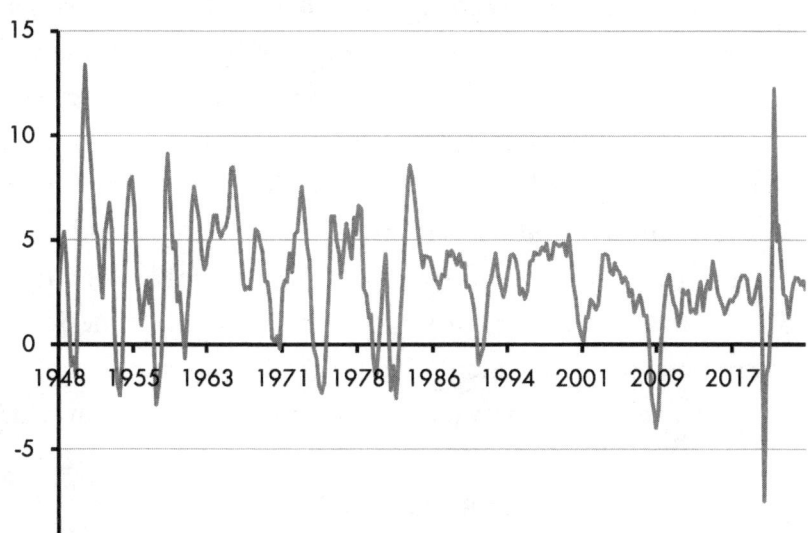

Over the long term, the economy can feel like a smooth upward ride. But in the short term, the economy often feels more turbulent as we cycle through periods of expansion and contraction.

Why do certain assets protect us in these specific environments though? Let's look at the four holdings of the Permanent Portfolio in turn.

1. **Stocks** tend to rise in the long run because corporate profits and earnings generally grow over time. This is your *expansion* allocation. As the economy does well, we should expect corporate profits to expand and value to accrue to stocks over time.
2. **Cash** (T-Bill and Chill) helps diversify a portfolio by adding a nominally stable income-generating asset to a portfolio. It protects against *recession* because it gives you nominal principal certainty when the world becomes uncertain.

3. **Gold** tends to rise in the long run because it is an industrial commodity used in many goods inputs. It is also viewed by many as a form of money and is therefore widely held by central banks and investors who view it as a monetary *inflation* hedge. This protects us from inflation because it's both viewed as a monetary alternative to fiat currencies and because it has embedded real economic utility.
4. **US government bonds** are similar to cash in that they add a safe income-generating diversifier with minimal credit risk. Long-term Treasury bonds are useful at times as they have a high degree of interest rate sensitivity and during a *deflation*, when interest rates are most likely to decline, they can appreciate significantly in value.

FUN SIDE NOTE

US government bonds are the ultimate safe haven because they're the instrument issued by the largest income-generating entity in human history, the US government. These bonds are ultimately supported by the income stream of US corporations and individual taxpayers. As long as the US government doesn't print so much money that it causes runaway inflation, the underlying productive capacity of the US private sector will continue to drive sufficient income to the US government, which makes its liabilities extremely safe, especially during deflationary shocks.

Importantly, as we touched on in Chapter 7, the US is likely to lose some of its *relative* reserve currency status in the coming 50 years, but for now this position is unmatched. If you want to say that all fiat currencies are dirty shirts then the US dollar is the cleanest dirty shirt by a large margin.

CHAPTER 9

So, the Permanent Portfolio isn't just based on sound economic reasoning, but there are sound fundamental reasons why the actual asset classes make sense as well.

BUILDING YOUR OWN PERMANENT PORTFOLIO

There's a well-known mutual fund that adheres to the principles of the Permanent Portfolio and adds a bit of extra diversification. You'll be shocked to learn that the fund is called the Permanent Portfolio Fund (ticker: PRPFX).

If you wanted to own a lower-fee version of this portfolio you could also construct it using low-cost ETFs. For example, you could adopt the pure Harry Browne allocation, as shown in Figure 9.3:

- 25% VT (Vanguard Total World) or VTI (Vanguard Total US Stocks)
- 25% BIL (SPDR T-Bill ETF)
- 25% IAU (iShares Gold ETF)
- 25% VGLT (Vanguard Long-Term T-Bond ETF)

Figure 9.3: The simple four-fund Permanent Portfolio

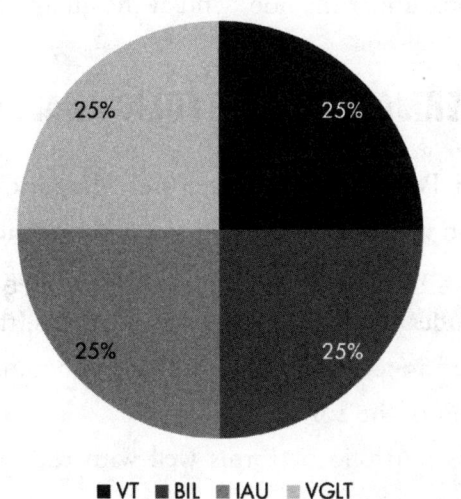

As it pertains to the four quadrants of risk, here's how that looks in Figure 9.4:

Figure 9.4: The four quadrants of the economic cycle with their corresponding assets

Risk: Recession Solution: Cash	Risk: Deflation Solution: US Government Bonds
Risk: Inflation Solution: Gold	Risk: Expansion Solution: Stocks

There it is. Nice and clean.

Now let's look under the hood and at the quant analysis.

PERMANENT PORTFOLIO ANALYSIS

The Permanent Portfolio analysis can only go back to 1970 because the price of gold was pegged in dollar terms before then. But even that historical view gives us a pretty good understanding of the portfolio because it includes the high inflation of the 1970s, the growth boom of the 1980s and 1990s, the tech and financial booms and busts, and the low inflation of the 2010s.

Overall, this portfolio performs well with real annual returns of

4.65% and volatility of 8.58%. Global equities returned 5.60% per year with 16.42% volatility over the same period. On a risk-adjusted basis, the Harry Browne Permanent Portfolio generates a 0.48 Sharpe and 0.93 Sortino ratio, good for a significant outperformance versus the broader global stock market, which had a Sharpe ratio of 0.37 and Sortino ratio of 0.52 over the same period.

It's worth noting that stocks aren't necessarily a fair benchmark here, but I am using them to reiterate just how strong the diversification is in the Permanent Portfolio. When compared to a global 60/40 Portfolio over the same period, the Permanent Portfolio looks even stronger with returns of 4.23% versus 4.51% for the 60/40 Portfolio, a Sharpe ratio of 0.52 versus 0.45, and Sortino ratio of 0.76 versus 0.63. So, this one beats global equities as well as a 60/40 mix on a risk-adjusted basis by a healthy margin.

Figure 9.5 shows a lower return, but much smoother ride across time for the Permanent Portfolio.

Figure 9.5: Permanent Portfolio performance

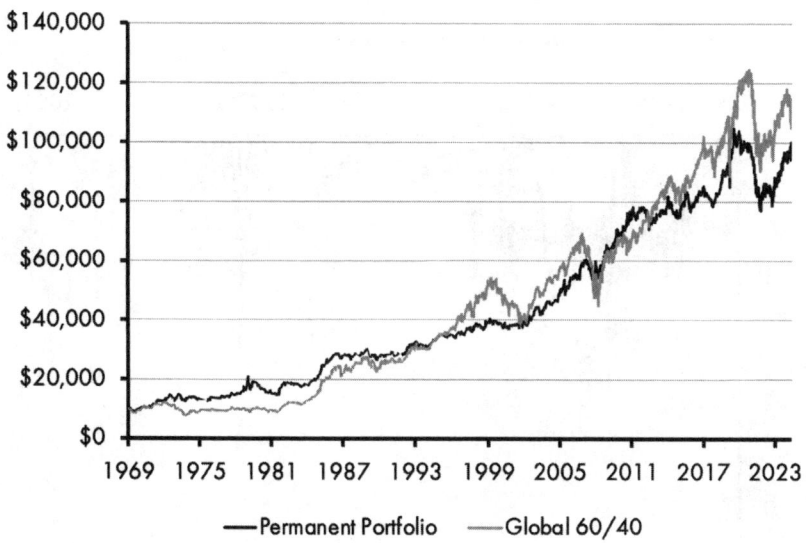

Table 9.1: Portfolio analysis

	PP	Global 60/40
Real Returns	4.23%	4.51%
Volatility	7.32%	9.64%
Sharpe Ratio	0.52	0.45
Sortino Ratio	0.76	0.63
Max Drawdown	−31.81%	−38.51%
Ulcer Index	8.26	12.33
Market Correlation	0.18	0.46

The portfolio's drawdowns are driven by extreme moves in stocks, gold, and T-bonds, but the inclusion of cash and its general diversification makes its drawdowns less severe on average than that of the global 60/40 Portfolio, as seen in Figure 9.6. The Ulcer Index of 8.26 is moderately high, but not as high as 60/40 on average. And with a correlation of just 0.18 you've got an asset allocation that will consistently look different from your traditional 60/40 or pure stock portfolio.

Figure 9.6: Permanent Portfolio drawdowns (%)

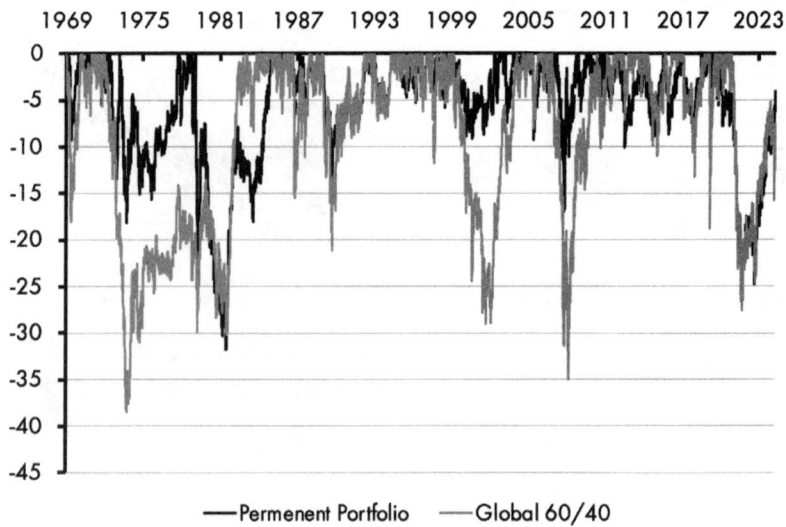

CHAPTER 9

PERMANENT PORTFOLIO PROS AND CONS

This one's interesting, huh? There's a logic to the underlying portfolio theory that is intriguing, and you don't get bogged down in some of the complexities of other all-weather approaches. The risk-adjusted outperformance is especially interesting given the simplicity of the allocation and the uncorrelated returns.

But what about the pros and the cons? Let's take a closer look. First, the bad news:

1. There's something elegant about the simplicity of the four-quadrant approach and its straightforward 25% allocations. But its basic approach might strike some investors as being *too* simplistic.
2. The insurance components in this portfolio could be overkill. For example, while recessions can be devastating, they are also somewhat rare as evidenced by the fact that the US economy has been expanding 82% of the time over the last 50 years (see Figure 9.7 below). Recessions are not the norm. Deflationary recessions are even more unusual, and we've only experienced one meaningful deflationary recession (the GFC) in the last 50 years.

Figure 9.7: US economic recessions

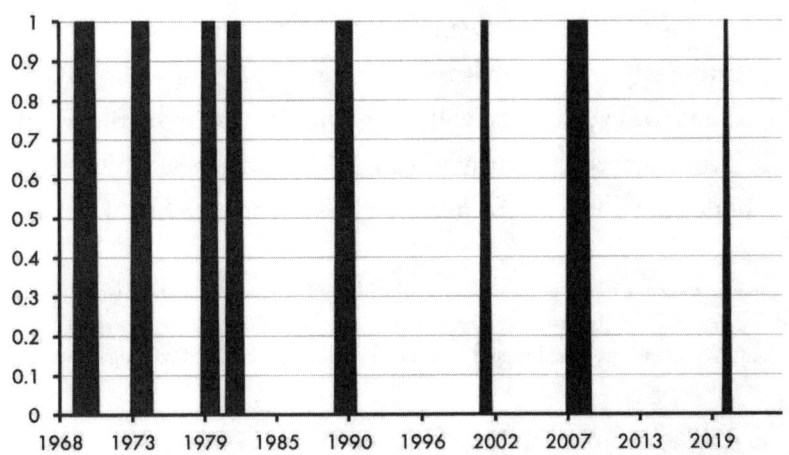

3. The most glaring weakness of the Permanent Portfolio is the small equity allocation of just 25%. You can argue that most investors should have a larger stock allocation since equities are likely to be among the highest expected return instruments we can own.

4. While gold has industrial uses that make it a relatively good inflation hedge, much of its value rests on the belief that it will continue to serve as a monetary hedge. I often note that gold has an embedded "faith put" in its price. That is, people buy it because they believe it's the ultimate form of sound money. But what if that perception changed? What if, for instance, Bitcoin completely replaced gold as the go-to store of value? In that scenario, gold might behave more like a typical commodity and lose much of its demand as a hedge against fiat currency. Is that likely? I don't know. But it's difficult to argue that this perception will persist forever based on hard evidence alone. As often noted, much of gold's monetary role depends on the assumption that because it's been seen as money in the past, it always will be.*

5. The portfolio's cash allocation is large and subject to persistent 0% or negative real return over time. Don't get me wrong – I like having a T-Bill and Chill component in a portfolio. But how much chilling does a person really need? A 25% cash allocation might be a bit too much relaxation.

6. The T-bond position is the highest duration bond instrument most investors will own. It will not beat cash by a large margin across most market cycles, but it will be significantly more volatile. Further, deflations are exceptionally unusual although generally devastating. T-bonds are an excellent hedge against deflation, but if deflation

---

* Larry Summers wrote a good paper in 1985 discussing gold and Gibson's paradox, and gold's tendency to correlate with real interest rates over time. Robert B. Barsky and Lawrence H. Summers, "Gibson's Paradox and The Gold Standard," NBER Working Paper Series (August 1985).

only occurs 1–5% of the time, does it really make sense to maintain a permanent 25% allocation as insurance for that scenario? Color me skeptical.

Alright, let's not be so critical. What about the pros?

1. The portfolio is diversified and can be implemented in a simple, low-cost and tax-efficient manner.
2. The portfolio is likely to be a good behavioral hedge as the allocation rationale is logical and intuitive.
3. This is a true one-stop-shop portfolio. It has bits of insurance, growth and liquidity. You can argue with the specific allocations and weightings, but it does meet almost all the needs an asset allocator might have over time. In theory, these four allocations could be enough to comprise an entire portfolio.

SUITORS FOR THE PERMANENT PORTFOLIO

This portfolio is best suited for investors who want the benefits of broad, multi-asset diversification in a simple, easy-to-follow structure.

To stick with it, you need to have an unwavering faith in gold as an asset class. And you also need to understand that the small equity component could leave you underexposed to cash-flow-generating, inflation-hedged instruments. Oh, and you need to be really comfortable with long-term US Treasury bonds, which have historically performed as a low return and very high volatility instrument.

As Harry Browne envisioned, this portfolio embraces a fail-safe approach – one that likely prioritizes downside protection more than most investors typically need. This is, in some ways, a doomsday bunker portfolio that has such a large insurance component that you are happy forgoing significant growth because you have a more resilient portfolio during downturns.

Perhaps most importantly, you need to really buy into the permanency of the allocation. These are volatile assets that won't always be exposed to the environments you're using them to protect you against. You cannot expect them all to be operating well at the same time. And that's the point. This portfolio works precisely because its four parts behave differently. To benefit, you need to be exceptionally patient and committed to its long-term strategy.

FINAL THOUGHTS

A Permanent Portfolio for all seasons sounds nice.

But what if you wanted something a little more customized for a situation that requires a high level of liquidity with the potential for high growth? You might want a portfolio that is not quite so permanent, but specifically structured across two distinctly different time horizons.

Well, let me introduce you to the Flying Ladder Portfolio. It has an awesome name which is derived from an even better story and we all know that your portfolio needs to have a cool name, so keep reading.

10

THE FLYING LADDER STRATEGY

ON December 15, 1968, Second Lieutenant John Slater found his US Marine Force Recon team surrounded by Vietnamese soldiers. The recon team had been on the ground no more than 48 hours before being compromised and in desperate need of extraction.

Given the challenging terrain of the Vietnamese jungle, the team required a helicopter extraction using a device known as the "Jungle Penetrator." The Jungle Penetrator was lowered from a helicopter on a winch and unfolded into a seat designed to fit a single person that could be hoisted up to safety.

The winch itself was only strong enough to hoist two men at most, but Captain Larry Adams was determined to save all seven men on the ground. The CH-46 helicopter made two trips under heavy fire, successfully extracting four men. As it returned for a third trip, Marine UH-1 Hueys provided cover, unleashing heavy fire on the enemy forces surrounding the recon team. Still, enemy troops were closing in dangerously on the remaining three Marines. The three men would have to board the Jungle Penetrator all at once, as the risk of a fourth trip was too high. As the helicopter lifted off, the winch struggled under the weight and was unable to reel the men into the aircraft, leaving them dangling beneath the chopper as it climbed hundreds of feet into the air. Captain Adams attempted to divert to a nearby sandbar several miles away for an emergency landing, but during the flight, one of the Marines lost his grip and tragically fell to his death.

After the failed extraction, Major Roger Simmons, Commanding Officer of First Force Recon, sought help from the army's elite Studies and Observations Group to find an alternative to the Jungle Penetrator that could improve the efficiency of the extractions. One of the solutions he devised was a giant swinging ladder that could hold an entire recon team. The Simmons Rig, as it would come to be known, was never approved for official use, but came to be known as the "lifesaver from the sky" after the ladder was used in a pinch to extract eight stranded Marines in January 1969.[24]

The Flying Ladder Strategy, as I've named it, is not nearly the heroic device that was used in Vietnam, but I've used it increasingly to help save retirement plans.

Here's how it works.

HOW THE FLYING LADDER STRATEGY WORKS

The Flying Ladder Strategy is what it sounds like – a bond ladder that's attached to a flying equity component. This operates much like a barbelled strategy where the bond and equity components serve distinctly different roles to help provide both principal stability and growth in one clean portfolio. It's called a barbell because the structure resembles an actual barbell with your holdings concentrated at the two extremes of the liquidity spectrum with little or nothing in between.*

I'd argue the Flying Ladder Strategy is best for someone who wants

---

* Barbells are also great for leg day.

the structure and stability of predictable cash flows from the ladder component, while still having a need or desire for long-term growth.

While something like the Buffett Portfolio is specifically geared towards growth, the Flying Ladder is designed to create a very stable income-generating bond ladder with an aggressively barbelled growth/flying component to help generate high returns that can help enhance the future funding of the ladder's income.

Let's dig into each component in more detail.

The bond ladder

A bond ladder is a structured portfolio of bonds with staggered maturities, designed to help investors diversify their exposure across different time horizons, or "rungs" of the ladder.

For example, a 10-rung bond ladder might involve purchasing 10 bonds with maturities ranging from one to 10 years. As each bond matures, you "climb" the ladder by reinvesting the proceeds into a new 10-year bond, effectively rolling the ladder forward. When the one-year bond matures, the existing rungs shift down, and you add a new tenth rung. This ongoing process helps maintain a consistently rotating fixed income portfolio unlike holding a single duration bond, which gradually shortens in maturity and increases reinvestment risk over time.

Bond ladders help create consistent income, near-term certainty and constant maturity, thereby helping you plan for short-term liability needs across time while remaining diversified out across longer time horizons. They have an advantage over alternatives such as constant maturity aggregate bond funds because they're disaggregated, providing you with liquidity access and avoiding homogeneous asset class risk that I discussed before.

The equity allocation

Within the Flying Ladder Strategy, the ladder is a constant feature. But it flies because you attach that ladder to a more aggressive equity allocation that helps generate higher growth. This gives the ladder the potential for more sustainability by helping the entire portfolio ascend higher over time.

The optimal way to implement the helicopter is to allocate this part of the portfolio to aggressive high-growth equities that help this component achieve a high rate of ascent. One idea here is to take the Forward Cap Portfolio or factor tilts and mix them with a custom bond ladder.

This strategy works by providing strong principal stability and consistent income through the ladder component, while also isolating the stock allocation in a way that allows for meaningful growth alongside the fixed income holdings.

By compartmentalizing the assets in a systematic ladder and segmented growth component, the investor can remain more comfortable with their aggressive equity allocation knowing that their near-term fixed income needs are taken care of.

BUILDING YOUR OWN FLYING LADDER STRATEGY

As discussed above, this portfolio has two barbelled components – the bond ladder and flying equity piece.

The bond ladder can be customized as needed, but I'll outline an easy way in which this can be done. For example, if you wanted to have a bond ladder with an average maturity of five years to meet income needs across 10 years, you would need to construct a 10-rung bond ladder. This could be done by buying 10 individual US government

T-bills and T-notes as outlined below. For the equity piece we want to construct an aggressive equity allocation with a diversified stock position that tilts to higher-risk growth.

For this case study we're going to use an example of a retiree who is 70 years old with a $1,000,000 portfolio who wants a steady stream of stable income of $25,000+ per year to supplement their Social Security income of $25,000 per year. If we assume an average interest rate of 4% the investor can achieve this by allocating 70% of their portfolio to the bond ladder and 30% of their portfolio to stocks.

As depicted in Figure 10.1, here's how this might look:

$700,000 or 70% fixed income:
- 1 Year T-bill at 3.5% interest: $70,000 or a 7% allocation
- 2 Year T-note at 3.6%: $70,000 or 7%
- 3 Year T-note at 3.7%: $70,000 or 7%
- 4 Year T-note at 3.8%: $70,000 or 7%
- 5 Year T-note at 3.9%: $70,000 or 7%
- 6 Year T-note at 4.0%: $70,000 or 7%
- 7 Year T-note at 4.1%: $70,000 or 7%
- 8 Year T-note at 4.2%: $70,000 or 7%
- 9 Year T-note at 4.3%: $70,000 or 7%
- 10 Year T-note at 4.4%: $70,000 or 7%

While you could spice up your Flying component with something like the Forward Cap Portfolio, I am going to keep our equity piece nice and simple for illustrative purposes. Let's use a domestic and foreign stock holding at global market cap weight with a tilt towards more aggressive growth-oriented positions.

This might look like this:

$300,000 or 30% equities:
- Vanguard Total US Stocks (ticker: VTI): $60,000 or 6%
- Vanguard Foreign Ex-US (ticker: VXUS): $60,000 or 6%
- Vanguard Technology (ticker: VGT): $60,000 or 6%
- Vanguard Small Cap Growth (ticker: VBK): $60,000 or 6%
- Vanguard Emerging Markets (ticker: VWO): $60,000 or 6%

Figure 10.1: The Flying Ladder Portfolio

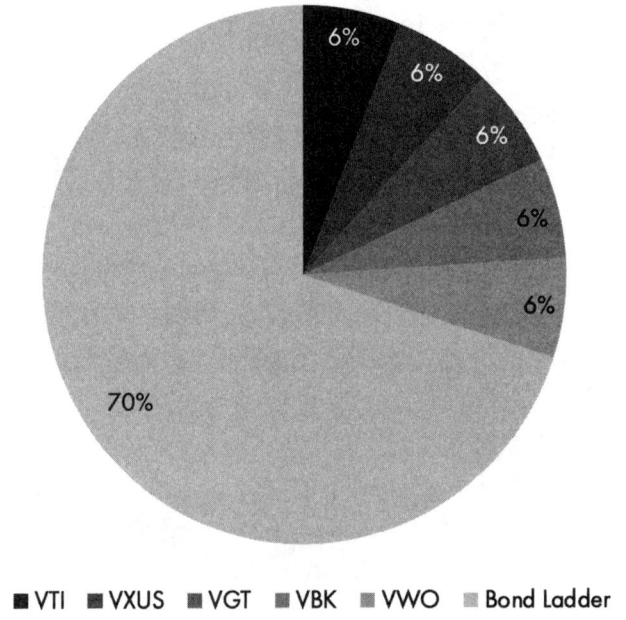

This gives the investor a secure and reliable income laddered over 10 years that provides approximately $28,000 of annual bond income as well as an aggressive growth component that will hopefully help fund further spending as the investor ages.

CHAPTER 10

FLYING LADDER STRATEGY ANALYSIS

This portfolio allows for flexible implementation based on individual needs, and its performance will vary significantly depending on how heavily you weight the ladder component versus how aggressively you position the growth side – the higher you want your "chopper" to fly. These tilts will push the portfolio's behavior closer to that of a higher-risk equity allocation or a more conservative bond ladder, depending on the balance you choose.

For our example above, which is relatively conservative given the large ladder allocation, we're looking at something that's very stable and relatively low-return. As shown in Figure 10.2, since 1995, this allocation would have generated about 4.21% annual returns with 6.09% volatility. The Ulcer Index, at 7.35, is very bond-like, but the equity slice helps it "fly" away from something like a pure bond portfolio.

Figure 10.2: Flying Ladder Portfolio performance

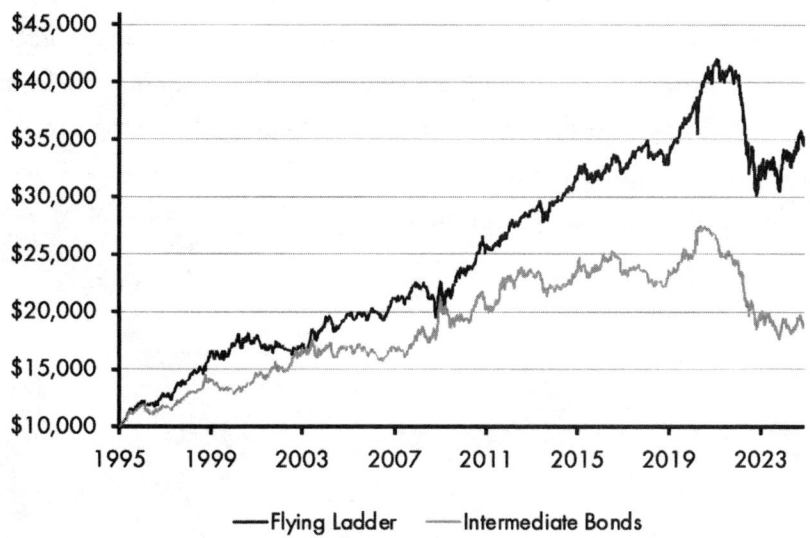

Table 10.1: Portfolio analysis

	Flying Ladder	Global Stocks	Intermediate Bonds
Real Returns	4.21%	5.57%	2.11%
Volatility	6.09%	18.44%	6.66%
Sharpe Ratio	0.74	0.40	0.37
Sortino Ratio	1.06	0.55	0.53
Max Drawdown	−28.28%	−58.88%	−35.95%
Ulcer Index	7.35	18.58	11.11
Market Correlation	0.19	0.88	-0.08

Looking at the strategy's max drawdowns (Figure 10.3) we see that with the exception of the Covid era, they tend to be relatively shallow, as expected. The low Ulcer Index shows us that these downturns tend to be highly tolerable given that they tend not to last too long. Keep in mind that the heavy allocation to bonds in our example, combined with the uniqueness of Covid, and the Fed lifting rates quickly from 0% to 5%, makes the drawdown look worse than it is likely to be in the future. And even during the Covid era the Flying Ladder experiences shallower drawdowns than a pure bond portfolio.

Figure 10.3: Flying Ladder Portfolio max drawdowns (%)

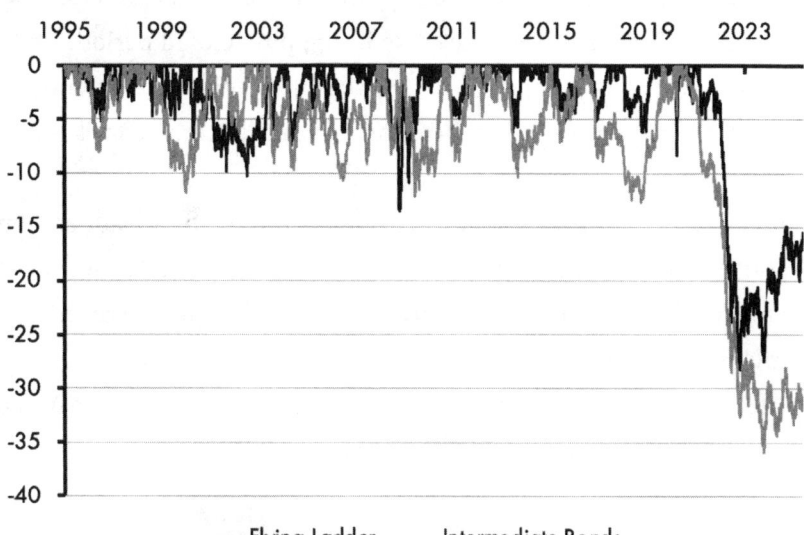

The equity piece alone does a nice job of flying here as it would have generated 6.80% per year as a standalone component, compared to 5.57% for the global stock market, with similar risk characteristics. Remember, we want an aggressive equity slice on its own, that hopefully outperforms broader stocks due to its more aggressive tilts, combined with the much more conservative bond allocation.

FLYING LADDER STRATEGY PROS AND CONS

What is good and bad about this portfolio? Bad news first:

1. Barbell portfolios aren't traditionally diversified across a broad range of asset classes – they're concentrated at the extremes. This structure offers diversification across risk profiles and time horizons, but not across asset types in the traditional sense. The

narrow positioning can expose investors to behavioral challenges – especially during periods of equity volatility or bond market shocks, like the inflation-driven rate spike in the post-Covid period.
2. This portfolio is comprised of only equities and fixed income, so you will face the risk that these instruments become correlated in the short term.
3. If you're living off the income generated from the bond ladder then you will have withdrawal risk if your ladder gets smaller over time and needs to be funded in future years with equity returns that might not be reliable.
4. The bond ladder requires ongoing attention, which may be overwhelming or impractical for some investors.

What about the good news?

1. This portfolio is diversified, low-fee, and tax efficient. It can be implemented in a simplistic manner.
2. The portfolio gives you a high degree of temporal certainty since the ladder is specifically designed to meet liquidity needs over a customizable time horizon.
3. The portfolio has a cool name with a cooler origin story. Just imagine yourself at a BBQ with your friends and someone asks you how you allocate your assets: "Oh, I use the Flying Ladder Strategy, it's a barbelled bond ladder with an aggressive equity tilt." You'll be the coolest guy at the party.

SUITORS FOR THE FLYING LADDER STRATEGY

The Flying Ladder Strategy is good for people who need reliable near-term principal stability and income, but also want a growth component in their portfolio to help make the bond ladder more viable in the long run. The ladder is the key component of this portfolio because it's the part that makes it the most useful. After all, you're not getting rescued from the market jungle without the ladder.

This portfolio could be especially helpful for retirees and others who are entering periods of near-term uncertainty. For the retiree who considers this portfolio you'd want to be someone who has a higher risk tolerance because the flying component will test your behavior at times. It could also be appropriate for a more aggressive investor who inverts the example above and creates a very aggressive equity allocation with a systematically structured bond ladder to serve as their bond portfolio.

This portfolio is flexible and can be customized, so it's not constrained to only doing retirement rescues, even if that's its best use case.

FINAL THOUGHTS

Well, there's your Flying Ladder. It might not help you survive the jungles of Vietnam, but it might just save you in a financial pinch by creating some much-needed structure and stability.

Speaking of aviation heroes – let's talk about a man named Taylor Larimore and how he went from jumping out of planes at the Battle of the Bulge to helping construct one of the most influential portfolios in investing history.

11

THE BOGLEHEAD THREE-FUND PORTFOLIO

As a former manager of the Wellington Fund and founder of Vanguard, John Bogle became one of the most influential people in modern finance. His focus on low costs and simplicity shook the industry to its core and revolutionized the way people allocate their assets.

Bogle was always an advocate for the small investor and championed the mutual fund company structure that helped democratize modern investment products. His influence inspired a well-deserved, cult-like group of followers known as the Bogleheads.

Perhaps the best known Boglehead is a man named Taylor Larimore, whom Bogle referred to as the "king of the Bogleheads." Larimore was a paratrooper in the 101st Airborne Division during the Battle of the Bulge in World War 2 and would go on to become a life insurance underwriter and chief of the financial division for the Small Business Administration in South Florida.

CHAPTER 11

Larimore became enamored with Bogle's work in the 1980s. He told me he was living in Miami at the time, and his wife, Patricia, was the highest-paid model in the city. For the first time in his life, he had what he considered a significant amount of money and began to question whether his Wall Street stockbroker was truly acting in his and his wife's best interest.

Around this time, he began obsessively reading about investments, the structure of mutual funds and especially low-cost index funds. Bogle's book *Bogle on Mutual Funds* completely changed Larimore's investment philosophy and convinced him that his broker was more interested in fees than investor returns.

Larimore spent much of the next four decades getting to know Bogle personally and working with him to bring these complex topics to the average investor. Larimore has become an expert in his own right and the famous Boglehead Forum, which Larimore has moderated for decades, is now one of the most informative and populated investment roundtables in the world.

In 1999, Larimore created a basic global allocation using four funds: a US stock fund, a foreign stock fund, an aggregate bond index, and a cash component. As interest rates declined and the value of a separate cash allocation diminished, he eventually reduced the portfolio to three funds. The result was a beautifully simple, low-cost, and broadly diversified portfolio that checked all the boxes of the Bogle investment philosophy. In fact, the idea was so elegant in its simplicity that it has become a widely adopted approach for DIY investors following a Boglehead approach.

BUILDING YOUR OWN BOGLEHEAD THREE-FUND PORTFOLIO

As you can probably guess, this one's pretty easy to construct. It is, as its name suggests, comprised of just three simple funds.

Larimore advocates taking three funds and allocating them across stocks and bonds in a proportion that is consistent with the investor's risk profile. The stock sleeve could be comprised of two funds that hold the global market cap of stocks and the bond piece should be a simple, low-cost total bond market fund. Larimore tends to prefer an overweight US stock position, but I am using an equal weight allocation for the sake of simplicity.

Figure 11.1: How the Boglehead Three-Fund Portfolio might look

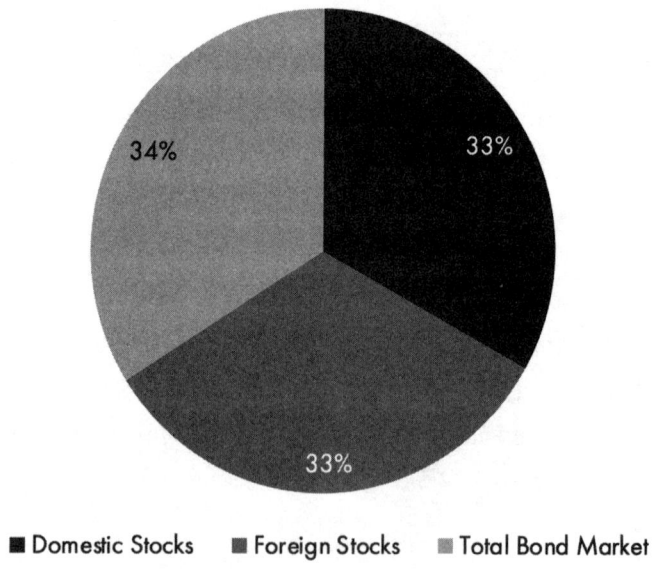

Doesn't get much cleaner than that.

In terms of specific funds, you can apply this with just three holdings – Vanguard funds, of course:

- 34% Total Bond Market (ticker: BND)
- 33% Total US Stocks (ticker: VTI)
- 33% Total Ex-US Stocks (ticker: VXUS)

Figure 11.2: Boglehead Three-Fund Portfolio

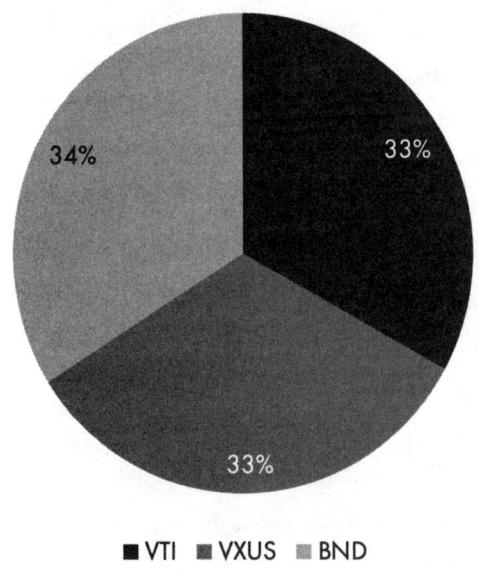

WHY THE BOGLEHEAD THREE-FUND PORTFOLIO WORKS

The Boglehead Three-Fund Portfolio is beautifully effortless while also being broadly diversified across low-cost fund options. Christine Benz, the Director of Personal Finance at *Morningstar*, has described the Three-Fund Portfolio as "the ultimate in elegant minimalism."[25]

The strategy works in large part because it's very close to the efficient market portfolio, the GFAP. It is a hugely diverse portfolio despite being such a simple structure. In Larimore's *own words*, he thinks this is the optimal portfolio for the following 21 reasons:

1. Avoids wasted time and the possibility of mistakes trying to pick the best of thousands of mutual funds and ETFs.
2. No individual stock risk.
3. Highest return with lowest risk.
4. Very diversified with over 20,000 worldwide securities (lower risk).
5. Very low expense ratios.
6. Very low (hidden) turnover costs.
7. Very tax efficient.
8. The many advantages of simplicity.
9. No advisor risk.
10. No fund manager risk.
11. No style drift.
12. No asset bloat.
13. No tracking error to cause abandonment of the strategy.
14. No fund overlap.
15. No front-running that reduces sub-index returns.
16. Automatic rebalancing within each fund.
17. No need for a portfolio tracking program.
18. Less worry. Never underperforms the market.
19. Easy to maintain for the owner, spouse, caregivers, and heirs.
20. More free time.
21. Mathematically certain to outperform most investors.[26]

There's not too much to analyze, but we'll run the numbers as always.

CHAPTER 11

THE BOGLEHEAD THREE-FUND PORTFOLIO ANALYSIS

This portfolio is not terribly complex and can be customized around an investor's particular risk profile, but Figure 11.3 and Table 11.1 demonstrate how the figures look assuming we used a simple three-fund allocation with 66% stocks and 34% bonds.

Figure 11.3: Three-Fund Portfolio performance

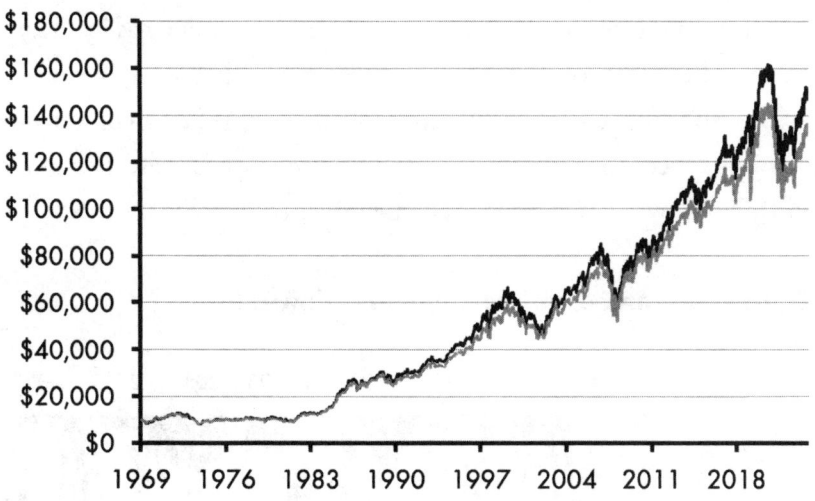

Table 11.1: Portfolio analysis

	Three-Fund	Global 60/40
Real Returns	5.02%	4.80%
Volatility	10.30%	9.75%
Sharpe Ratio	0.47	0.47
Sortino Ratio	0.67	0.67
Max Drawdown	-39.74%	-37.65%
Ulcer Index	12.77	11.79
Market Correlation	0.51	0.47

Given its simplicity, the performance is better than you might expect. Over the period from 1970 to present, the Boglehead Three-Fund Portfolio would have generated 5.02% annual returns with 10.30% volatility, while the global 60/40 Portfolio generated 4.80% annually with 9.75% volatility.

On a risk-adjusted basis, the Boglehead Three-Fund Portfolio looks surprisingly good. The global 60/40 Portfolio and the Three-Fund Portfolio generated the same risk-adjusted return over the period, with a Sharpe ratio of 0.47 and Sortino ratio of 0.67. Further, the Ulcer Index for the Boglehead Three-Fund Portfolio was just 12.77, compared to 11.79 for the global stock market, only modestly worse.

This isn't just a basic and low-stress portfolio based on maintenance and implementation needs. It has also been a relatively low-stress portfolio to own based on its drawdowns, as seen in Figure 11.4.

Figure 11.4: Three-Fund Portfolio drawdowns (%)

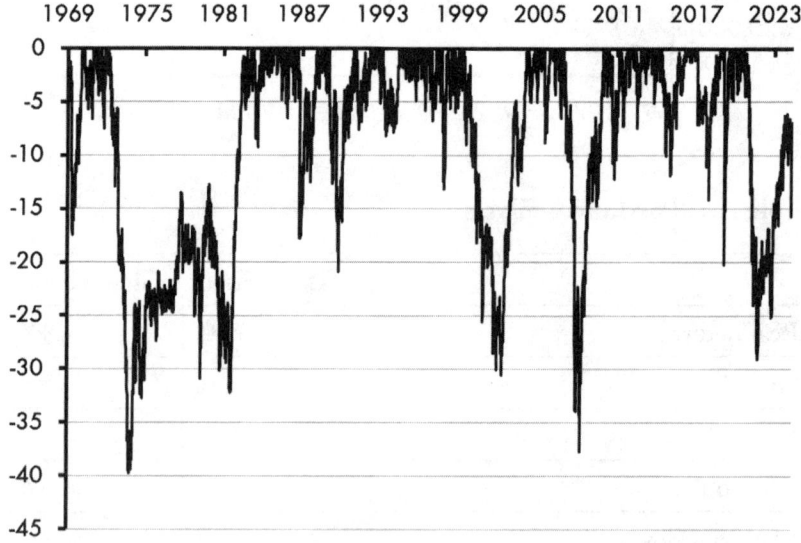

CHAPTER 11

THE BOGLEHEAD THREE-FUND PORTFOLIO PROS AND CONS

This one might be simple, but that doesn't mean its pros and cons are. First the bad news:

1. This portfolio is arguably too simple, which we'll dig into below.
2. Because of its simplicity the portfolio will not always be diversified given it is only comprised of stocks and bonds.
3. Three funds could create some behavioral hurdles. There's a certain discomfort in owning just a handful of funds. I am generally a believer in the idea that less is more, but that is not always true in asset management. One fund, for instance, is not usually sufficient for many reasons we've already discussed. Three funds might also not be enough depending on certain circumstances. There is a fine line in asset management between avoiding excessive complexity and creating just the right amount of sophistication to meet your financial needs.
4. You likely need a fourth allocation here to provide for cash and emergency reserves. The aggregate bond component has a duration of six years and an average effective maturity of 8.4 years, which exposes it to meaningful interest rate and principal risk in the short term. An aggregate bond fund alone is not a sufficient source of liquidity.

Now the good news:

1. You read 21 pros directly from Larimore. I'll spare you the rinse-and-repeat.

SUITORS FOR THE BOGLEHEAD THREE-FUND PORTFOLIO

The Boglehead Three-Fund Portfolio is especially good for people who want simplicity and ultra-low costs. There's nothing fancy going on here so this won't be intriguing to someone who likes more bells and whistles, or wants to shoot for the moon. The portfolio also has a moderately long time horizon given that it has no cash component. This simple portfolio is best for patient people who know not to tinker with it and who want to adhere to a more "passive" methodology.

FINAL THOUGHTS

Well, that's about as straightforward as it gets. But we all know that the world is a complex place and with all the behavioral biases we're confronted with we might require some embedded guardrails to help navigate the roller-coaster ride of the financial markets.

What if we could take the principles of John Bogle and apply them in a behaviorally robust "stay the course" portfolio that took more of a contrarian view on things?

The Countercyclical Rebalancing Portfolio is up next and it's about as pure a play on behavior as you're going to find.

12

THE COUNTERCYCLICAL REBALANCING PORTFOLIO

IN a 2018 interview John Bogle, the father of passive indexing, described how he managed his own investments in an *active* manner at times:

> We seem to come down to, for most investors, an idea that something like 65% stocks, 35% bonds is an intelligent allocation. Now, we know stocks are almost certain to do better in the long run just because of the nature of the capital markets, and so we said we want to do something to give us a little, you know, anchor to windward, dry powder, call it what you will, to protect you against behavioral mistakes and to give you some stability in your account and usually more income, although not much more today.
>
> So if it's 65/35 and for whatever sound, unemotional reason you can come up with, and the market looks substantially

overvalued, don't worry about if it gets 20% overvalued or 25% overvalued or undervalued by the same amount. But if it seems to get out of line by a substantial amount, take the 65 to 50. Take the 35 to 50 and be 50/50. But the idea of an all-or-nothing approach, 'Well, I sold all my stocks yesterday.' *eyeroll* You're going to have a long, hard investment lifetime. Who can do that?[27]

While Bogle was a strong advocate for simplicity and low-cost investing, he wasn't dogmatic about maintaining zero activity in a portfolio. He wasn't an efficient market purist and recognized the importance of behavioral finance in financial planning. His commitment to low-cost investing was balanced by his philosophy of "staying the course." He understood that some level of activity – such as rebalancing – could help investors remain comfortable with their portfolios and improve success rates over time.

Bogle was behaviorally active with his own money. During the Nasdaq bubble he said that he took his typically 70/30 stock/bond allocation to 30/70. He wasn't trying to beat the market, he simply wasn't comfortable holding 70% of his portfolio in stocks when valuations were so elevated. The fact that he happened to time the market well was part luck and partly sound behavioral management. But the point is Bogle wasn't playing the "all-in" or "all-out" game like so many people do with their portfolios. He was staying the course even though he tilted the portfolio at times.

Bogle wasn't the only smart indexing guru who was an advocate of rebalancing in a more adaptive manner. Nobel Prize winner William Sharpe, the creator of both CAPM and the Sharpe ratio, wrote a wonderful paper back in 2009 titled "Adaptive Asset Allocation Policies."[28]

Sharpe's focus was on the way that a 60/40 Portfolio will deviate from its underlying actual market caps over time and yet rebalances back to its fixed target with no regard for what actually happened in the markets. For example, during the 1990s, US stocks more than doubled in value. Rather than allowing for a higher equity allocation to reflect their growing share of total financial assets, a 60/40 Portfolio would have repeatedly rebalanced away from stocks. Sharpe argued that a more efficient approach would be to rebalance in a way that more closely tracks the evolving market portfolio, rather than anchoring to an arbitrary 60/40 split.

It's interesting to consider Bogle and Sharpe side by side. While Sharpe is a more efficient market theorist, Bogle takes a more behavioralist view. They often arrive at similar conclusions, but through a very different lens. Sharpe would argue for tracking the total market portfolio, letting asset weights shift with market capitalizations. Bogle, on the other hand, might advocate for overbalancing away from the total market portfolio if it helps an investor stay more behaviorally grounded. So, just as he did, Bogle would want us to overbalance to bonds in the late 1990s for behavioral reasons. As noted earlier, this kind of behavioral tilt effectively inverts the GFAP – and, as we now know, would have delivered superior returns during that period.

While neither Sharpe nor Bogle ever formally endorsed a countercyclical strategy, we can extrapolate from their own management and rebalancing research that they would have agreed with something more adaptive than just a static 60/40 Portfolio all of the time.

WHY THE COUNTERCYCLICAL REBALANCING PORTFOLIO WORKS

This is another strategy that isn't necessarily designed to beat the market. If anything, it's aimed at creating a sound behavioral hedge so that you stick with your financial plan over time. It gradually shifts your stock exposure to better align with your comfort level and risk tolerance, helping you stay invested through different market conditions. While we might hope it leads to better risk-adjusted returns, the primary goal is to improve long-term outcomes by helping you stay the course – avoiding the temptation to jump in and out of the market.

The basic thinking behind this type of strategy is simple: when stocks rally, their higher prices often come with a greater risk of lower future returns. Conversely, when stock prices decline, their expected future returns tend to rise.

The valuation issue that Bogle mentions can be compounded at times. For example, we've already discussed the way in which your risk exposures in a stock/bond allocation are not balanced. But this imbalance can be exacerbated at the worst possible times. For instance, if you hold a 60/40 Portfolio in a year like 2007, you are exposed to far more risk in the 60% equity slice than you are in a year like 2009, because stocks are oftentimes less risky when they decline in value significantly.

While stocks are inherently more volatile than bonds, stocks are also much riskier in certain environments when compared to their historical average volatility. This is typically true at market extremes during big booms and busts. A countercyclical strategy can help you maintain discipline by adjusting exposures as risks increase or fade throughout economic and market cycles.

Further, most rebalancing can be considered countercyclical to some extent. When your 60/40 asset mix turns into 70/30 because the equities outperform the bonds, you might choose to rebalance the portfolio back to your original target allocation of 60/40. This is a countercyclical maneuver in the sense that you're reducing exposure to the more inherently procyclical instrument. The trick is in finding the level of rebalancing that is right for you.

CHAPTER 12

BUILDING YOUR OWN COUNTERCYCLICAL PORTFOLIO

Building the Countercyclical Rebalancing Portfolio ("Countercyclical Portfolio" for short) can be tricky because it requires some sort of systematic rebalancing model in a dynamic manner. Bogle cited high equity valuations as the main reason for his discomfort in 1999. While valuations can be relatively predictive of long-term returns, they don't consistently exhibit short-term countercyclical behavior.

For example, the popular Shiller CAPE (Cyclically Adjusted Price-to-Earnings) ratio, which is designed to assess whether the stock market is overvalued or undervalued relative to historical norms, has been in a mostly higher trend for 45 years (see Figure 12.1). There has been no reliable way to use this metric on its own as a rebalancing tool. This was especially true in the last 30 years, when valuations soared during the tech bubble and only mean-reverted back to levels that would have been near-record highs in prior periods. Since then, valuations have remained elevated or continued drifting even higher.

The challenging part is designing a systematic approach that stays true to Bogle's core principles while also applying a sensible countercyclical rebalancing strategy. Lucky for you, I've spent an unhealthy amount of time over the past decade thinking about exactly that – so let's dig in.

Figure 12.1: Shiller CAPE ratio

FUN SIDE NOTE

Why have valuations been so high in recent years? There's considerable debate about this, but I've concluded that it's mostly due to increasing corporate margins. Technology, lower inflation and public policy have facilitated an increase in corporations' cash flow over the last 30 years. Companies are operating more efficiently than ever and capturing a larger share of domestic income. As a result, equities have grown to represent a larger and more influential portion of overall financial assets – driven by this structural shift in corporate efficiency.

I've explored this concept through a variety of methodologies over the years and have found that incorporating valuations, credit spreads, and other macroeconomic indicators can help construct a sufficiently procyclical index – one that serves as a foundation for

CHAPTER 12

building a Countercyclical Portfolio. This index is maintained by my firm, Discipline Funds, and it also informs the approach we use in our own countercyclical strategies and can be implemented inside the Defined Duration strategies, discussed later.*

When I was originally trying to replicate Bogle's approach, I found that valuations were too procyclical to utilize reliably. What you really want is a signal that behaves more like a sine wave over time – something that zigs when the stock market zags, and vice versa and also does so consistently across time. But to build that, you need to go beyond valuations and incorporate a more sophisticated set of indicators. Some people like Dan Rasmussen, the Founder of Verdad Capital and author of *The Humble Investor*, advocate for building a Countercyclical Portfolio using credit spreads. This is a clever addition, but the problem with credit spreads in solitude is that they're countercyclical but would leave you underweight stocks for very long periods of time as credit spreads spend a lot more time at lower levels than they do at higher levels (which would oftentimes leave you too conservative for too long). Credit spreads are a better buy signal than they are an effective hold signal.

That said, if you're looking for a very simple and systematic way to implement a countercyclical strategy, you can just follow credit spreads and apply a model where you're buying more equities when credit spreads increase and reducing exposure when credit spreads decline.**

I found that when you combine four metrics – valuations, credit spreads, the yield curve, and the unemployment rate – you create a much more reliable countercyclical index. This makes sense because credit spreads are very sensitive to economic activity while the yield curve and unemployment rate tend to be much less sensitive. In

---

* For those interested, you can find more details on the "Your Perfect Portfolio" page at www.ria.disciplinefunds.com/your-perfect-portfolio.

** This data on credit spreads is publicly available, such as via the St. Louis Fed's FRED website (fred.stlouisfed.org/series/BAMLH0A3HYC).

particular, metrics like the unemployment rate evolve over longer time horizons, adding a layer of structural stability and diversity to the index. Together, these variables create a more balanced and fundamentally grounded framework.

Ahhh, but here's the next challenge. We want the portfolio to lean aggressive at times, never *too* aggressive. After all, this is a behavioral portfolio and if you found yourself at 100% stocks after the market dropped in 2008, only to watch it fall another 27% in the first three months of 2009 (as it did), you haven't managed risk – you've amplified it. Through your rebalancing you've compounded the very behavioral risks the portfolio was meant to reduce. Fortunately, the solution has already been offered... by Bogle himself.

To reduce the risk of outsized stock market risk we can throttle the rebalancing process by setting boundaries – just as Bogle suggested – between 70/30 and 30/70. These bands ensure the portfolio never shifts into an excessively aggressive position. Figure 12.2 illustrates how this works in practice using my four metric index.

Figure 12.2: Four-metric countercyclical index

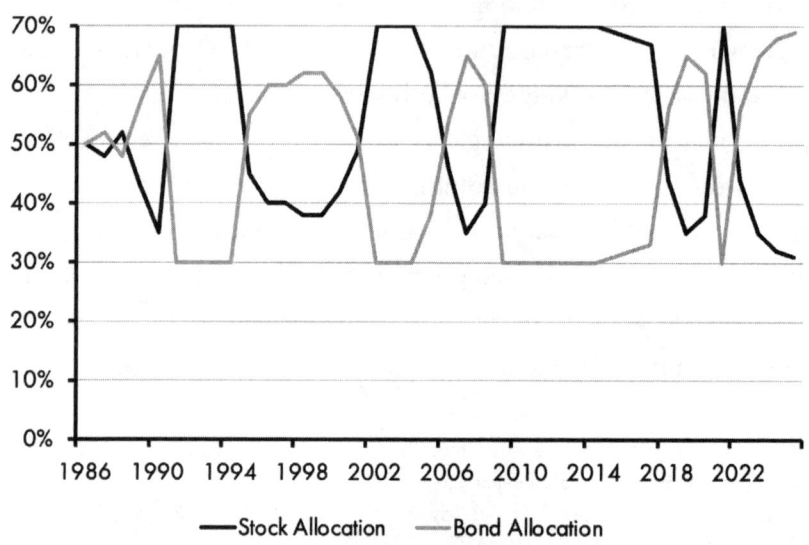

To build a Countercyclical Portfolio, you can use any broad stock and bond index that aligns with the signals, parameters, and allocations discussed above. I'm personally partial to using global equities and domestic fixed income within this portfolio. For example, you could build your own Countercyclical Portfolio using the following ETFs, which, as of 2025 would be weighted as shown:

- Vanguard Total Domestic Stocks (VTI): 17%
- SPDR Foreign Developed Stocks (SPDW): 12%
- Vanguard Emerging Markets Stocks (VWO): 5%
- Vanguard Short-term Government Bonds (VGSH): 30%
- Vanguard Intermediate Government Bonds (VGIT): 25%
- Vanguard Long-term Government Bonds (VGLT): 11%

This aligns with the market capitalizations of global stocks and US government bonds, but reweights the relative stock versus bond holdings to try to better control for the risks between the two asset classes. I also prefer to take the bond piece one step further and control for duration risk inside the bonds, but that's overcomplicating things for the sake of this text.

If you're interested in how our customized Countercyclical Index might fit into your personal strategy, feel free to reach out – I'm always happy to help others think through how to apply these concepts in a practical way.

THE COUNTERCYCLICAL PORTFOLIO ANALYSIS

I've always appreciated this concept as a form of multi-asset portfolio that aims to create balance, without all the complexity of something like a traditional Risk Parity strategy. It works well as a contrarian approach, designed to zig when others zag, especially at market extremes when sentiment becomes highly stretched. While it may be behaviorally difficult for many investors to increase risk during periods like 2009, this kind of allocation would have systematically tilted more aggressive at that time, shifting toward 70% stocks as valuations declined and opportunity increased.

Will this outperform something like the traditional 60/40 Portfolio? That's hard to say, especially since its average allocation tends to hover closer to 50/50, as I've implemented it. However, one of its strengths is that it's grounded in an empirically driven, contrarian framework. Unlike the 60/40 Portfolio – which offers no specific rationale for its 60% stock allocation – the Countercyclical Portfolio provides a more tangible basis for adjusting exposure. That structure can make it easier to stick with the strategy, especially when markets feel overextended or out of sync.

In terms of its hypothetical performance this one does well, especially when it matters most. The portfolio generates 5.51% average annual returns with volatility of 9.52% while the global 60/40 Portfolio generated 5.39% per year with 10.15% volatility.

Figure 12.3: Countercyclical Rebalancing Portfolio performance

Table 12.1: Portfolio analysis

	Countercyclical Portfolio	Global 60/40
Real Returns	5.51%	5.39%
Volatility	9.52%	10.15%
Sharpe Ratio	0.57	0.53
Sortino Ratio	0.81	0.76
Max Drawdown	−25.94%	−33.65%
Ulcer Index	8.24	8.65
Market Correlation	0.41	0.46

The Ulcer Index for the Countercyclical Portfolio is 8.24, roughly similar to the global 60/40 Portfolio at 8.65. The bigger difference occurs during drawdowns, with the global 60/40 Portfolio falling 33.65% versus the max drawdown of 25.94% for the Countercyclical Portfolio.

Figure 12.4: Countercyclical Rebalancing Portfolio drawdowns

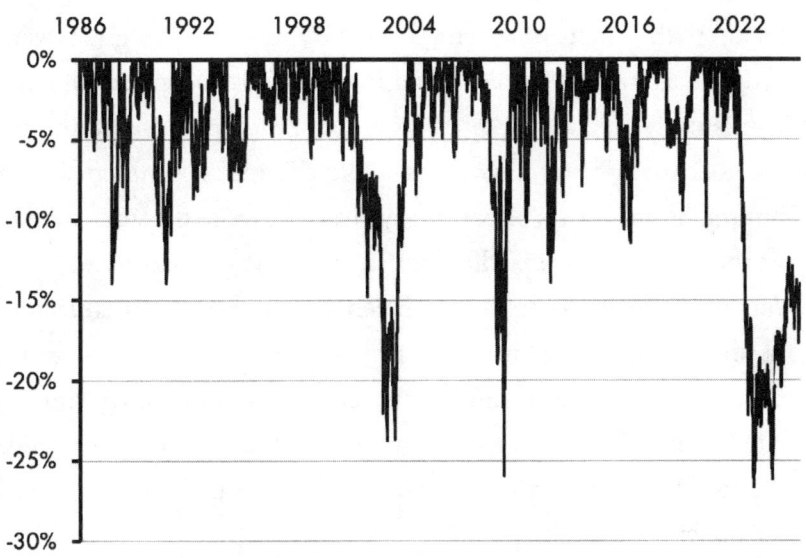

One thing to keep in mind with this portfolio is that it will likely underperform during big bull markets as you move underweight stocks, but it will often make up for it during a bear market. There are trade-offs in this approach that may or may not suit your behavior.

THE COUNTERCYCLICAL PORTFOLIO PROS AND CONS

I'm biased because I created the countercyclical index and love everything Jack Bogle ever did, but it's not all good news on this one. Here's the bad news:

1. This is not a beat-the-market portfolio. While it's designed to keep your behavioral biases in check, it could go through periods where you're underweight stocks during major rallies, or overweight stocks during extended periods of negative sentiment. If you're not a conservative investor, you could experience the wrong kind of behavioral bias from this portfolio in the form of anxiety about being left behind in a rally.
2. Picking the best countercyclical metric isn't straightforward. Procyclical indicators like valuations and credit spreads do not consistently predict market highs or lows. Incorporating additional macroeconomic variables helps make the index more consistent, but might not always be countercyclical relative to the stock market. As the old saying goes, "the stock market isn't the economy."
3. You could incur some tax inefficiencies using this structure in a taxable account since it involves more aggressive rebalancing over time. In contrast to a simpler strategy like 60/40, you're shifting allocations in a more pronounced way, which can trigger taxable events. That's one reason to consider sticking with an annual rebalancing schedule.

4. While this approach creates better balance than a traditional 60/40 Portfolio, it's still limited to stocks and bonds, so you may need outside assets to achieve broader diversification. I generally calculate a 50/50 stock/bond portfolio as having a duration similar to a 10-year instrument. So, this portfolio should be viewed as having a time horizon that's not short term, but also not especially long.

What about the good news?

1. For a moderately active strategy, this portfolio is relatively easy to construct and manage – it only requires a handful of funds and a simple annual rebalancing schedule. While determining the right signals and associated allocations may take some thoughtful planning, the ongoing maintenance is straightforward. This portfolio is diverse and low-fee.
2. The portfolio is designed to be behaviorally resilient, helping investors remain grounded during periods of heightened market stress. For those able to resist the pull of fear of missing out, it can provide a sense of stability – particularly during extremes like the market peaks of 1999 or the troughs of 2009, when many others may be acting irrationally.
3. The portfolio aims to achieve a similar objective as Risk Parity by rebalancing in a way that helps offset the stock market's outsized risks, especially during the most challenging periods.
4. This is a great portfolio for the investor who is consistently struggling with behavioral biases and concerns about how to implement a more systematically contrarian style of allocation without succumbing to the all-in or all-out bias. Using a quantifiable and systematic approach will help you remain more disciplined by relying on data outputs instead of emotions.

SUITORS FOR THE COUNTERCYCLICAL PORTFOLIO

The Countercyclical Portfolio is best suited for conservative investors or those who tend to be more emotionally sensitive to the booms and busts of the market. It's designed to generate more stable returns over time, even if that means accepting lower relative returns during extended bull markets.

This portfolio appeals to investors who are skeptical of complex strategies like Risk Parity but still want a more balanced approach within a straightforward stock/bond framework.

It's also a strong fit for those who want to stay consistently invested, as it remains fully allocated to stocks and bonds at all times. However, it may not be ideal for very aggressive investors or those seeking broader diversification beyond traditional equity and fixed income asset classes.

FINAL THOUGHTS

I practically twisted my brain into a noodle designing the custom index for this portfolio. At times, I wished I had a neurologist to help me stop overthinking it. And that brings us to our next portfolio.

William Bernstein, an actual neurologist, is up next with his aptly named No-Brainer Portfolio. Bernstein is a literal genius, so you're going to want to keep reading.

13

THE BERNSTEIN NO-BRAINER PORTFOLIO

I HAD the great honor of interviewing William Bernstein, one of my personal investing heroes, for this chapter. His website, "Efficient Frontier," is a bottomless gold mine of financial insight and research. A lot of the concepts in this book are things I learned from Bill.

Bernstein began his career as a neurologist and built his wealth in the medical field. He then got interested in how best to allocate his own savings when he became suspicious that a financial advisor might not have his best interests at heart.

Bernstein didn't just learn about how finance and investing works. He immersed himself in understanding the field and became a legendary thought leader and eventually a financial advisor himself. Over time he arrived at many of the same conclusions that Taylor Larimore and the Bogleheads did – diversify, minimize taxes and fees, and keep it simple.

A strategy that Bernstein has become known for is called the

Bernstein No-Brainer. But the version you've seen online isn't exactly his preferred approach — so let's take a closer look at how he actually thinks about building a No-Brainer Portfolio.

Here's my interview with Bill.

★★★

CR: Can you share the historical context and inspiration behind the No-Brainer Portfolio, and your broader approach to asset allocation?

WB: The No-Brainer is an old portfolio that I played around with in the electronic versions of *The Intelligent Asset Allocator (TIAA)*, which first came out in 1995. I came up with it in response to a journalist inquiry. That said, it's a fine portfolio for someone who's highly risk-tolerant; it is, after all, 75% stocks. Far, far more important than one's precise allocation, beyond selecting the overall stock/bond mix, is sticking with it. A "suboptimal" portfolio you can stick with is better than an "optimal" one you can't.

CR: How did your personal journey as an investor influence the development of the No-Brainer Portfolio, and how has your perspective on it evolved over time?

WB: The backstory is simple: I live in a country without a functioning social safety net and I realized I was going to have to save and invest on my own for retirement. I proceeded the way I thought anyone with scientific training would: reading basic texts, the peer-reviewed literature, and building models. That wasn't easy for a small investor in the 1990s, and by the time I had finished I realized that I had done something that small investors could use, and I finally got *TIAA* published. History is an important part of investing, and it was the part of the writing I enjoyed the most, so I've also written four history books.

I picked the portfolio about 30 years ago. There's nothing special about it, beyond that it's reasonably well diversified, has an aggressive

75/25 stock/bond split, and the stock portion is 67/33 domestic/foreign [as seen in Figure 13.1]. My books generally start with very simple portfolios, similar to the above, and work up to tilted ones with up to a dozen or so stock asset classes. I don't think I've recommended the "no-brainer" for a long time.

Figure 13.1: Bernstein's No-Brainer

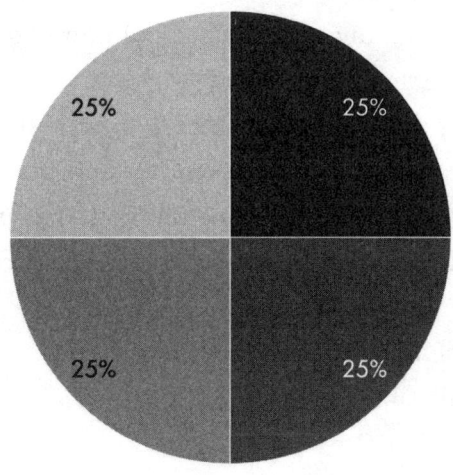

■ Large Cap Blend ■ Small Cap Blend ■ International Stocks ■ Short-Term Bonds

FUN SIDE NOTE

Bill has written some incredible history books, including:
A Splendid Exchange: How Trade Shaped the World
The Birth of Plenty: How the Prosperity of the Modern World was Created
Masters of the Word: How Media Shaped History from the Alphabet to the Internet
The Delusions of Crowds: Why People Go Mad in Groups

CR: Who most influenced your development of the No-Brainer Portfolio? Was there any academic or factor-based reasoning?

WB: Probably the most influential was Brinson's *Determinants of Portfolio Performance* from over 30 years ago that talked about portfolio optimization, as well as Markowitz, and Fama and French's research which supports tilting. But, as I've implied above, it's not possible to pick "optimal" portfolios in advance. Better to pick something reasonable and stick with it.

CR: Do you have any criticisms of the portfolio or aspects you might consider altering in the future?

WB: Nope, my thinking about asset allocation hasn't changed much in the past 20 years. Here is my current recommended allocation for the stock part of a portfolio. These percentages, of course, get diluted down with bonds to taste for risk tolerance, capacity or need.

- 37.5% US total market
- 12.5% US small value
- 10% REITs
- 2.5% energy stocks
- 2.5% precious metals stocks
- 10% European
- 10% Pacific
- 5% developed market small value
- 7.5% emerging market
- 2.5% emerging market small value

Will this do any better than the one-third each of US large, US small, and foreign recommended in the original No-Brainer? I haven't the foggiest. As I said, that's unknowable in advance, and sticking with your allocation is more important than the actual allocation.

★★★

Bernstein is really speaking my language with all this talk about how the potentially suboptimal portfolio you stick with is likely to be superior to the optimal portfolio you abandon.

Of course, the most interesting part here is that even though Bill likes the original No-Brainer Portfolio, it's clear that he has a more nuanced appreciation for the need to customize beyond the simplest of allocations.

For instance, I know that Bill is sometimes a little bit critical of the Boglehead Three-Fund Portfolio for its lack of cash liquidity. That is easily solved with one position, but Bernstein also knows that an investor might need to go a bit beyond something that looks like a very simple No-Brainer.

I also like his emphasis on the role of bonds in a portfolio. Bernstein likes to highlight that the purpose of bonds is not to generate high returns. They are for providing principal stability and income across very specific time horizons. This is one reason why he isn't a huge fan of corporate bonds or junk bonds. Like myself, he believes these instruments oftentimes look like stocks in disguise due to their credit risk and potential for permanent principal losses.

Another thing that Bill has mentioned in his work is that he's a big fan of owning Treasury Inflation Protected Securities (TIPS) for the bond allocation when you're drawing down a portfolio and trying to create greater certainty of consumption in the future. He likes building out custom TIPS ladders for this purpose. He says:

A TIPS is risky in the short term and riskless in the long run, which is precisely the opposite of, and complementary to, a T-bill, which is riskless in the short term but, because of reinvestment rate volatility, risky in the long run.[29]

I appreciate that description and it's a very useful way to balance the risks of bonds in a portfolio. Bill likes using bonds in an asset-liability matching approach that isn't all that different from my Defined Duration Strategy (see Chapter 20). He argues TIPS are the only instrument that can give you absolute certainty of meeting future inflation-adjusted consumption when structured over a bond ladder. Based on this broader understanding of Bill's approach I've created what I call the "Updated No-Brainer Portfolio."*

Let's start digging into this entire portfolio in more detail.

HOW THE UPDATED NO-BRAINER PORTFOLIO WORKS

The Updated No-Brainer Portfolio is another very broadly diversified portfolio that focuses on capturing as much of the market's returns as possible while also minimizing taxes, fees, and activity. At the same time, it's more sophisticated than what we've seen with some of our other indexing strategies. In fact, the Updated No-Brainer Portfolio has quite a lot of tilting going on. Will that work? As Bill notes, we don't really know, but it's grounded in the same sound logic that underpins the Boglehead Three-Fund Portfolio and the Factor Investing Portfolio.

Bill's overall approach is also somewhat similar to the Flying Ladder in that it's structured as two very distinctly different pieces serving very different needs. In short, the stock component of the Bernstein No-Brainer Portfolio is based on broad diversification with empirically supported factor tiling. And then our bond slice is based on sound judgment of how bonds should best be utilized and the

---

* The Updated No-Brainer Portfolio is based on Bill's work, but he endorses much more customized approaches in his own work.

proper instruments that can be used to match certain income and spending needs over time.

So, this portfolio works because it's diversified, low-cost, and can be personalized to meet someone's financial planning needs.

BUILDING YOUR OWN UPDATED NO-BRAINER PORTFOLIO

The Bernstein No-Brainer Portfolio has two very specific components that serve different purposes. Bill uses bonds as an income and financial planning tool to help an investor try to match certain assets with future liabilities. And then he builds a stock portfolio along with this bond component to help generate growth.

The bond component is pretty clean and we're going to focus on using T-bills and TIPS, as Bill discussed earlier.

The stock component is where Bill gets a little fancier and does a decent amount of tilting both to factors, sectors, and regions. Although the portfolio can be customized, we're going to assume a starting point consistent with the original 75/25 stock/bond target. Based on this, the Updated No-Brainer Portfolio would look something like Figure 13.2.

Now we're talking. As you can see, our perfect portfolios are building on one another as we expand the approaches and begin to integrate them with one another. Now let's dig into the analysis of this portfolio.

Figure 13.2: The Updated Bernstein No-Brainer

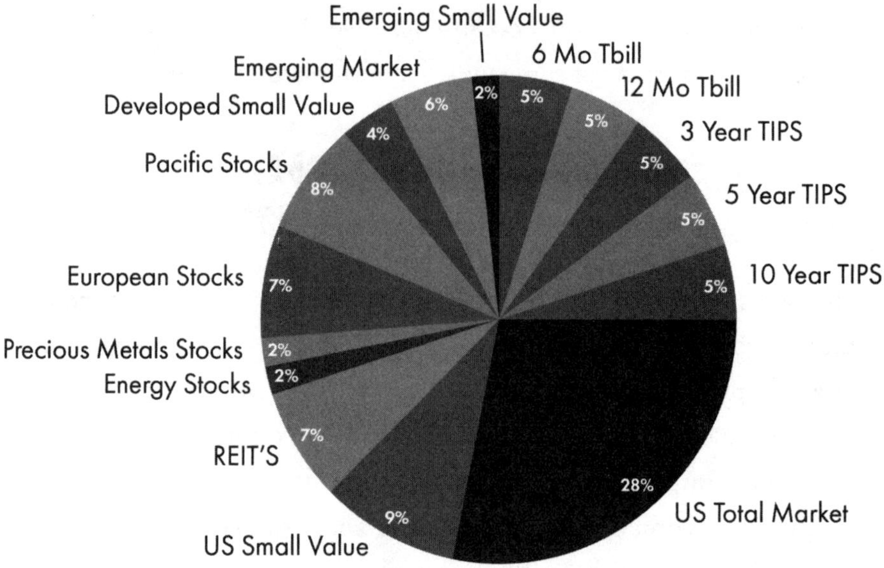

Pie chart segments:
- Emerging Small Value: 2%
- 6 Mo Tbill: 5%
- 12 Mo Tbill: 5%
- 3 Year TIPS: 5%
- 5 Year TIPS: 5%
- 10 Year TIPS: 5%
- US Total Market: 28%
- US Small Value: 9%
- REIT'S: 7%
- Energy Stocks: 2%
- Precious Metals Stocks: 2%
- European Stocks: 7%
- Pacific Stocks: 8%
- Developed Small Value: 4%
- Emerging Market: 6%

UPDATED NO-BRAINER PORTFOLIO ANALYSIS

The Updated No-Brainer Portfolio can be customized to meet an investor's needs, but we'll run our analysis here using our Updated No-Brainer holdings within the 75/25 stock/bond weighting that is consistent with the overall weighting of the Original No-Brainer Portfolio. Our analysis begins in 1997, as TIPS were not issued before then, but this still provides a meaningful period for evaluation.

Despite being comprised of 25% TIPS and T-bills, the Updated No-Brainer Portfolio does surprisingly well, earning 4.95% average annual returns, compared to 5.20% for the global stock market over the same period. It achieves this return with 11.98% volatility, compared to 18.84% for the global stock market. Granted, this was an especially good period for bonds, but the equity piece of the portfolio still performs well over the same period. Keep in mind that while we're comparing the Updated No-Brainer Portfolio to an all-stock portfolio, it's important to note that with its 75/25 allocation, it's likely to fall somewhere between a 100% Stock Portfolio and a traditional 60/40 Portfolio in terms of aggressiveness and risk. Global 60/40 returned 4.35% per year with 10.21% volatility over this same period so the No-Brainer does well compared to both global stocks and global 60/40. This is visually clear in Figure 13.3:

Figure 13.3: Updated No-Brainer performance

Table 13.1: Portfolio analysis

	Updated No-Brainer	Global Stocks
Real Returns	4.95%	5.20%
Volatility	11.98%	18.84%
Sharpe Ratio	0.42	0.37
Sortino Ratio	0.59	0.52
Max Drawdown	-44.85%	-58.88%
Ulcer Index	13.87	19.20
Market Correlation	0.60	0.89

Drawdowns and risk metrics are also much more favorable for the Updated No-Brainer Portfolio, with a Sharpe ratio of 0.42 compared to 0.37 for stocks. A Sortino ratio of 0.59 compared to 0.52 shows that it protects better for downside volatility, with a max drawdown of 44.85% compared to 58.88% for global stocks, as seen in Figure 13.4. Its Ulcer Index of 13.87 compares with 19.20 for global stocks and is consistent with a portfolio that will be more behaviorally robust.

Figure 13.4: Updated No-Brainer drawdowns (%)

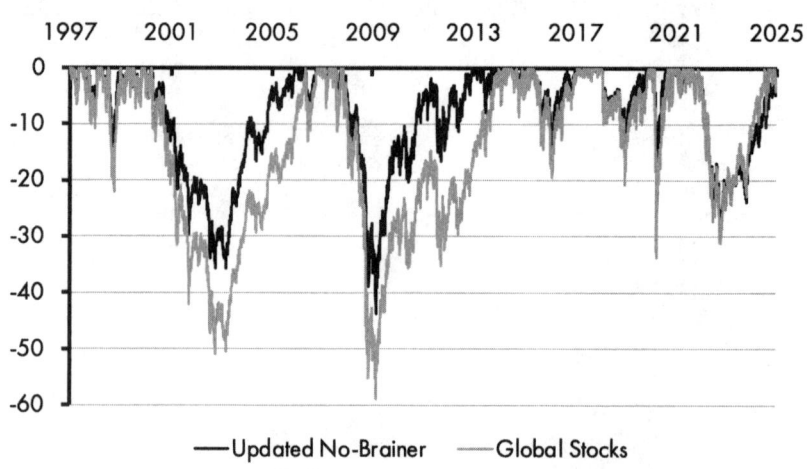

There's a lot going on here, but it obviously works well. Let's get into the pros and cons.

UPDATED NO-BRAINER PORTFOLIO PROS AND CONS

Let's get the bad news out of the way first, as usual:

1. The baseline No-Brainer is aggressive so as Bill noted you need to be someone with a relatively high risk tolerance. This has an element of the Flying Ladder Portfolio when used with the TIPS ladder, so you need to compartmentalize the roles of the ladder relative to the equity sleeve.
2. There's a lot going on here between the TIPS ladder and the numerous tilts. Some of those tilts are also so small that it raises a valid concern over how meaningful they are and whether they're worth the added annoyance of seeing them every day. This may not be suitable for the investor who wants to keep things simple.
3. There's not a great deal of evidence that this type of portfolio is much better than the Three-Fund Portfolio outside of the bond slice. That is, are all those stock tilts better than just owning what Taylor Larimore recommends with two equity funds?
4. I go back and forth about TIPS. The argument is that you will generate a more reliable inflation-adjusted fixed income stream. But the problem there is that inflation is measured at a national level and experienced at a local level. National TIPS aren't guaranteed to give you purchasing power protection. Further, TIPS are largely an interest rate bet. If rates go down, plain vanilla Treasuries will do better. And if rates go up then TIPS will do better over specific

time periods. You need to be aware that you're making a bit of an interest rate bet when you buy TIPS versus straight Treasuries.
5. The portfolio is only stocks and bonds so in environments where equities and fixed income become highly correlated, you'll feel undiversified.

And what about the good news?

1. The portfolio is simple, all things considered. Especially if you're not using the TIPS ladder. And the stock tilts, while arguably excessive, do give you the potential to generate a little extra return.
2. The Updated No-Brainer Portfolio improves on the fixed income piece of the Three-Fund Portfolio in a big way. Especially if you're drawing down your portfolio and trying to attain more certainty than what you'll get in the total bond position of the Three-Fund Portfolio.
3. The more sophisticated investor might like having all these stock tilts that give them a little more optionality and potential for superior returns.
4. Although the portfolio doesn't have pure play inflation hedges like gold or commodities, it does tilt to some more specific hard asset classes and inflation hedges like REITs, energy stocks, precious metals, and TIPS. Bill is getting some inflation hedging in there without having to own more costly inflation hedges.

SUITORS FOR THE UPDATED NO-BRAINER PORTFOLIO

The Updated No-Brainer Portfolio is ideal for the investor who wants a little more nuance and potential return from their portfolio. While Bernstein is a Boglehead, he also understands the importance of customization and adding some layers where it makes sense. The portfolio is right for the person who likes the idea of the Three-Fund Portfolio, but finds it a bit too simple for their personal needs or desires.

It's also worth noting that this portfolio requires the right temperament. While the TIPS/T-bill ladder is designed to provide stability, the 75% stock allocation will still feel like a roller coaster at times. Since most of the portfolio's risk comes from its equity exposure, it's important to recognize that a 75% stock allocation will likely take some hard hits along the way. That's why this portfolio works best when tailored to match your specific risk profile.

FINAL THOUGHTS

An Updated No-Brainer Portfolio from a brainiac who also happens to be an expert about the human brain. Pretty cool.

But what if you don't want to overthink things? What if you'd rather just clip coupons, skip the academic mumbo jumbo, and focus on that sweet, sweet cash flow?

Well, in that case you're going to like the dividend-oriented strategies that are behind Door #14. You might be surprised about where these strategies came from and how they're likely to evolve in the future.

14

DIVIDEND INVESTING AND ANTI-DIVIDEND INVESTING PORTFOLIOS

WARREN BUFFETT was far from being the first activist investor – 334 years before Buffett Partners was formed a group of activist shareholders revolted against the directors of the Vereenigde Oost-Indische Compagnie (VOC), also known as the Dutch East India Company. The VOC was the world's largest corporation at the time and dominated the global spice trade. As the company grew increasingly large and complex, its shareholders became tired of the various inefficiencies that cropped up and they demanded greater oversight and control.

In 1610, Isaac Le Maire, a former director of the VOC who had been barred for fraud, established a short position in the company's shares and began a relentless public attack, accusing the VOC of mishandling shareholder funds. Le Maire had an axe to grind and hoped to drive the share price low enough that other shareholders would redeem and force an eventual liquidation of the company. This would enable Le Maire and his partners to initiate competing companies that could take over the VOC's monopoly on the spice trade.

Le Maire's efforts appeared to be working until the VOC outed his syndicate and convinced the government to ban short selling. Le Maire and his partners spent much of the next few years trying to cover their debts and ultimately went into hiding. But while his efforts failed, the directors conceded in part by paying a dividend to shareholders, paid in spice at a value of 75% of the nominal capital. A cash dividend soon followed.[30]

The VOC went on to pay a dividend for over 100 years and it was a consistent sign of the company's financial prowess until its ultimate demise in 1799.

Throughout early stock market history dividends were a key symbol of financial strength. It was one of the ultimate symbols that a firm had a strong and healthy balance sheet because, as Peter Lynch once said, "A company cannot fake that which it does not have." Dividends continue to be a symbol of company health to this day.

WHY DIVIDEND INVESTING WORKS

Who doesn't love a stream of sweet, sweet cash? That's the appeal of any dividend-paying strategy. You get to clip those coupons and watch the cash flow into your portfolio. It makes intuitive sense: as the old saying goes, two in the hand is worth one in the bush. It's the same reason people gravitate toward safe bonds, but with dividends, you get the added potential for upside through stock price appreciation.

Dividend-driven strategies are, at their core, fundamentally driven. That's because stock returns are comprised of dividends plus capital appreciation and while capital appreciation is nice, your stock market returns aren't real until you sell the shares and realize the gains. So, there's a lot of uncertainty around unrealized capital appreciation. Dividends, on the other hand, give you a more tangible return.

Dividends are typically paid out of a company's net income or retained earnings and often signal strong or stable profitability. Like the VOC, many dividend-paying firms generate consistent cash flow, allowing them to regularly return a portion of their profits to shareholders. This means that owning dividend-paying stocks can provide not just a steady stream of income, but also exposure to companies that are financially sound and capable of sustaining those payouts over time.

This is especially true in diversified index funds where you can reduce single entity risk and own a stream of dividends coming from many different entities. With a dividend-paying ETF you can virtually eliminate single entity risk and get your low risk coupon payments. In short, owning dividend-paying stocks works because dividends only flow if the firm itself is working.

WHY ANTI-DIVIDEND INVESTING WORKS

The story is more complex though and while I appreciate the allure of dividends they're by no means a free lunch. This is where the anti-dividend view comes into play.

Dividends remain very popular as seen in Figure 14.1, but firms are increasingly starting to return capital via share repurchases. There's quite a bit of controversy and misunderstanding around this topic so it's worth spending a little time on this.

Figure 14.1: Net US corporate dividend payments ($bn)

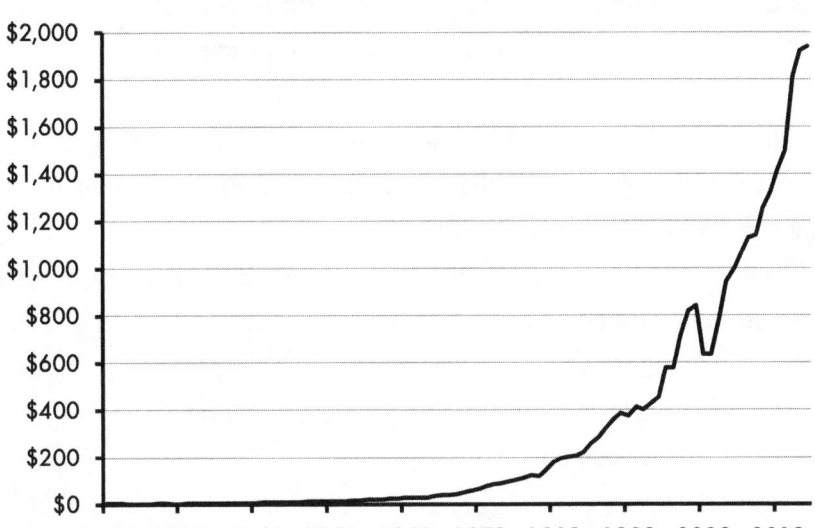

When a company pays a dividend, the shareholder incurs taxes whether they wanted the income or not. In effect, the company is creating a tax liability for its investors. But what if a company could return capital to shareholders without immediately triggering that tax bill? In other words, what if investors could choose when to realize the tax liability? That's essentially what a stock buyback, or repurchase, accomplishes.

A stock buyback involves the corporation using some of its cash to repurchase outstanding shares that were previously issued. For example, if the corporation initiates a buyback for $100, then shareholders receive $100 of cash from the corporation when they sell their stock back to the company. The corporation pays $100 of cash to the shareholders (just like they would with a dividend) and retires some portion of stock that was previously issued. If a shareholder is selling the stock at a long-term capital gain rate they might receive more favorable tax treatment than they would if they had received a dividend. And regardless of tax rate, the firm is using the repurchase to allow shareholders to determine whether they even get a tax bill in the first place by giving them the option to sell or not.

In short, dividends and buybacks are both ways of returning cash to shareholders, but the buyback puts the tax control in the hands of the shareholders. Pretty fair, huh?

In his 2012 annual shareholder letter Warren Buffett went over this topic in some detail describing the four ways that firms can handle cash:

1. Reinvest in the company (i.e., pursue organic growth).
2. Acquire other companies.
3. Repurchase shares.
4. Pay dividends.[31]

He then explained that he prefers to repurchase shares in Berkshire when they're selling at a discount to intrinsic value because dividends don't treat all shareholders fairly due to the uneven tax treatment and the fact that different shareholders prefer different size payouts.

This is similar to what billionaire investor Ken Fisher calls "homegrown dividends."[32] Fisher is an advocate of using capital appreciation to sell an investor's shares opportunistically over time to create your own form of dividends at superior tax rates and to better align with personal needs.

CHAPTER 14

FUN SIDE NOTE

People sometimes confuse dividend income with bond fixed income. These things are not the same and they should not be utilized the same way. While stock dividends can be a signal of financial strength they are by no means stable in the same way that bond-like income is. And that's because the underlying principal value of the securities is wildly different.

We often hear the financial media compare something like a 3% yielding five-year government bond to the 3% dividend yield of the S&P 500. You might say these things are similar in that they both pay reliable income. But the main point of owning bonds in a portfolio is to create certainty of principal over time with income. We know, for a fact, that a five-year US T-note yielding 3% will mature at $100 in five years while having paid out 3% all along the way. There is no uncertainty of principal or income in this instrument over five years.

The stock market is a completely different animal. You might get 3% dividend payments along the way and persistent negative *total* returns across the same five-year period. You have no certainty of principal in the stock market, even over five-year periods. Dividend-paying stocks, while likely to be more stable than non-dividend paying stocks, are not an apples-to-apples income and principal stabilizer in the same way that government or investment-grade bonds are.

It's also worth noting that, in truly perilous economic environments like the GFC, dividend-paying stocks do not protect you and some of the safest stocks like utilities fell by 60% or more, in part because dividend-paying firms often cut or halt their dividends during recessions.

Buybacks are not a free lunch though. Despite putting more power into the hands of shareholders, the existing shareholders incur a certain degree of added risk because management is making an asset allocation that may or may not be in the best interest of shareholders. Firms should always try to maximize reinvestment in their own firm by putting money back into organic growth or acquisitions, but firms like the VOC or more modern-day firms like Apple end up with such enormous cash hoards that they end up returning cash to shareholders in what equates to the firm saying: "Here, you reallocate this because we've reinvested all of our cash as wisely as we believe we can and we think you might have a better use for this."

Reinvesting cash in a business is difficult, especially when you're a large, successful firm. Some people are quick to say buybacks are "financial engineering" that drives up stock prices, but if we look at some publicly listed buyback ETFs such as the PowerShares Buyback Achievers Fund (ticker: PKW), it's unclear that firms repurchasing shares exhibit any sort of superior performance when compared to the broader market. In fact, they look nearly identical, as reflected in Figure 14.2.

Figure 14.2: Buyback Funds versus S&P 500

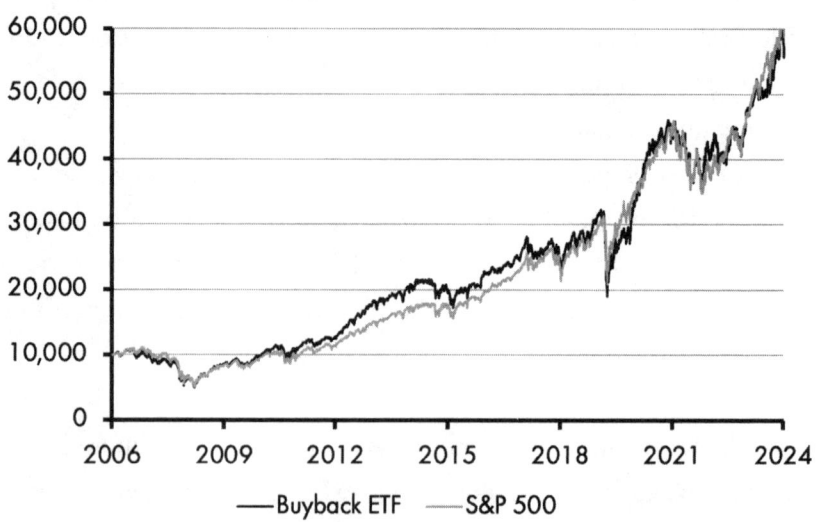

And so this brings us to an interesting conclusion. From a pure return-on-investment perspective, the difference between buybacks and dividends appears inconclusive at best, but we know for a fact that the buyback investors benefit from superior tax treatment.

At the same time, some of the criticism of buybacks is fair. When firms borrow money to buy back shares, offset new dilution, or buy back shares well above intrinsic value, they are potentially doing their existing shareholders a disservice. While there are certainly instances of this, there is no clear evidence that buybacks are definitively good nor bad in and of themselves.

Further, an interesting thing is happening in the US capital markets as buybacks grow in popularity – dividends are no longer the reliable symbol of financial strength they once were as buybacks are increasingly being used to send the signaling effect: "Hey you, we have cash and we're buying back our shares because we think our shares are undervalued!"

So, the value of buybacks is inconclusive relative to dividends, but the good news is that we don't have to pick just one. We know that people like cash in the hand, but people also hate taxes. So, what if you could have your cake and eat it too? This is where the seemingly conflicted views can be used to complement one another.

In 2005 William Priest wrote a paper titled "The Case for Shareholder Yield as a Dominant Driver of Future Equity Returns." This idea focuses on building strategies around firms that return capital to shareholders through all the available methods. This helps capture the traditional signal of financial strength that shareholders have relied on for hundreds of years while also capturing the valuation signal that buybacks often reflect.

Meb Faber of Cambria Investments has expanded on this concept in recent years and points out that dividend strategies miss two key indicators of strong cash flow:

1. Net share repurchases.
2. Debt paydown.

Using this we could calculate total shareholder yield as shown in Figure 14.3.

Figure 14.3: Shareholder yield calculation

$$\text{Shareholder Yield} = \frac{\text{Cash Dividends} + \text{Net Share Repurchases} + \text{Net Debt Reduction}}{\text{Market Capitalization}}$$

Cambria uses an example as follows. Consider a firm that pays cash dividends of $1,000,000, repurchases shares of $150,000, issues $30,000 of new shares and implements $1,000,000 of net debt reduction. If they have a market cap of $30,000,000 then their total shareholder yield would be:

Figure 14.4: Shareholder yield calculation example

$$\text{Shareholder Yield} = \frac{\$1,000,000 + (\$150,000 - \$30,000) + \$1,000,000}{\$1,000,000 \times \$30} = 7.07\%$$

As you can see this formulation does a good job of capturing the way in which firms return capital to investors.

CHAPTER 14

BUILDING YOUR OWN (ANTI) DIVIDEND PORTFOLIO

There is no shortage of dividend and income-oriented ETFs out there. Broadly diversified dividend ETFs like Schwab US Dividend Income (ticker: SCHD) or Vanguard High Dividend Yield ETF (ticker: VYM) are great options. Blending it with something like Vanguard International High Dividend Yield (ticker: VYMI) would give you a more globally diversified allocation.

As mentioned before, you could also get pure play buyback firms via the PowerShares Buyback Achievers Fund (ticker: PKW).

And if you wanted to explore an option that does all the above you might research Cambria Shareholder Yield ETF (ticker: SYLD) which focuses on all three ways of returning cash to investors.[33]

(ANTI) DIVIDEND PORTFOLIO ANALYSIS

Dividend, repurchase, and shareholder yield funds do not exhibit reliable forms of alpha. They are best thought of as income-paying funds that will have a high correlation with their related market.

Many of these dividend-specific funds will also look like value or quality factor funds because the dividend focus tends to be consistent with firms that have similar attributes to value and quality factors. So they've tended to underperform or correlate with the broader market over time.

One that was especially memorable for me (because I owned it at the time) was the iShares Dividend Select ETF, one of the earliest dividend ETFs. This fund has significantly lagged the market over time with just 5.70% real returns versus the total market's returns of 7.82%, as shown in Figure 14.5.

Figure 14.5: Dividend Select versus total market stocks

The thing that made this fund so memorable to me was the way it performed in 2008 during the GFC. As seen in Figure 14.6, this fund fell 63% from peak to trough, more than the broad market. Its problem was that it was loaded with seemingly safe dividend-paying stocks in the finance and utilities sectors. And when the crisis hit many of those firms halted their dividends, which exacerbated the selling. This is one reason why it's very important to think of dividend-paying stocks as a different animal than something like US government bonds. They cannot be relied upon to be safe at the times when safety is most desired.

If we look at this more broadly, in Figure 14.7 we see that newer funds like Vanguard Dividend Appreciation (ticker: VIG) and Schwab US Dividend ETF (ticker: SCHD) do a better job of tracking the market, but still comparatively look more like value and quality factors.

Figure 14.6: Dividend ETF drawdowns (%)

Figure 14.7: Dividend fund performance

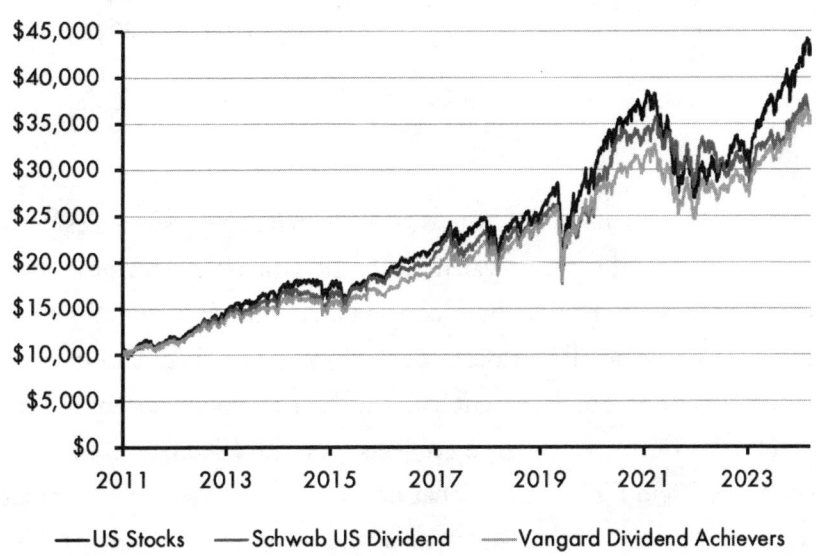

Cambria's Shareholder Yield ETF is an interesting new entrant to the shareholder yield world and the purest play on capturing the concept. Although it's relatively new the fund has captured more of the total market return when compared to funds like SCHD and VIG, as depicted in Figure 14.8.

Figure 14.8: SYLD versus VTI

I should also note that these income-generating strategies have become more and more prevalent and, unfortunately, oftentimes prey on investor ignorance of these concepts. As noted, dividend-paying stocks do not generally outperform the broader market. And they are not a reliable bond replacement. But this hasn't stopped dozens of Wall Street firms from creating shiny objects that are called names like "the Safe 100% Yield ETF." I made that up, but there are so many of these funds out there now that advertise attractive yields by using options or other complex strategies. They often sound appealing because of the income, but in practice they tend to underperform because they're using expensive overlays to get that extra income.

I know we all like income and purportedly high returns, but double and triple check these when you come across them. Heck, send them to me for an independent assessment if you'd like. There are only a few things in this world that make me happier than helping people sidestep a shiny looking investment object that is actually a high-fee landmine.*

(ANTI) DIVIDEND PORTFOLIO PROS AND CONS

Let's talk about the good news and the bad news. Bad news, you're up to bat:

1. These are all-stock strategies and, as I noted earlier, we shouldn't confuse the safety of stocks for the safety of bonds. This portfolio could be good for the stock-specific portion of your allocation when used to build a total income portfolio.
2. Dividend-focused strategies incur income by definition, so you'll want to be aware of the tax implications.
3. Dividend-paying stocks don't demonstrate a strong tendency to outperform the broader market. So, not only are you incurring more taxes along the way, but you're not outperforming either. This might make some people wonder why they'd focus on dividends when they could own a similarly diversified total market fund and implement something like Fisher's home-grown dividends.
4. Beware of the types of dividend funds you consider. It's become very popular in recent years for new funds to promise huge yields.

---

* Things that make me happier include leg day, triple fudge brownies, and "warm hugs" from my daughters. If you have young kids who watch *Frozen* all day you know what I mean.

These funds are usually paying big dividends out of principal or trying to generate income by selling options or implementing other expensive and risky alternatives. These funds rarely beat correlated indices, but almost always have high(er) fees. As the old saying goes, if it seems too good to be true it probably is.

And what about the good news?

1. People love income. And if income keeps you invested then that's great. You have to find what you like and stick with it. If income helps you achieve behavioral robustness then this is a good thing.
2. There is a compelling argument that the shareholder yield approach generates superior returns when compared to pure dividends. This could be magnified after taxes given the inherent tax focus of the strategy.
3. I talk a lot about duration and time in my methodologies. One way to reduce duration and increase certainty in a portfolio is to generate income. Capital appreciation is great and all, but dividends are high-probability, short-term profit payouts, while capital appreciation is far from being high-probability in the short term. Any strategy that helps you boost certainty is worth considering.

SUITORS FOR THE (ANTI) DIVIDEND PORTFOLIO

Dividend portfolios and shareholder yield portfolios are great for people who want steady income and don't love getting it only from bonds. Shareholder yield funds are arguably more reliable and updated ways of owning firms that are returning cash to shareholders due to their own underlying financial strength.

Many of these funds will frame themselves as market-beating, but I'd argue they're more behavioral than anything else. That is, they're likely to generate returns similar to or lower than the broader market, but if the income or signaling effect helps you stay the course or better plan for your expenses then these are good for you.

In general, these types of strategies are most suitable for someone who's a little more conservative and perhaps in retirement or nearing retirement. Since income and shareholder yield can be more consistent with value and quality, it's a good option for people who want a little more certainty in their equity slice when compared to something like an aggressive growth fund.

Taxes could play an important role in these strategies so if you earn a high income or are in a higher tax bracket you might consider more tax-efficient ways of generating income.

FINAL THOUGHTS

Firms that pay out consistent dividends, like the VOC, tend to be firms that have positively trending revenues and profits. These positively trending financials give investors certainty and help provide them with a stable stream of income.

But can we use trends that don't relate to either dividends or factors to predict market prices? And would such a strategy be useful?

Behind Door #15 is a strategy called Trend Following and this one's really fascinating.

15

THE TREND FOLLOWING PORTFOLIO

IN late 1987 I followed my father into the Loudon County Virginia Courthouse where he was arguing a case on behalf of a teenage boy. I twiddled my thumbs patiently waiting for him to finish until a loud scream filled the courtroom and the boy jumped into my father's arms in celebration as he was absolved of a noise violation. The judge slammed his gavel and called for order.

Given his reaction I was convinced my dad had saved this boy's life and as the two of them walked my way the overzealous boy wasted no time in giving me a high five that still hurts to this day. This was the first time I would meet my friend Michael Covel, the most important advocate of what has famously become known as Trend Following.

The next time I would see Covel was when I was a young stockbroker at Merrill Lynch. We were having lunch in Tyson's Corner, Virginia, and he handed me one of the first ever published copies of *Trend Following*, an intriguing book that described a relatively unknown investment strategy. By then, he was a totally different person than the raucous boy I had met long ago, and he stoically explained the basic idea of the strategy and the many fascinating people who had become fabulously wealthy from it.

Like the older, trend-evolved Covel, the strategy was unemotional and stoically systematic, but still reflected a glimmer of the young Covel in that it was considered a contrarian, Wild West part of the investment world. It had the added benefit of performing especially well in circumstances when other asset classes did not. It did not just trend with the market, but tended to move one way when bigger asset classes, like stocks, moved the other direction.

I read the book in a single day and was lucky enough to have access to one of the most famous trend followers Covel wrote about. Merrill had begun offering an investing program in partnership with an investor named John W. Henry. I knew the name primarily because, as an avid Yankees fan growing up, I recognized the man who had just purchased my arch-nemesis, the Boston Red Sox.

FUN SIDE NOTE

I want to brag about my amazing dad. He once defeated Chuck Norris in a lawsuit. As a result of this the only two men who ever defeated Norris are Brien Roche and Bruce Lee.*

I called up the team that had constructed the investment program and I grilled them on the intimate details of the strategy. I had been hired to be a salesman, but I found myself being sold and I was

---

* I kid. Chuck Norris was just a paid spokesperson for a firm my father was involved in litigation with. And Chuck only lost to Bruce Lee in a movie, but none of this diminishes the amazingness of my dad.

hooked on Trend Following. Who knew that my love affair for Trend Following would grow from my hatred of the Boston Red Sox?

The Trend Following story is much older than J. W. Henry or Covel. In fact, one of the best-known Trend Followers was the most famous stock market speculator in history, Jesse Livermore. In his 1940 book *How to Trade in Stocks* Livermore distilled his process into a single paragraph:

> It may surprise many to know that in my method of trading, when I see by my records that an upward trend is in progress, I become a buyer as soon as a stock makes a new high on its movement, after having had a normal reaction. The same applies whenever I take the short side. Why? Because I am following the trend at the time. My records signal me to go ahead![34]

Livermore famously won and lost more money than most of us can ever imagine, and his losses ultimately resulted in a severe decline in mental health and suicide. Although Livermore was an original Trend Follower, he also had a knack for doubling down on ending trends. This compounding of risk helped teach modern-day Trend Followers the most important rule of all – the trend is your friend until it ends.

WHY TREND FOLLOWING WORKS

Trend Following refers to a broad range of strategies that implement time series momentum. Time series momentum focuses on a single asset's past returns to determine the trend of the instrument. This is different from the momentum factor, which uses a cross-sectional measure of momentum. A cross-sectional momentum approach takes a particular instrument (typically stocks only) and compares the past performance to the momentum of other correlated assets. This relative momentum helps determine whether an instrument has strong momentum when compared to similar instruments, as opposed to the pure Trend Following strategy which focuses on the absolute momentum of a singular instrument relative to its own past performance.

While Trend Following is distinctly different from the momentum factor, it works for similar reasons. There tends to be behavioral reasons for assets to move in a trend as investors feed on herd behavior. In the case of Trend Following, the goal is often to bet on small trends with the hope that they turn into larger ones. This is why Trend Following often results in huge asymmetric and uncorrelated returns. Because they're buying uncorrelated assets, trend followers often benefit from extreme market moves where a small trend, like the 2008 stock market downturn, turns into a crash. This is where Trend Following really shines and provides its outsized uncorrelated returns.

Research shows that Trend Following has worked for hundreds of years and has consistently exhibited uncorrelated returns throughout history (see Figure 15.1). Hurst, Ooi, and Pederson showed in 2017 that the trends are especially interesting in periods of great turmoil.[35]

Figure 15.1: 100+ years of Trend Following

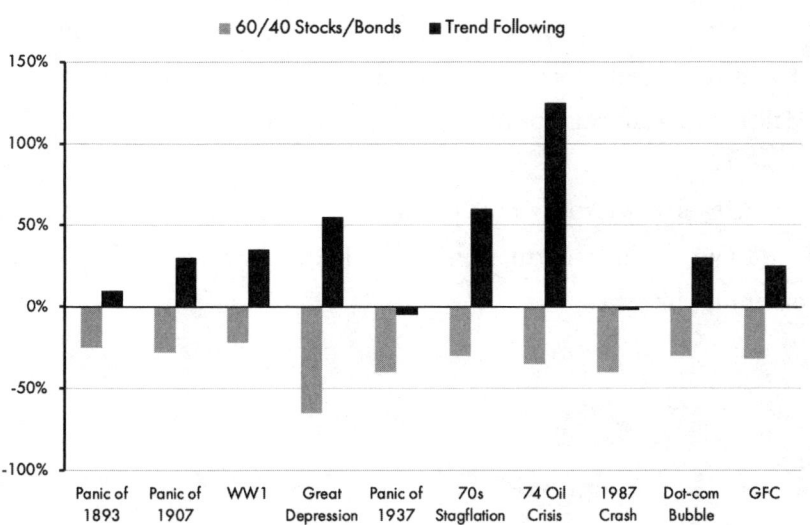

They created an equal weighted index across one-, three- and 12-month time horizons using 67 markets and found that trend strategies generated net annual returns of 8.6% (adjusted for inflation), with positive returns in every decade since 1880. More importantly, they found virtually no correlation to stocks and bonds. They concluded:

> [A] large body of research suggests that price trends exist in part because of long-standing behavioral biases exhibited by investors, such as anchoring and herding [and I would add to that list the disposition effect and confirmation bias], as well as the trading activity of non-profit-seeking participants, such as central banks and corporate hedging programs.

The theory says that behavioral biases such as herding lead to sustained trends:

> The intuition is that most bear markets have historically occurred gradually over several months, rather than abruptly over a few days, giving trend followers an opportunity to position themselves short after the initial market decline and profit from continued market declines. In fact, the average peak-to-trough drawdown length of the 10 largest 60/40 drawdowns between 1880 and 2016 was approximately 15 months.

Uncorrelated returns that perform especially well when we most need them. Sounds useful, huh? Let's dig into how we can implement something like this.

CHAPTER 15

BUILDING YOUR OWN TREND FOLLOWING PORTFOLIO

There are hundreds of different ways to skin this cat because Trend Following doesn't constrain us to a particular market or instrument. That's one of its benefits – it's a "go anywhere" type of strategy. You might be long oil and short interest rates one month, only to find yourself long pork bellies and short fart jars the next day. Just kidding, you can't short fart jars even though there was a market for them in 2021 during the heyday of the NFT craze. You get my point though – these strategies can go anywhere and it's the unconstrained nature of Trend Following, within a rigid systematic style of trading, that makes it so interesting.

I talked to Covel about why Trend Following works and he emphasized that it's because so much of what passes for "fundamentals" is nonsense. When you're Trend Following, you're using a pure price signal. There's no fundamental analysis required and so you're not relying on accountants, analysts, or backward-looking data to forecast anything. You're just using price trends.

But within that seemingly simplistic approach you're building a strict set of systematic rules. Rules are important because, as legendary investor Jim O'Shaughnessy writes in *What Works on Wall Street*, "If we can remove emotion and subjectivity from our investment strategies, we can beat the market in the long run." When you're Trend Following you're taking the behavior and the fundamentals out of the equation and simply trading a systematic price methodology. This can improve performance by reducing the potential for catastrophic mistakes. And while this might appear dissimilar to many of the strategies in this book, the general principles of Trend Following are consistent with most of the broader themes we've discussed, including:

1. **Focus on trends, not predictions**: Trend Following is all about riding the momentum of market trends rather than trying to predict market movements. It is essentially a version of extrapolative expectations wrapped around a rigorously systematic trading approach.
2. **Use clear rules**: Covel emphasizes the importance of easy-to-follow rules without complex analysis or predictions. This means focusing on basic technical indicators and avoiding overcomplicating the strategy.
3. **Risk management**: Proper risk management is crucial. This includes setting stop-loss orders to limit potential losses and determining position sizes based on your risk tolerance and goals.
4. **Discipline and consistency**: Stick to your strategy and rules without letting behavior drive your decisions. Stay the course with your systematic approach!
5. **Diversification**: Spread your investments across different markets and asset classes to reduce risk and increase the chances of capturing trends in various sectors. Diversify your trends so you increase the odds of capturing the big trends.
6. **Patience**: Trend Following requires patience, as trends can last for long periods, and it's crucial not to jump in and out of positions too quickly.

I would recommend reading Covel's books, not only because they explain how to implement the strategy at a more customizable level, but also because they're a fantastic historical read on the topic.

That said, there are numerous different ways to implement this strategy using publicly available funds. A few that you might consider doing more research on include:

- iMGP DBi Managed Futures Strategy ETF (ticker: DBMF)
- Simplify Managed Futures Strategy (ticker: CTA)
- First Trust Managed Futures Strategy Fund (ticker: FMF)
- KraneShares Managed Futures (ticker: KMLM)
- Arrow Managed Futures Strategy Fund (ticker: MFTNX)
- Virtus AlphaSimplex Managed Futures (ticker: ASFYX)
- AQR Managed Futures Strategy Fund (ticker: AQMIX)
- AQR Managed Futures Strategy HV Fund (ticker: QMHIX)

TREND FOLLOWING PORTFOLIO ANALYSIS

We're going to use the KMLM Index, one of the longer existing Trend Following indices and one that is also tracked by real-time funds for this analysis. Their fee-adjusted historical data begins in 1992 so we're somewhat limited by the historical data on trend analysis.

You'll notice something very interesting here – this strategy is almost inversely correlated with global stocks in the short term, even though they both trend higher in the long term. In fact, over the last 45 years you'd have ended up in nearly identical places despite very different paths, as seen in Figure 15.2. While both approaches generated about 5% annual real returns, they did so with almost no correlation. Their volatility profiles are quite different, with Trend Following generating 13.55% volatility per year and global stocks generating 18.85%.

Figure 15.2: Trend Following performance

Table 15.1: Portfolio analysis

	KMLM Index	**Global Stocks**
Real Returns	5.34%	5.41%
Volatility	13.55%	18.85%
Sharpe Ratio	0.46	0.39
Sortino Ratio	0.65	0.54
Max Drawdown	−38.00%	−58.88%
Ulcer Index	19.00	17.78
Market Correlation	−0.16	0.88

This Trend Following index achieved its returns with far smaller but longer lasting drawdowns (see Figure 15.3). That's due to the boom and bust nature of the trends being captured here. As noted, you're often capturing these very large asymmetric trends where a small trend builds into a major one and then, as Jesse Livermore learned, often mean reverts. Again, the trend is your friend until it ends. This emphasizes the importance of rules-based trading and having stop losses or systematic sell signals.

Figure 15.3: Trend Following max drawdowns (%)

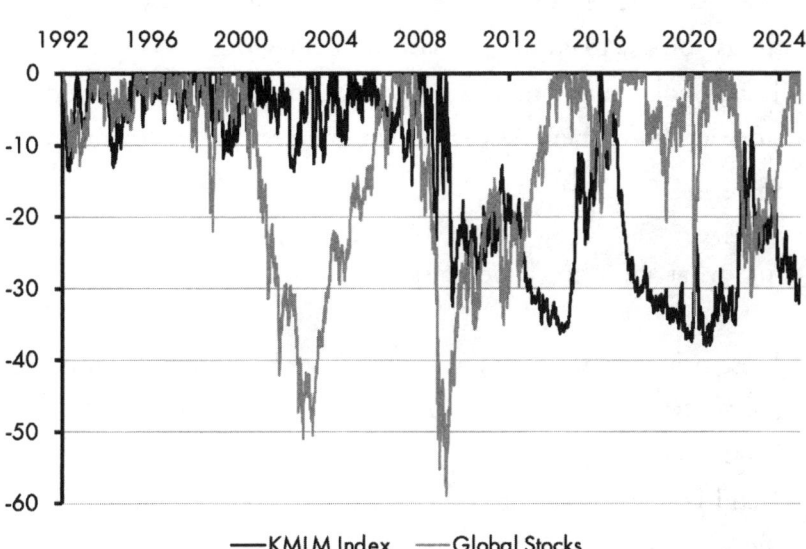

TREND FOLLOWING PORTFOLIO PROS AND CONS

I've got good news and bad news for you here. Of course, I'll break the bad news to you first.

1. This is, by design, a trading strategy. And we all know the math of the markets by now. The more active you are, the more likely you are to reduce overall returns. Trend Following also tends to operate in negative-sum markets where you don't have the benefit

of patiently waiting on capital appreciation from corporate cash flows. Markets like futures are constrained to specific time horizons which make them zero-sum or negative-sum games in the aggregate during that time horizon.
2. There's no guarantee that Trend Following will generate positive returns in the long run because we're not always dealing in cash-flow-generating assets like stocks and bonds.
3. The taxes and fees are usually unkind. Double check any specific funds you use to ensure the fees aren't egregious.
4. Trend Following strategies can go through long periods of sideways movement, especially in markets where there are no exaggerated trends.

And what about the good news?

1. These strategies are truly uncorrelated. It's hard to find consistently uncorrelated strategies, but Trend Following is one of the few that fits the bill.
2. Trend Following strategies aren't just uncorrelated, but tend to be the least correlated when it matters most. For instance, during the bear markets of 2002, 2008, and 2020.
3. These strategies don't rely on bull or bear markets or understanding fundamental analysis. There's no forecasting of economic or financial conditions.
4. Trend Following strategies are purely rules-based. There are no behavioral biases involved because the systematic nature of the strategy removes human emotion from the equation.
5. I like to think of these kinds of strategies as insurance. As I've noted, insurance is something you own and don't expect a positive sum return from in the short run. But, in certain unexpected environments, insurance pays out a huge asymmetric positive

return. Trend Following strategies are often similar. They can go years without showing much of a trend, but when big trends become pronounced (typically during big market swings like market crashes), Trend Following funds shine as those little trends suddenly turn into larger ones that lead to big returns.

SUITORS FOR THE TREND FOLLOWING PORTFOLIO

These strategies are volatile and unreliable in the short term, requiring an investor who is both patient and risk-tolerant. They also demand an appreciation for the role of unusual, uncorrelated assets and insurance.

In practice, the investors who adopt these approaches are those who understand how such strategies can function as part of a broader allocation and complement other assets.

FINAL THOUGHTS

Unemotional strategies are great. I am a big advocate of making your entire portfolio systematic to protect you from your own worst enemy. But I also know that investing requires a certain degree of activity and emotion. And if a little emotion helps you stay in the game then by all means introduce some emotion.

In the next chapter we're going to discuss the pros and cons of politically biased investing and what's come to be known as ESG investing. This one might ruffle a few feathers, so please keep reading, but remember to send all hate mail to the current Chairperson of the Federal Reserve and not me!

16

THE VICE AND VIRTUE PORTFOLIO

THE behavioral portfolios we've discussed so far are mostly about helping you stay comfortable with a portfolio because the markets are volatile and unpredictable.

But what if you're someone who wants to invest in strategies where you can make money and *feel good* about how you make that money? It's time to look at virtuous portfolios which help you stay the course by feeling better about what you're invested in.

Can you have your cake, eat it, and feel good about yourself too? Let's see.

★ ★ ★

As I'll explain later, I am generally inclined to default towards picking the simplest and most diverse portfolio that aligns with your personal goals. I don't recommend deviating too much from that portfolio because excess activity can create unnecessary taxes, fees, and performance frictions.

But there's a lot to be said for managing a portfolio so that you're personally comfortable with it rather than just adhering to a set of textbook mantras. After all, as Bernstein taught us earlier, the suboptimal portfolio you can stay loyal to will likely perform better than the theoretical optimal portfolio that you are constantly chasing (and changing).

As low-cost indexing has become more readily available, we are able to customize portfolios to meet our personal needs and wants. Vice And Virtue investing can be thought of as customizing a strategy to take advantage of the things we have personal preferences for. This approach has become popular as political narratives influence where dollars are allocated. Themes like climate change, social responsibility, and corporate governance are increasingly important to many investors, and entirely new asset classes have been created to meet the increasing demand for this movement. So-called ESG (environment, social, and governance) strategies have attracted hundreds of billions of dollars in recent years with the intent to help investors build a more virtuous portfolio for themselves.

I write this chapter with some hesitancy because I generally feel that we should not allow our vices, virtues, and politics to heavily influence our portfolios. That said, I am not here to tell you how to allocate your portfolio. I am here to remind you to never miss leg day and to help you find a portfolio you can stay loyal to. The point is, if you feel strongly that your allocation is more viable because it aligns with your personal views then this sort of strategy could be an essential piece in helping you stay the course.

But before we get into the specifics, I am going to outline my general view on these strategies so you can assess whether this makes sense for you or not.

ESG INVESTING IN PERSPECTIVE

The basic goal of ESG investing is to construct index funds and portfolios that are more socially acceptable. For instance, you might think that Exxon Mobil (XOM) is hurting the environment, so you construct a portfolio that doesn't own that stock. Makes sense.

Or does it? Let's take a moment to review some of the big themes from ESG investing and assess their validity.

ESG investing is more active investing that will increase the probability of lower future returns

We know that the more active average investor must, by definition, earn a lower average return than the less active average investor.

Let's say you don't like XOM and similar energy components in the S&P 500. What you're doing if you decide to exclude these firms from your portfolio is saying, "I think the other 90% of firms in the index will perform better than the index as a whole." This is active investing by another name. And the odds are you're incurring higher taxes and fees along the way when compared to a comparable alternative.

More fundamentally, as Cliff Asness once wrote:

> What happens when one group of investors, call them the virtuous, simply won't own a segment of the market (the sin stocks)? Well, in economist terms the market still has to "clear." In English, everything still gets owned by someone. So, clearly the group without such qualms, call them the sinners, have to own more than they otherwise would of the sin stocks. How does a market get anyone, perhaps particularly a sinner, to own more of something? Well it pays them! In this case through a higher expected return on the segment in question. This may

be unpleasant but it is just math (like math could ever be unpleasant). In the absence of extra expected return the sinners would own X of the market segment in question. The only way to get them to own X+Y is to pay them something more. Now, assuming nothing else changed, how does the market assign this sinful segment a higher expected return? Well by according it a lower price. That is, if the virtuous decide they won't own something, the sinners then have to, and they have to be induced to through getting a higher expected return than otherwise. This in turn is achieved through a lower than otherwise price.[36]

Perfectly stated. And this leads me right into a second (and fundamental) point.

The secondary market is a bad place to enact change

The intelligent defense of ESG is "by reducing the demand for a stock we can increase its cost of capital and impact the company's operating performance." This is true to *some* degree, but I think the impact is overstated. For instance, the firms in the S&P 500 are all large, established companies that have more than enough capital to finance their operations. They typically aren't using the secondary equity markets to fund their operations. In fact, most firms have so much capital that they've been net buyers of stock in the last 50 years. So, this thinking is a bit backwards.

A good analogy for this is to think of public secondary markets like horse betting. We can bet on the horses, but secondary market purchases are just private exchanges between third-party ticket owners, not cash issuance to firms. As a result, betting on the horses doesn't change the outcome of the race. The cash from our betting isn't buying the horse's hay, paying for training, or providing the stable. Similarly, our secondary market purchases and sales are mostly shuffling ownership among investors and not directly financing or even impacting the firm's daily operations. The company, like the horse running in a race, does not care who owns the shares or bets and it doesn't meaningfully impact the outcome of the race.

ESG investing can put more money in the hands of bad actors

A smart indexer decides to own all the firms in the market because we don't know which firms will perform better or worse. When you reduce exposure to certain firms because they aren't aligned with your moral views then you increase the odds that you'll earn a lower return.

This means that someone else is earning a higher return and potentially investing more of that money into the causes you don't believe in. You are, in essence, choosing to earn a lower return, thereby funding the very types of people you might disagree with.

No one knows what a "sin stock" really is

The reason I called this chapter "The Vice *And* Virtue Portfolio" is because we do not actually know what vices and virtues are, in the context of firms. The only reasonable definition of a company that is "immoral" is something that is illegal. Aside from that, a company that operates a legal business is simply providing a service for someone who doesn't view that business as morally contemptible.

For instance, I own an old Ford F-100 that uses gasoline. I don't drive it much, but when I do I either get looks of contempt or a million thumbs-up (almost exclusively from other men, which always makes my wife laugh). Sometimes I fill that truck up using XOM gasoline. Some people might find this morally contemptible. There's nothing wrong with that opinion, but there are also millions of people in this world who don't find gas-powered engines to be immoral. One person's vice can be another person's virtue.

This concept gets even more interesting when we consider the way that companies provide their services across time. For instance, XOM is now one of the leading firms in exploring alternative energies. What if, in 100 years, they are the market leader in renewables and no longer engage in fossil fuel production? By selling XOM you would have reduced your exposure to a firm that is innovating and producing beneficial changes in the world because your behavioral biases led you to believe that XOM is *currently* an immoral company. This is part of what makes active stock picking so hard. We can't predict how firms will change and how society will view their businesses across time. What's a sin stock to you today might not be a sin stock to someone else today or even to you tomorrow.

I am all for investing morally, but I think it should be done in a way that we can maximize the impact and, the fact is, the best place to enact change is in the **real** economy and not secondary markets. In fact, trying to boycott a stock in the secondary market could be counterproductive to your financial goals which could hurt your ability to do good. So, if you disagree with a firm like XOM then don't buy their gasoline. But refusing to buy their stock will have little to no impact on their actual business and that's what will drive their stock price ultimately.

I say you can have your cake and eat it too here. You can own a firm like XOM inside of an index fund, earn the returns, use those returns to fund the moral operations you prefer, and you can boycott XOM's operations in the real economy if you want to. It's the best of all worlds.

Okay, I'll get off my soapbox, but hopefully we all understand the logic behind why ESG investing might not be as great as it seems.

WHY VICE AND VIRTUE STRATEGIES WORK

As Cliff already discussed, these strategies don't work to generate superior returns. Or at least it's very unlikely that they'll do that over any extended period.

At the same time, the textbooks aren't always right because the economy is driven by people – people with big emotions. And as I will keep drilling into your head, the suboptimal portfolio you stick with is likely to be better than the optimal portfolio you constantly chase. So, if your moral justification for owning the S&P 499 (ex-XOM) results in you being more comfortable and disciplined then that's wonderful. I think it's great to have conviction and then follow that conviction. But you need to be aware of all the biases you're probably succumbing to in the process of implementing this strategy.

Let's get on with the portfolio construction, okay?

BUILDING YOUR OWN VICE AND VIRTUE PORTFOLIO

Building your own ESG portfolio requires a decent bit of customization to meet your personal needs. The surest way to align a portfolio to your personal needs is to use a custom indexing solution or work with a financial advisor who uses a custom indexing platform. Good options (which might require an advisor) include:

1. Canvas Custom Indexing (canvas.osam.com)
2. Schwab Direct Indexing (www.schwab.com/direct-indexing)

The alternative is to go direct to the ETF options and choose one that aligns with your personal views. This might require a decent

CHAPTER 16

amount of research. Some of these are very generally aligned with the broader ESG movement. Here are some of the larger choices:

1. iShares USA ESG Select (ticker: SUSA)
2. iShares ESG Aware MSCI EAFE (ticker: ESGD)

VICE AND VIRTUE PORTFOLIO ANALYSIS

I won't belabor the aforementioned point. Even though this strategy is relatively new, we can see that these strategies do not typically generate higher returns than the overall market. In fact, they tend to underperform and based on the assessment of the SUSA ESG Select ETF they correlate very highly with any corresponding benchmark (see Figure 16.1).

Figure 16.1: ESG performance

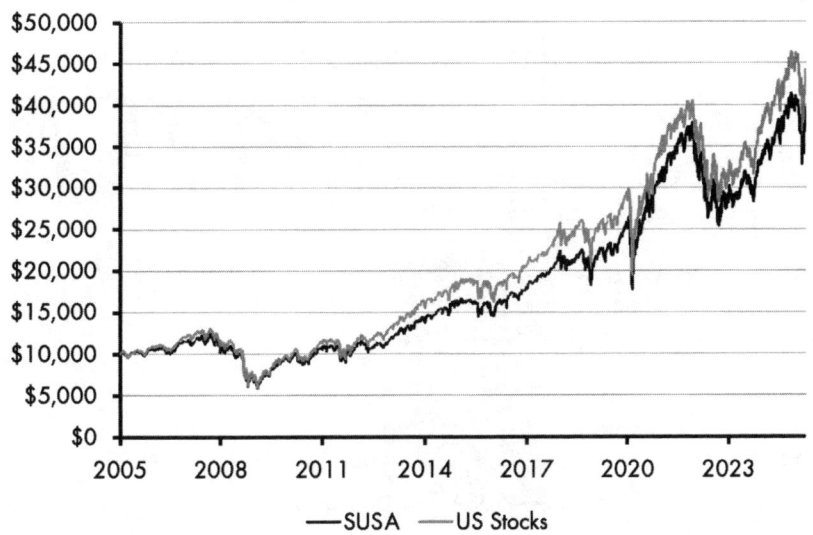

Table 16.1: Portfolio analysis

	ESG	US Stocks
Real Returns	7.04%	7.65%
Volatility	18.57%	19.24%
Sharpe Ratio	0.51	0.55
Sortino Ratio	0.71	0.75
Max Drawdown	-54.70%	-55.93%
Ulcer Index	14.50	14.30
Market Correlation	0.95	1.00

The drawdowns (see Figure 16.2) and Ulcer Index are also very similar across the biggest ESG fund and the total US market.

Figure 16.2: ESG max drawdowns (%)

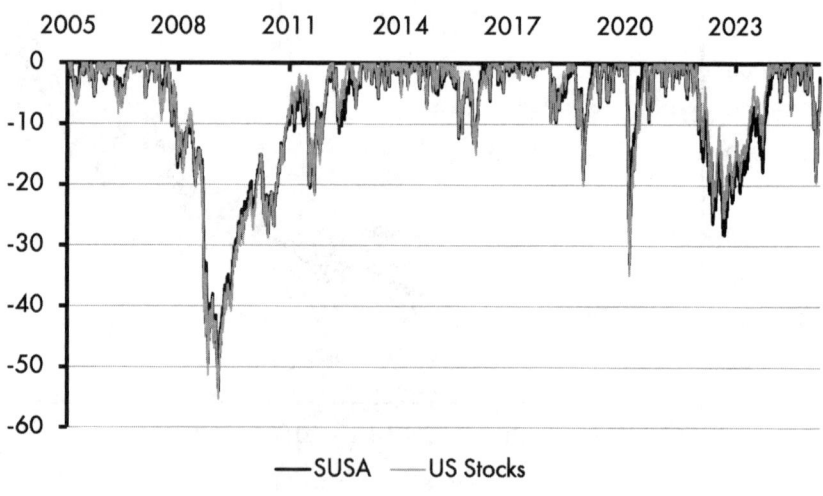

These look a lot like what I'd refer to as closet index funds. That is, they're not implementing some sort of unique alpha tilt or anything like that and mostly reflect a correlated index fund, typically with higher fees.

Okay, so you're not necessarily going to get superior performance here or even decrease correlation, but you will get something very similar to the broad market that might align with your personal views.

VICE AND VIRTUE PORTFOLIO PROS AND CONS

As always, we've got good news and bad news. First the bad:

1. I would describe the Vice And Virtue Portfolios as behavioral portfolios. They aren't likely to outperform the market and they shouldn't be sold under that false pretense, but if they help you stay behaviorally disciplined then they're certainly better than the alternative reality where you're stuck sitting in cash or some other inferior option.
2. The virtuous portfolio is subjective. You have to embrace the bias that's inherent in this particular strategy.
3. Many ESG portfolios are very broad by design and might not fully align with your personal views.
4. The custom indexing solutions give me anxiety and can be a tax nuisance because you end up holding 499 (or however many) positions and a more complex tax situation as a result. It's complexity cloaked as a simple solution.

Now the good news:

1. These portfolios can be implemented in a very diverse, tax- and fee-efficient manner. Something like SUSA costs just 0.25%, which is very reasonable.
2. You can get exposure to this strategy using a custom indexing service. This would allow you to remove specific items you disagree with as opposed to adhering to a broader ESG implementation.
3. These are strictly behavioral portfolios designed to help you allocate capital in a manner that keeps you fully invested by being more morally comfortable with what you are investing in.

SUITORS FOR VICE AND VIRTUE PORTFOLIOS

These portfolios are best for people who are interested in a politically and morally palatable portfolio. This portfolio isn't for the investor seeking to beat the market and in fact you have to understand that this type of portfolio will likely underperform broader indices.

FINAL THOUGHTS

I don't generally like to mix politics and investing, but the two worlds inevitably overlap more than we'd like. So ESG investing can be a good way for someone to try to blend their politics with their investing in a way that's more personally comfortable. There's nothing wrong with that assuming you understand exactly what you're doing.

Speaking of politics – let's talk about one of the most politicized figures in macroeconomics. John Maynard Keynes is best known for his political influence via economics, but did you know that he was highly influential in forming one of the most famous investment strategies currently in use? That's right, the Endowment Portfolio is up next. So buckle up.

17

THE ENDOWMENT PORTFOLIO

THE Endowment Portfolio story starts long ago with someone who was better known as an economist than an investment manager – John Maynard Keynes. While Keynes is most famous for having changed the field of macroeconomics with the publication of *The General Theory of Employment, Interest and Money*, he was arguably a much better portfolio manager than economist.[37]

Keynes managed the King's College endowment from 1921 until he died in 1946. Before Keynes, endowments relied on heavy allocations to real estate and fixed income-style instruments. One of Keynes's great insights was that stocks were a long-term instrument which should be utilized inside endowment funds that have inherently long time horizons for parts of their portfolio. While other UK fund managers largely shunned stocks, Keynes shed huge portions of the endowment's real estate portfolio in favor of a 33% allocation to public stocks.

Keynes was a first-mover on the public equity frontier and the fund's 16% annual returns from 1921–1946 trounced not only the UK equity markets, but other endowments as well.[38]

After Keynes died, the allocation followed roughly in the path of the other large trends we've discussed in portfolios, such as the 60/40 Portfolio, where public equities came to dominate these large diversified.

Keynes is often attributed with four general concepts that guided his investment philosophy:

1. Focus on equities for growth.
2. Avoid market timing.
3. Maintain a long-term focus.
4. Have a value bias.

Keynes was highly influential in the institutional asset management world because of these views. As Elroy Dimson once noted:

> As a result of his experiences and his advocacy for equities as the preferred asset class for long-term investors, the great economist had a considerable influence on the US endowment model.[39]

This thinking had a huge impact on a young man named David Swensen who was tapped to take over the Yale endowment fund in 1985 when he was just 31 years old.[40] Swensen was heavily influenced by Keynes, but added his own twist. Instead of transitioning endowments from real estate to public equities like Keynes did, Swensen relied heavily on transitioning the endowment from other diversifiers to private equities and venture capital-style allocations. Swensen's view was that public equities, while still attractive, did not expose the investor to the same degree of mispricing that private equities could. He wrote:

While illiquid markets provide a much greater range of mispriced assets, private investors fare little better than their marketable security counterparts as the extraordinary fee burden typical of private equity funds almost guarantees delivery of disappointing risk-adjusted results.

Median results for venture capital and leveraged buyouts dramatically trail those for marketable equities, despite the higher risk and greater illiquidity of private investing. In order to justify including private equity in the portfolio, managers must select top quartile managers. Anything less fails to compensate for the time, effort, and risk entailed in the pursuit of nonmarketable investments.

Swensen saw this unloved sector as an opportunity, much like Keynes saw public equities as an opportunity in the early 1900s. Over the course of the next 30 years, Yale's endowment transformed from a largely bond and public equity fund to a much broader mix of public/private equities and alternatives. Swensen passed away in 2021, but his enormous impact on finance is far from forgotten.

Figure 17.1 shows the evolution of Yale's endowment allocations.

FUN SIDE NOTE

Keynes is often thought of as the creator of big government economic policy, but Keynes was an avid capitalist who was vocally critical of the socialist movement in the early 1900s. While he was an advocate of countercyclical budget deficits during economic recessions, Keynes was also an advocate of budget surpluses during booms. Some people say "we're all Keynesians now," but his actual economic approach hasn't been followed in developed economies in a very long time.

Figure 17.1: Evolution of endowment allocations

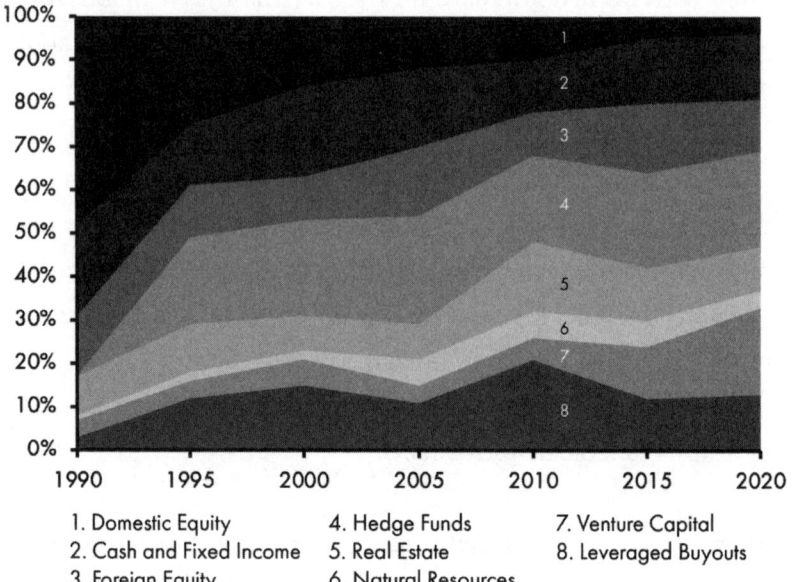

1. Domestic Equity
2. Cash and Fixed Income
3. Foreign Equity
4. Hedge Funds
5. Real Estate
6. Natural Resources
7. Venture Capital
8. Leveraged Buyouts

HOW THE ENDOWMENT PORTFOLIO WORKS

The Endowment Portfolio takes the basic building blocks of something like the GFAP and adds numerous diversifiers, with an emphasis on private markets including private equity, hedge funds, real estate, commodities, and others.

Figure 17.2 shows how the Yale Endowment Portfolio was allocated at the time of David's passing.

The items that really jump out are a small allocation to bonds and cash, and a 60% allocation to venture capital, private equity, and absolute return (hedge funds). This was part of Swensen's belief in an illiquidity premium. He said:

> Intelligent acceptance of illiquidity and a value orientation constitutes a sensible, conservative approach to portfolio management.

Figure 17.2: Yale endowment asset allocation (2021)

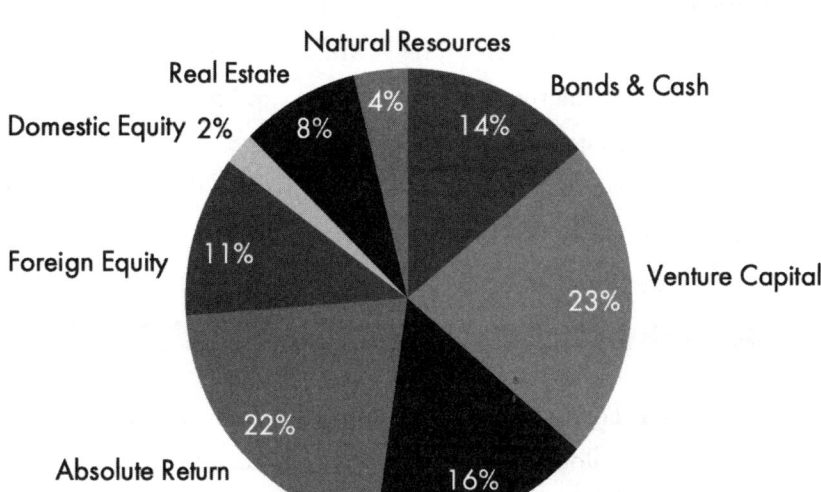

The basic theory of an illiquidity premium is that you can lock up capital to allow it to be targeted to higher-return, long-term allocations, which will reduce the trading costs created by short-term-oriented investors. By giving the strategy more time to achieve its goals you sacrifice short-term liquidity for long-term returns.

Further, because these strategies can be more complex, they have higher embedded costs that can only be offset by aligning them with the right long-term investor.[41] It makes sense, assuming of course that you allocate to the right projects.

The key takeaway from this is that Swensen really leaned into the long-term nature of a specific asset allocation, adopted the Keynesian value approach, and then took the focus on corporations one step further by adding private equities to a public equity portfolio. And that makes sense for an endowment because they are inherently long-term entities so they should have a heavy emphasis on more long-term and more illiquid assets.

The key reason why this strategy works is because it leans very heavily into the productive capacity of public and private equities. At the same time, the strategy maintains a high degree of diversification across other uncorrelated assets. This is probably the most diverse portfolio we'll study in this book.

BUILDING YOUR OWN ENDOWMENT PORTFOLIO

The Endowment Portfolio is difficult to replicate because the majority of the portfolio is allocated in privately held assets like venture capital, private equity, and hedge funds. Swensen had almost 40% of the portfolio allocated in venture capital and private equity at the time of his death. That's a big figure and replicating that would be very difficult given that Swensen had resources most of us do not.

In his 2005 book, *Unconventional Success*, Swensen outlined a straightforward way to implement an alternative portfolio. The allocation was outlined as follows:

- 30% Domestic stocks
- 15% Foreign stocks
- 5% Emerging market stocks
- 20% REITs
- 15% Government bonds
- 15% TIPS

This is a very rough approximation of what Swensen actually did with the endowment approach, but it's an easily replicated Swensen portfolio that could be implemented using the following funds, as shown in Figure 17.3.

Figure 17.3: Building the *Unconventional Success* Portfolio with funds

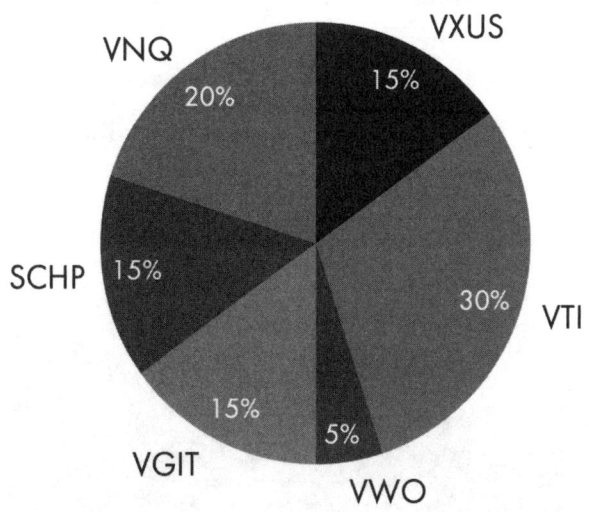

The actual Endowment Portfolio is much more complex and revolves largely around assets that are hard to access in public markets. The private equity and venture slices are especially hard to replicate. If you wanted to explore some ways to get private equity exposure you might consider some of the following options:

- AngelList (www.angellist.com)
- We Funder (wefunder.com)
- Equity Zen (equityzen.com)

Combined with a larger allocation of private equity access you could add in the *Unconventional Success* allocation for something that more closely replicates the Swensen portfolio.

Perhaps the private assets are too daunting for you and you'd like to build an Endowment Portfolio using publicly available funds. If you held a gun to my head and asked me to do that I'd probably come up with something like the allocation shown in Figure 17.4, which I'd call the Poor Man's Endowment Portfolio (which, ironically, requires you to be a rich accredited investor).

Figure 17.4: The Poor Man's Endowment Portfolio

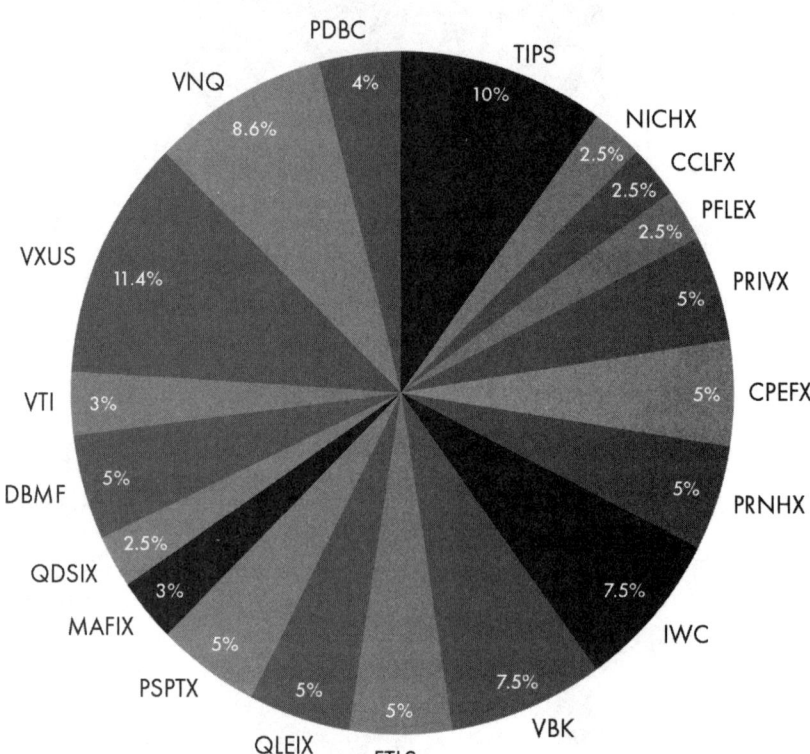

The goal here is to better replicate investments in private equity, private credit, and hedge funds using publicly available funds (some of which require accreditation and therefore might need to be removed depending on the investor's access to such funds).

A few of these funds are a relatively new fund style called interval funds, which can access private markets by locking up the redemption schedule. This creates more transparency than some private funds, but also adheres to Swensen's illiquidity premium by locking up funds for longer periods than you'd see with an open-end mutual fund which has daily redemptions.

Here are the allocations and specific funds as outlined:

Bonds and alternative income
- TIPS ETF or TIPS ladder 10%
- Variant Alternative Income Fund (ticker: NICHX) 2.5%
- Cliffwater Corporate Lending (ticker: CCLFX) 2.5%
- PIMCO Flexible Credit Fund (ticker: PFLEX) 2.5%

Venture capital and private equity alternatives
- The Private Shares Fund (ticker: PRIVX) 5%
- Cascade Private Capital Fund (ticker: CPEFX) 5%
- T.Rowe New Horizons Fund (ticker: PRNHX) 5%
- iShares Micro-Cap ETF (ticker: IWC) 7.5%
- Vanguard Small Cap Growth ETF (ticker: VBK) 7.5%

Absolute return alternatives
- First Trust Long/Short Equity ETF (ticker: FTLS) 5%
- AQR Long-Short Equity (ticker: QLEIX) 5%
- PIMCO StockPLUS Absolute Return (ticker: PSPTX) 5%
- Abbey Capital Multi-Asset (ticker: MAFIX) 3%
- AQR Diversifying Strategies (ticker: QDSIX) 2.5%
- iMGP DBi Managed Futures Strategy (ticker: DBMF) 5%

US and foreign public equities
- Vanguard Total Stocks (ticker: VTI) 3%
- Vanguard Total Stock Ex-US (ticker: VXUS) 11.4%

REITs
- Vanguard REIT ETF (ticker: VNQ) 8.6%

Natural resources
- Invesco Diversified Commodities (ticker: PDBC) 4%

That. Is. A. Lot. Even though this is my replication of an approximate Endowment Portfolio, I would be remiss if I didn't say that I am skeptical of this construction. Not only does it not reflect the actual way Swensen accessed private markets, but it is arguably way too diverse and at risk of *diworsification*, high fees, and tax inefficiencies. The biggest problem with something like this is that even though it's extremely diverse, you're not getting the moonshot potential that Swensen would get with venture capital. That's a huge difference-maker.

But if you're finding that many of the portfolios in this book are too simple for you then perhaps something overly complex will get you on a path you prefer? In that case maybe there are some interesting ideas in here.

If you're looking for something a little leaner and cleaner in one package then you might consider Cambria's Endowment Style ETF (ticker: ENDW). This fund replicates the endowment strategy by taking a target allocation of 50% equities, 20% fixed income, 15% real assets (REITs, TIPS, Commodities and commodity equities), and then alternatives (Trend Following strategies mostly). The equities are globally diversified and tilted to various factors including value, momentum, and Trend Following and levered to a target allocation of 70%. The use of leverage in this fund is interesting because it helps to better replicate the higher expected returns we might expect in venture capital and private equity. It's a very new fund, but Cambria is one of the thought leaders in the endowment model space so they're worth paying attention to.

CHAPTER 17

THE ENDOWMENT PORTFOLIO ANALYSIS

It's virtually impossible to analyze this portfolio in an objective manner because we're not cleanly replicating the Swensen Portfolio or the large endowments. The vast allocation to private equity makes it virtually impossible for us to copy and analyze objectively. Further, the short track record of many of the funds included in my Poor Man's Endowment Portfolio limits our ability to assess its historical performance.

So we'll have to make do with what we have. Swensen's *Unconventional Success* allocation is easy to replicate and implement, even if it doesn't truly reflect the complex methodology he used to allocate assets.

The portfolio Swensen outlines ends up having a very high correlation with a global 70/30 stock/bond portfolio. It is interesting, however, that Swensen starts with a much heavier equity emphasis.

Figure 17.5: *Unconventional Success* **Portfolio performance**

Table 17.1: Portfolio analysis

	Unconventional Success	70/30 Stocks/Bonds
Real Returns	7.50%	7.25%
Volatility	13.55%	12.65%
Sharpe Ratio	0.49	0.49
Sortino Ratio	0.68	0.68
Max Drawdown	−43.51%	−39.58%
Ulcer Index	9.02	8.30
Market Correlation	0.67	0.62

In terms of its drawdowns we also get very similar results when compared to a global 70/30 (see Figure 17.6).

Figure 17.6: *Unconventional Success* **Portfolio drawdowns (%)**

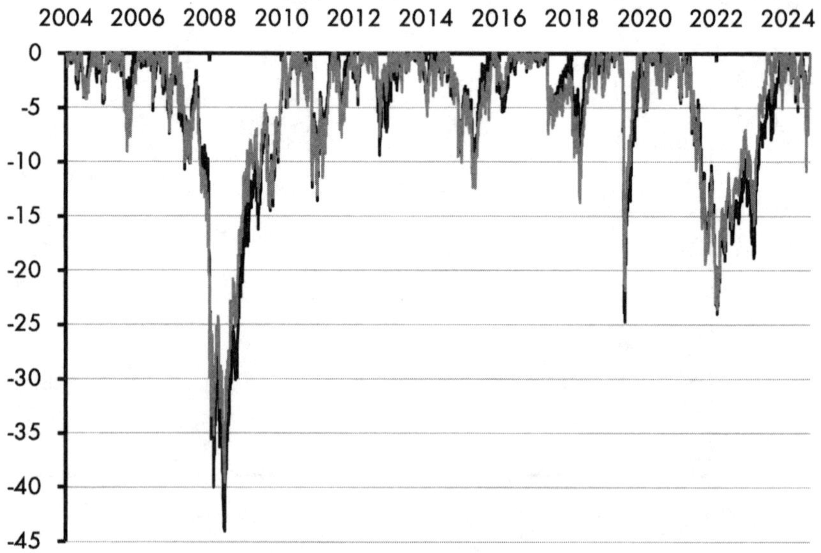

In short, the *Unconventional Success* Portfolio doesn't display highly differentiated characteristics when compared to relatively basic indexing strategies. All of this reinforces the point that this strategy works best when it's maximizing its access to the same kind of private market assets that Swensen focused on.

In my view the *Unconventional Success* Portfolio is overly simplistic and doesn't really reflect the more sophisticated ways the endowment model is designed to work. Because of this you should explore more customized ways to access this style of asset allocation. That means personalized private equity approaches meshed with something like the *Unconventional Success* Portfolio, using a packaged ETF or exploring the Poor Man's Endowment Portfolio in more detail.

THE ENDOWMENT PORTFOLIO PROS AND CONS

I've got good news and bad news. Let's get the bad news out of the way:

1. As stated above, this portfolio is hard to replicate. We don't have access to the investments that Swensen did given the scale and network that was available to him. If you want to replicate this portfolio you need to do it indirectly.
2. There's a strong argument that most of us cannot afford to invest like an endowment because we don't have the time horizon of an endowment. These funds will likely outlive every single person who reads this book. While you have short-term liabilities and expenses, an endowment has the luxury of thinking very long term.
3. There's increasing evidence that private market investments don't consistently outperform their public market counterparts, especially when we consider taxes and fees. Endowments have come under significant criticism in the last decade over their poor performance,

which is largely attributable to the high-fee allocations they often have in things like hedge funds, private equity, and venture capital.

And now the good news:

1. These strategies are ultra diverse.
2. Private placements can give you unique potential for uncorrelated returns and the moonshot potential is far greater in private markets than in public markets.
3. The *Unconventional Success* Portfolio can be implemented in a very simple, diverse, and tax/fee efficient manner.
4. In my opinion the big lesson from this portfolio is that we should all learn more about the private equity slice of the allocation. That is, after all, the defining feature of Swensen's approach.

SUITORS FOR THE ENDOWMENT PORTFOLIO

I really like the core elements of this portfolio and the broader philosophy of thinking long term and staying diversified. But this approach is only appropriate for a specific segment of your portfolio, or a very specific type of investor who is incredibly patient, doesn't mind illiquidity, and can access these types of investments.

To replicate the Endowment Portfolio cleanly, you need to implement the private equity components of the portfolio. Otherwise, you're not really capturing the essence of the illiquidity and long-term premiums that Swensen advocated. But that requires a uniquely sophisticated type of investor.

CHAPTER 17

FINAL THOUGHTS

That might not be the most practical portfolio for you to implement. And if you're looking for something highly practical then you're going to like our next one.

Retirement Bond Tent Strategies are up next – they are extremely pertinent for anyone nearing retirement or anyone seeking some shelter for a specific piece of their portfolio.

18

RETIREMENT BOND TENT STRATEGY

Ahh, retirement. That period in life where you finally get to kick back and stop worrying about everything. Right? RIGHT? Not necessarily.

As someone who has advised hundreds of retirees over the course of my career, I've found that retirement is often the most difficult psychological financial period you'll ever encounter.

It's not that retirement is a big hurdle itself. It's easy to stop working so you can focus on things you enjoy. But it's a huge transition for many people because you go from having had a purpose your whole life while growing your nest egg to suddenly transitioning to finding a different purpose while watching your nest egg potentially shrink as you live off it. At the same time, you have to grapple with the fact that your income is now shrinking and that cash flow you had before can no longer be relied on to fund your expenses. This can be a big psychological hurdle for many people to overcome.

I mentioned earlier that I like to think of your job and your income as a part of your bond portfolio. If you make $100,000 per year you can think of this as though you have the equivalent of a $1,000,000 bond allocation that pays you 10% per year. You have an asset (your job) and it pays you a fixed income every year. This is why it can make a lot of sense to be very aggressive when you're young and working. You effectively have a large fixed-income allocation already so you can afford to take more equity market risk.

When you retire, that synthetic bond allocation either disappears or it shrinks significantly. All of a sudden your relative equity allocation increases. And this is where the psychological hurdles and sequence-of-returns risk can become magnified.

What's an investor to do?

One strategy to consider is a Retirement Bond Tent. Let's dive into it.

WHY RETIREMENT BOND TENT STRATEGIES WORK

Michael Kitces wrote a research piece in 2016 discussing a concept called a "bond tent."[42] It took a very different view on retirement asset allocation when compared to traditional financial planning approaches. In the traditional model, your bond allocation roughly follows your age (see Figure 18.1).

This makes sense on its face. As you get older you should reduce your stock market exposure and increase your bond exposure because you're running out of time to navigate the excess volatility of the stock market. You add more bonds to throttle the stock market risk and therefore create more near-term certainty in your financial planning.

Figure 18.1: The age-in-bonds rule

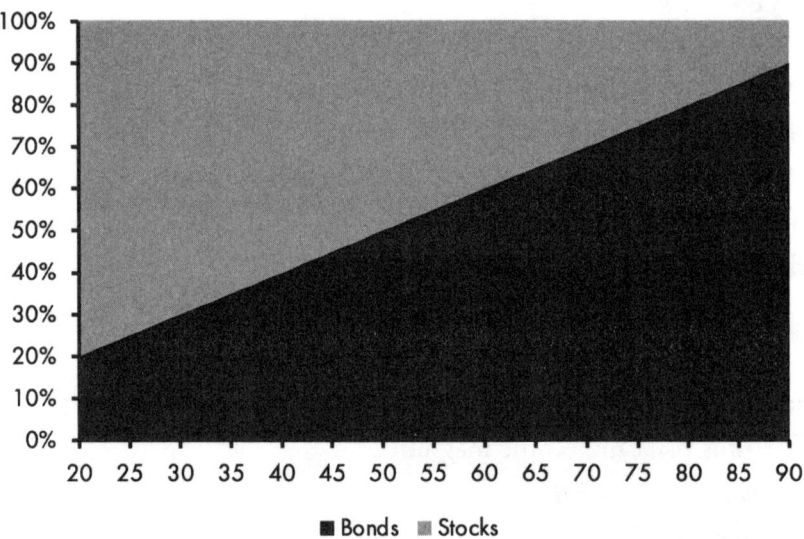

The problem with this concept around retirement is that life isn't one smooth glide path into retirement. It's generally a very abrupt start/stop type of sequence. For example, if you retire on January 1 of the year you turn 65, your wages abruptly shrink or disappear. If you think of your job as that bond allocation, you suddenly have a huge disparity in your stock/bond allocation. I don't think most investors consciously think of it this way, but they intuitively feel it this way. That creates a huge amount of uncertainty for many investors. Especially if your retirement income sources are not significant.

Kitces' solution to this problem is to build a "bond tent" where, in the years leading up to retirement and in early retirement, you boost your bond allocation more than what the age-in-bonds rule would say. The bond tent is designed to create more income and stability around your retirement transition so you can more comfortably navigate those unpredictable years around retirement. Then as you get older you reduce the size of the tent and your relative equity allocation should begin to increase. Figure 18.2 shows what this looks like.

Figure 18.2: The Kitces bond tent

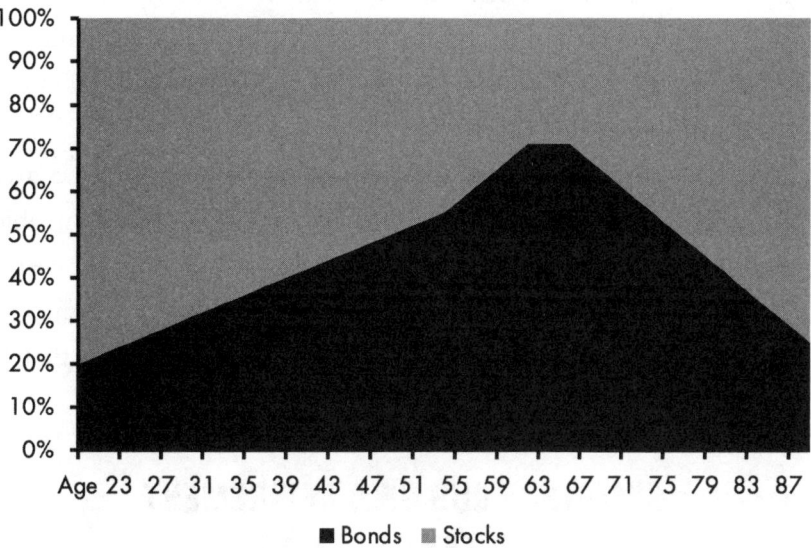

Most people think the riskiest part of your retirement years will be the point where you're very old and potentially running out of money. But the biggest risk usually comes around retirement age when your sequence-of-returns risk is largest.

For example, if an investor retires at 65 with a portfolio of $1,000,000 that is growing at 7% per year with a 60/40 stock/bond allocation, they can comfortably withdraw $50,000 per year (adjusted for inflation). But what if they retire just as a severe bear market hits and their portfolio declines 10% annually for the first three years? This investor is suddenly looking at a portfolio value that is around $594,000. If they continue withdrawing $50,000 annually, they're now taking out 8.4% of their portfolio each year and their financial plan is much more likely to fail. This investor may have to go back to work, take more risk, alter their living standards, or win the lottery.

Worse, what about the psychological turmoil? And what if this investor makes the worst mistake of all by reducing their stock exposure during the bear market, as so many investors often do? This is why sequence-of-returns risk is so important to understand. As Morgan Housel says, tails drive everything around us, and this is the ultimate retirement tail risk.

Yes, this is an oversimplified and extreme example, but it's a scenario that can and does play out in real life. And it's very easily avoidable by insulating yourself around those precarious early retirement years.

In short, the Retirement Bond Tent works because it's designed to build a protective envelope around the period of retirement that is most difficult to navigate.

BUILDING YOUR OWN RETIREMENT BOND TENT STRATEGY

The Retirement Bond Tent is highly customizable and depends heavily on personal circumstances.

In general, you can construct a Retirement Bond Tent quite simply. Let's use a hypothetical 20-year-old college graduate who follows the age-in-bonds rule up until they're 55:

- Years 20–55: Increase bond allocation in accordance with the age-in-bonds rule.
- Years 55–62: Escalate the rate of bond reallocation by 2% per year so that you reach about 70–71% by the age of 62.
- Years 62–67: Maintain the tent at 71% bonds.
- Years 71+: Reduce your bond allocation by 2%+ per year as you

withdraw funds and allow the higher expected returns to accrue in your stock market allocation.

An alternative option is to maintain any other strategy you like until you near your retirement years. For instance, if you're an aggressive investor with a high income perhaps you maintain a 100% stock allocation from 20–55. At this point you initiate the above stages by making all retirement plan contributions to the bond allocation only. Over a 10-year period, your only asset allocation goal is to get that bond allocation to a point where it's meeting your retirement income needs. If necessary, this could require selling some stocks and reinvesting the cash in bonds.

Implementation of the bond tent is highly dependent on personal circumstances so consider the actual asset allocation process in the context of your own needs. As we've discussed in earlier chapters, this sort of strategy would mesh well with our Flying Ladder Portfolio or any strategy that has a heavy bond emphasis with strategically structured bond ladders or fixed income components.

RETIREMENT BOND TENT STRATEGY ANALYSIS

Analyzing the Retirement Bond Tent strategy against a benchmark or index is challenging because the allocations shift based on the investor's age. This means you can't easily tie the portfolio's composition to specific time periods in the market, making direct comparisons difficult if not impossible. And in any event, this is very much not a "beat the market" portfolio as it is specifically structured as a behavioral portfolio and planning tool. You don't need to worry about how the broader market is performing when this strategy makes its moves, because the allocation is specifically designed to shield you from short-term volatility and the psychological mistakes it often provokes during the worst possible moments.

RETIREMENT BOND TENT STRATEGY PROS AND CONS

You know the drill:

1. The first bit of bad news is that the bond tent doesn't provide broad exposure to alternative assets. If you require greater diversification then you need to either reduce your stock allocation or consider incorporating high-quality bond alternatives. One solution here is to consider an "insurance tent." I've mentioned that instruments like cash, gold, and managed futures have attributes like insurance. If you wanted a twist on the "bond" tent concept you might consider adding an insurance tent to bolster the bond tent.
2. The bond tent requires a decent bit of upkeep. Your stocks are likely to outperform your bonds over time and if you're living off the income in the bond portfolio then you'll constantly need to monitor the bond allocations to avoid the stock allocation from growing ever larger. You need to be a bit hands-on.
3. All that rebalancing requires flexibility, so if you can implement this strategy in non-taxable accounts then that's smart. Otherwise, the added activity will incur higher taxes and fees.

And what about the pros?

1. This is an eminently sensible portfolio for anyone entering retirement who is losing significant income.
2. I really like how the equity piece is allowed to grow later in life because, depending on your portfolio size and withdrawal rate, the

odds of running out of money are low and the time horizon for the portfolio is therefore getting, strangely, *longer*. That's because the portfolio is likely becoming a multi-generational portfolio, so the beneficiary's asset allocation and risk profile suddenly comes into play.
3. This is a great behavioral portfolio as it helps solve a real-world problem for investors transitioning into retirement.

SUITORS FOR RETIREMENT BOND TENT STRATEGIES

If you're entering retirement or in early retirement you should absolutely consider this sort of strategy. I've been using the bond tent concept in client accounts for a long time and have personally witnessed its benefits. For anyone who has any behavioral uncertainty as they near retirement this is a very good option to consider.

FINAL THOUGHTS

This strategy covers a more personalized period of someone's life as they get closer to retirement. And that's part of why your perfect portfolio has to be adaptive to some degree – your life is going to change and your portfolio will need to adjust with it. A bond tent can be a great way to build more security as you near an uncertain part of your life.

Speaking of adaptive retirement-based portfolios, let's talk about some of the most popular time-based portfolios around. Target Date Portfolios have become a popular option in most retirement plans, so let's look at whether they might be perfect for you.

19

TARGET DATE PORTFOLIOS

IN the early 1990s, two advisors from Wells Fargo Investment Advisors (now Barclays Global Investors), Donald Luskin and Lawrence Tint, identified a problem with many retirement accounts – the investors didn't pay much attention to them and as a result often ended up with overly aggressive portfolios during their uncertain retirement withdrawal years.

To respond to this dilemma, the advisors devised a methodology by which a retirement portfolio could automatically reduce its risk as the investor neared retirement. They called this the LifePath Portfolios and the strategy roughly followed the age-in-bonds rule. By following this automated strategy, an employee with a retirement plan could pick a single fund and contribute to a diversified portfolio of stocks and bonds knowing that the portfolio would be more aggressive during their accumulation years and become less aggressive as they neared retirement and entered their decumulation years.

While seemingly obvious today, the strategy was a game changer at the time and would go on to become one of the most popular retirement plan choices.

WHY TARGET DATE FUNDS WORK

Target Date Portfolios should be considered as another behavioral portfolio. They're not designed to beat the market or optimize for alpha. They're designed to help an investor build a simple and diversified portfolio that helps them stay the course and plan for retirement. Most importantly, a Target Date Portfolio doesn't require a lot of upkeep, which makes it especially popular in retirement accounts and 401(k)s. The investor can set it and forget it and still know that they're on track for retirement without having to consistently tinker with and monitor an allocation.

Most target date funds follow a phased approach to rebalancing that matches your career arc. Figure 19.1 shows what they typically look like.

Figure 19.1: Phased target date approach

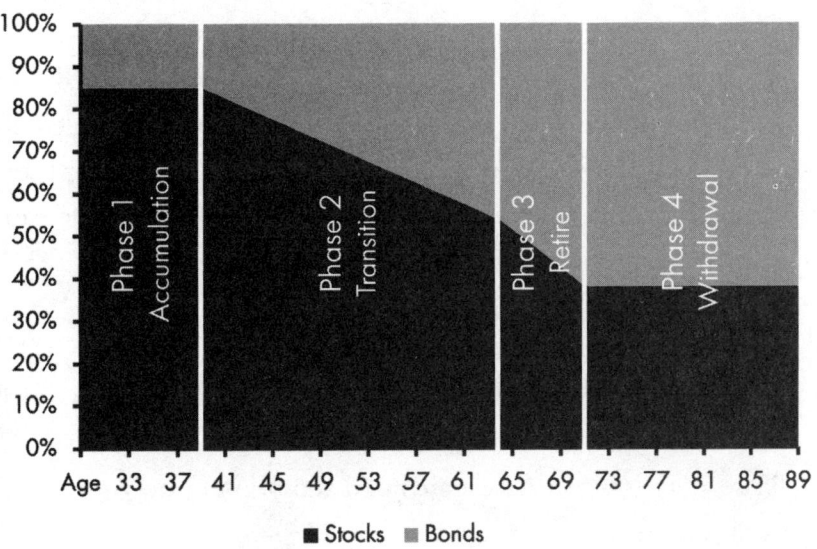

The key factor in a Target Date Portfolio is that it reduces sequence-of-returns risk by becoming more conservative as you near retirement. You choose a fund which matches your expected retirement year and the portfolio systematically becomes more risk-averse as you get closer to that date, and then typically becomes even more conservative as you navigate the early retirement years, until leveling off during the withdrawal phase.

Target date funds just make sense. They work because they take a diversified and low-cost portfolio and then systematically rebalance it so you can focus on what you do for a living and still know that your retirement plan is aligned with the likely changes in your risk tolerance based on age and retirement target.

BUILDING YOUR OWN TARGET DATE PORTFOLIO

There are two ways to build your own Target Date Portfolio. Option one is to consider target date funds from a low-cost fund family like Vanguard or Fidelity. They currently offer funds covering every five years from 2025–2070. You can simply select the fund that matches your retirement year and call it a day. No need to overthink it.

The other option is to build something more customized and rebalance it on your own. For instance, if you took the Boglehead Three-Fund Portfolio you would simply build out a plan using three funds and rebalance it over time to match the customized glide path you prefer. It might look something like this:

- Phase 1 (age 30–40): 85/15 stocks/bonds.
- Phase 2 (age 40–63): Increase bond allocation by 1.3% per year until you reach a 55/45 stock/bond allocation.
- Phase 3 (age 63–71): Accelerate bond allocation by 2.25% per year until you reach 37/63 stocks/bonds.

- Phase 4 (age 71+): Maintain 37/63 stock/bond allocation.

This can be done using any of the multi-asset portfolios we've discussed in this book.

TARGET DATE PORTFOLIO ANALYSIS

These aren't the sexiest portfolios, but let's run some figures anyhow.

To see how this works in practice we can look at the actual Vanguard 2020 Target Date Fund which followed a path approximately similar to the above four phases and is currently helping retirees who retired in 2020 and now have a 37.4% stock allocation with a 62.6% allocation in bonds.

Figure 19.2: Vanguard 2020 Target Date Fund

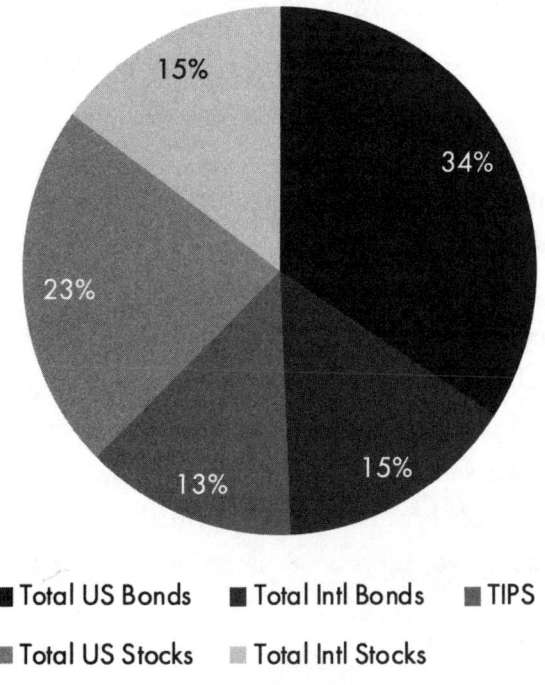

When compared to a 60/40 Portfolio we see that the 2020 TDF underperforms by a bit (Figure 19.3), which is to be expected given that the fund has been underweight stocks leading into 2020.

Figure 19.3: Vanguard 2020 Target Date Fund performance

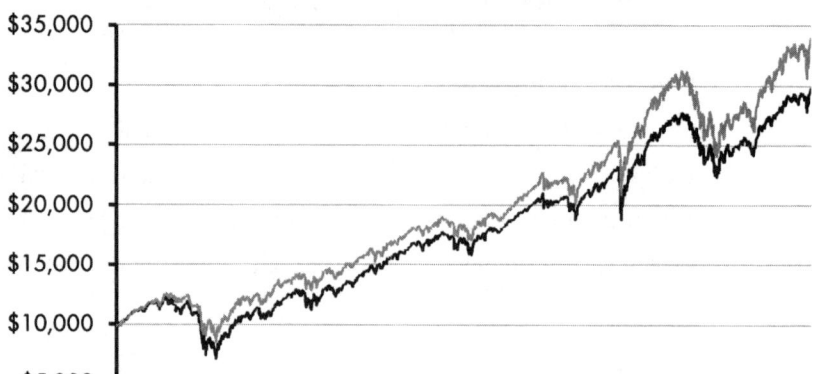

Interestingly, this fund also experienced a bit of sequence-of-returns risk, as its inception came close to the GFC. So, its more aggressive starting allocation hurt it upfront. But remember, this fund's target retirement year was 12 years later so the fund still achieved its more long-term goal of growing nicely and then helping to provide a little better principal protection around the target retirement year in 2020.

As Figure 19.4 shows, the fund mitigated drawdowns during the Covid market crash because it had systematically reduced its stock allocation as compared to its 2008 allocation.

Figure 19.4: Vanguard 2020 Target Date Fund drawdowns (%)

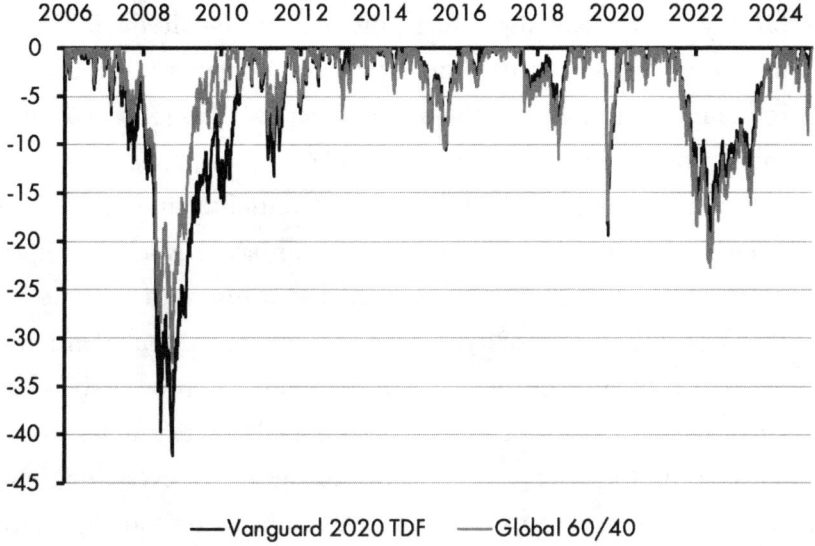

Overall, these funds do what we'd expect them to do as they're more aggressive at initiation and become less aggressive as they approach their target.

TARGET DATE PORTFOLIO PROS AND CONS

C'mon. You know how this works by now. Bad news first:

1. Target Date Portfolios will generally become cautious in retirement and then remain that way. As we discussed in the bond tent chapter, this might not be optimal because your allocation doesn't need to remain cautious throughout your entire retirement. In fact, as we noted in the bond tent strategy, TDFs might be doing something that imperfectly aligns with your behavior and retirement goals by too closely following the age-in-bonds rule.

2. The strategies are often homogeneous so your stocks and bonds are all in the same diversified mix of assets. As a result, if you withdraw funds you are essentially selling a bit of everything in the portfolio instead of just selling the liquid cash component you need. This is one reason to consider the option where we disaggregate it into something like the Three-Fund Portfolio.
3. Target date funds came under a lot of criticism in 2008 due to sequence-of-returns risk. Many TDFs will have a stock allocation of up to 40–50% at retirement age. If you just so happen to be on the verge of a 2008-type environment when you're entering retirement then a TDF with that allocation might prove to be a less effective behavioral hedge than you'd hoped. Therefore, it's worth considering the TDF allocation in the context of everything else you have going on to make sure you're not being too aggressive headed into retirement.
4. Most TDFs will have a 15–30% bond allocation in the early years of the fund. There's a reasonable criticism that this isn't optimal for the investor who's in their accumulation years because this bond allocation isn't providing them with reliable principal stability and isn't large enough to sufficiently hedge the stock volatility, so it operates as a pure return-drag relative to a more aggressive option.
5. Some TDFs have relatively high fees and should be avoided. These are incredibly simple portfolios and should always be implemented using a low-cost fund wrapper.

And now the good news:

1. TDFs are simple, low-cost and diversified. They require virtually no upkeep, and the investor barely has to lift a finger to manage it.
2. TDFs are excellent behavioral hedges. Although we can nitpick the age-in-bonds rule or the sequence-of-returns risk, these portfolios

do a fine job of establishing a target date and then managing the risk into that date.

SUITORS FOR TARGET DATE PORTFOLIOS

These portfolios are great in 401(k)s and other retirement accounts. They're not ideal for people who want to be more hands-on with an account, or people who are already in retirement. So, if you're someone in your 30s, 40s or 50s looking for a very easy solution for a retirement fund then these are great options. You probably can't go wrong with something like this in a 401(k) plan.

FINAL THOUGHTS

I'm a big fan of time-based investing strategies that help you obtain greater clarity of your assets across specific time horizons. And while target date funds do a nice job of achieving this, I've developed my own methodology for trying to improve upon this approach.

Yes, that's right. My current favorite portfolio is up next. I love it and I hope you will too.

20

DEFINED DURATION STRATEGY

LIKE many strategies in this book, the Defined Duration Strategy grew out of personal experiences. In this case, my personal experience. It's designed to solve for the ultimate problem in life – *time*.

Before I had children, my asset allocation was typically aggressive and long-term oriented. When it came to financial planning, my life was simple as it was just me, my wife, the most incredible Aussie Shepherd that ever existed and a flock of chickens.* I had one primary time horizon to consider and that was the time horizon my wife and I would navigate together. We both earned good incomes and so our portfolio had a long-term time horizon and we could afford to be very aggressive.

We had our first daughter just weeks before the Covid crash of 2020, and our portfolio fell significantly. I wasn't sleeping, the news was saying millions could die, and to top it off, my mother-in-law got trapped with us after the travel ban. My morning routine consisted of

---

* I always knew I was destined to be surrounded by chicks at some point in my life. I just didn't think it would be literal chicken chicks.

crying in the shower for 30 minutes before screaming into a sock for another 10.[*] Although we never realized the losses in the downturn, it was the first time in my life where my asset allocation felt irresponsible. After all, I now had a whole new time horizon to worry about – my daughter's time horizon.

I had spent much of my career helping other investors navigate difficult timelines, especially around retirement. But this was the first time where I felt like I was not well equipped to navigate a financial plan with multiple time horizons. Ironically, I'd spent the past 15 years studying pension funds and banks – institutions that are experts at managing time-based assets and liabilities. If you're familiar with my research, you probably know banking is a topic I've spent far too much time writing about. On the surface, banks are boring – but underneath, their portfolios are often intricate exercises in timing.

When banks allocate assets they have an inherent asset-liability mismatch. In other words, banks typically borrow short and lend long, which can leave them with the difficult portfolio management problem of trying to smoothly manage deposit outflows while holding a portfolio of longer-duration assets as most loans are. Banks have a temporal conundrum in their balance sheets that forces them to be overly aware of any mismatch that could create capital constraints.

NOT SO FUN SIDE NOTE

You might recall the Silicon Valley Bank panic in 2022. SVB had a huge asset-liability mismatch where they held billions in long-duration bonds and started having an excessive amount of short-term withdrawals. This imbalance forced them to consider selling some of their bonds at

---

[*] To be clear, the crying wasn't due to the newborn baby or Covid, but entirely due to my mother-in-law being trapped with us.

a loss, which would erode their capital cushion. The mismatch is what ultimately caused their demise.

When I began to think about this in more detail it occurred to me that banks face the same problem that every investor in the world does. We all have an inherent asset-liability mismatch. We earn income in the short term and use it to manage near-term expenses. At the same time, we hold long-term assets like stocks and bonds that produce uncertain returns – and rely on those assets to fund future, unpredictable liabilities like weddings, retirement, and other major life events.

I began to wonder if the way we allocate assets is fundamentally incomplete. I'd been trained to perform risk profiles for clients and then choose instruments to diversify across asset classes. But investors aren't just seeking diversification of instruments – they're looking for diversification across instruments *and* time. And in the end, isn't time what we're really trying to manage? We shouldn't be focused solely on beating the market or diversification of assets alone. Instead, we should aim to build financial planning-based portfolios that increase the certainty of meeting future financial needs across all the different time horizons we encounter in life.

Remember that Ken French quote: "risk is uncertainty of lifetime consumption." Bingo. Our asset allocation should be constructed to optimize our ability to navigate future consumption.

After I stopped screaming into socks, I wrote a paper in 2022 titled "Defined Duration Investing." The goal was to create a model for asset management that not only diversified portfolios across asset classes, but also across time horizons – so investors could better understand how specific assets align with specific financial goals in the future. For example, bond investing is incredibly clean because you know the key variables:

- A bond has a fixed time horizon.
- A bond has a fixed payout.
- A bond has a specific credit quality.

If you buy a 12-month T-bill yielding 4%, you know exactly what your asset is providing relative to any future liabilities you might incur. You know the return, the time horizon and the principal stability of the instrument over the time period.

This is why the strategy of bond laddering is so useful. If you hold one-, two-, and three-year bonds, you've created a laddered temporal asset allocation that gives you a nearly precise ability to understand what your future cash flows will look like.

But what if you could introduce other assets like stocks or commodities into the ladder? Then you could create a temporally allocated portfolio that included the assets that have the most temporal uncertainty. After all, we don't really know the duration of the stock market or commodities, and it's that uncertainty that makes them the most difficult to plan around.

The Defined Duration Strategy tries to solve this problem by quantifying the time horizon of the stock market (and any asset) to give us a better perspective of the time horizon over which those instruments can be reasonably relied upon to generate certain returns. We can then blend those assets together or match them specifically to a financial plan so that the investor aligns assets and expected liabilities. You can also apply this to William Sharpe's "arithmetic of active management." That is, if all investors held assets across their appropriate time horizons, they would earn higher returns by reducing frictions along the way. You can't squeeze more yield from a 10-year bond by trading it every 10 minutes. And in fact, the more investors trade that instrument, the lower their aggregate returns will be due to the various costs of doing so.

If, on the other hand, investors held assets across their appropriate time horizons they'd earn higher average returns. In other words, the average investor who holds their assets to maturity will earn a higher after-tax and after-fee return when compared to the average investor who tries to trade that asset in an attempt to earn more than it is designed to generate across its lifetime. The Defined Duration Strategy is designed to apply appropriate time horizons to certain assets thereby helping the average investor earn higher returns by holding the assets across appropriate time horizons.

In building out the model for this approach I took a concept from Bill Bernstein. Bernstein once proposed that you could quantify the "duration" of stocks by identifying a "point of indifference" – the point at which an investor would be indifferent to a drawdown because the asset has reached a real break-even point.

For example, if the stock market were to fall 50% in a worst-case scenario but is expected to earn a 5% real return annually, the investor reaches indifference when the asset's value recovers to a positive real return. In this case, that recovery takes 14.21 years. If you had bought global stocks at their peak in 2007 and they earned 5% real returns annually, you'd be indifferent to the GFC loss after 14.21 years. That's the stock market's "defined duration" – the time frame over which you can reasonably assess the asset's performance relative to your sequence-of-returns risk and ability to plan future consumption with very high confidence.

If you recall the data from Essential Principle #8, you'll remember that the probability of positive returns for the stock market over a 10- to 20-year period is around 90–99%. So this time horizon aligns with both historical and statistical expectations.

Admittedly, this approach is probably a bit conservative as it assumes a severe max drawdown scenario, but in investing we should plan for the worst and hope for the best. Of course, the inputs here are dynamic by design. You would have to modify the expected max drawdown and expected returns as market conditions change. And typically, as stocks decline in value, we should expect the potential max drawdown to be reduced while the expected future return increases, and vice versa.

More importantly, although we're attempting to apply precise time horizons to instruments, we know we're also providing a general framework for how to think about certain assets. Stocks are long-term instruments and can be thought of as being similar to a multi-decade bond that will pay an average coupon of 5% real returns if you are willing to hold it for 15–20 years. They should never be thought of as daily, monthly, or even annual instruments because they cannot mathematically distribute all their profits consistently over such brief time horizons and therefore do not generate reliable short-term returns.

This methodology also allows us to quantify the defined duration of any instrument or multi-asset strategy. For example, if we input the 60/40 Portfolio into this model and assume a max drawdown of 30% (the 2008 downturn) and expected 3% annual real returns, then the defined duration of this instrument would be approximately 12 years. This makes intuitive sense: an aggregate bond index has a defined duration of around five years, and if you blend that with an 18-year instrument (the defined duration of global stocks as of 2025), you arrive at an aggregate instrument with a defined duration that is longer than bonds but shorter than equities. As I've noted before, this is the beauty of the 60/40 Portfolio. It blends the long duration of equities with the shorter duration of bonds, resulting in more stable and reliable returns. But even the 60/40 needs to be thought of as a somewhat longer duration instrument because stocks skew its principal sensitivity heavily.

The most interesting conclusion from this model is that many of the "alternative" assets we've discussed in this book end up having characteristics that are similar to insurance. Insurance typically has a low or negative expected real return, but when triggered it generates a huge asymmetric payoff. Doesn't that sound a lot like long-term Treasury bonds, options, gold, Trend Following, or managed futures?

As we've discussed throughout this book, these instruments often have highly asymmetric returns in very specific environments. T-bonds generate strong asymmetric returns in deflations, gold performs best in periods of high inflation, managed futures and Trend Following excel during market anomalies, and far out-of-the money options can produce large payoffs in extreme tail risk events. In contrast, core assets like cash, intermediate-term bonds, and stocks tend to offer more stable, broadly reliable behavior over time, making them foundational building blocks. Alternatives, on the other hand, act more like long-term insurance, providing protection when those core assets face unusual or adverse conditions.

Table 20.1 shows how the defined duration time horizons look across different instruments as of 2025.

But it's important to emphasize that durations are not static. For example, Figure 20.1 shows the traditional duration of a 10-year T-note. This is crucially important for an investor who is sensitive to price changes because it means that a lower yielding bond will not protect you as well from potential rate increases and their coinciding principal losses. A 1% yielding T-note in 2020 is vastly riskier than a 5% yielding T-note in 2025 because its starting interest rate will not protect you to the same degree from potential interest rate risk in the short term.

CHAPTER 20

Table 20.1: Asset class durations (as of 2025)

Asset Class	0–3 Years	3–7 Years	7–15 Years	15+ Years	Insurance
T-bills	0.25				
2-year note	1.75				
Bond aggregate		4.84			
10-year T-note		5.85			
GFAP			9.45		
60/40 Portfolio			12.75		
T-bonds				16.25	
Global equities				18.21	
Gold					29.50
Commodities					38.75

This negative impact is especially harmful in bond funds like a bond aggregate where, not only has duration drifted higher and higher in recent decades, but longer duration government bonds have become an increasingly large component in the index over time, rising from 25% of the holdings in 1975 to 40% at present. This is why the bond market is one place where it makes a good deal of sense to be more active. If you simply "take what the market gives you" then you're being fed a constant meal of low yield and long duration interest rate risk from the government, which can expose you to excess principal risk over time and lower risk-adjusted returns. This is one of several major flaws in aggregate bond funds, as they rebalance back to a cap weighting that is dominated by what the government issues.

Figure 20.1: Traditional duration of 10-year T-note

Although this evolving duration dynamic is most obvious in bonds, the same general thing happens in all markets over time as asset prices boom and bust. The bond market happens to be one of the easier places to control it because you can explicitly dial back the temporal sensitivity of the instrument. We don't have the same luxury in the stock market where all the instruments are functionally longer in duration, however, we can still see clear evidence that indicators such as high valuations tend to correlate with lower future risk-adjusted returns, as shown in Figure 20.2. We learned in the Countercyclical Rebalancing chapter that valuations alone aren't good short-term return predictors, but if you're behaviorally sensitive to short-term volatility it makes sense to manage the risk around the instrument using some sort of countercyclical model.

Therefore, in multi-asset instruments (like a 60/40 stock/bond portfolio), it is sensible to control for duration risk across all instruments, assuming you're using the instrument to create stability over a 10–12-year time horizon. That is the beauty of rebalancing back to 60/40, after all – you're throttling the procyclical growth of the 60% slice whenever it grows above 60% exposure which helps avoid its defined duration from growing longer. Defined Duration Investing will inevitably require a certain degree of strategic rebalancing in the strategy as you're creating specific temporal targets using some inherently uncertain temporal instruments.

Figure 20.2: CAPE versus 10-year Sharpe ratio

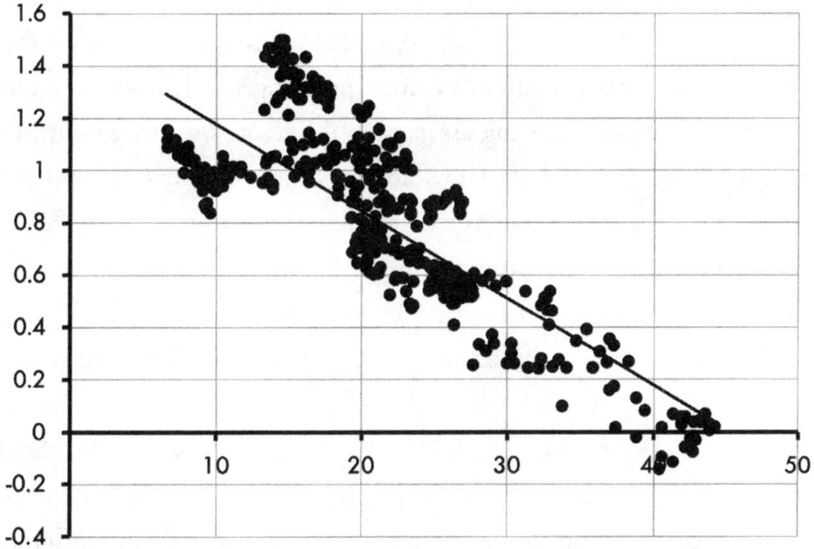

WHY DEFINED DURATION INVESTING WORKS

Defined Duration Investing (DDI) is a financial planning and behavioral strategy similar to what researchers have called "liability-driven investing" or "time segmentation" strategies. However, DDI goes a step further and specifically quantifies the time horizon of the assets in the portfolio to try to create greater certainty and clarity over the specific time horizons we're targeting. Traditional bucketing strategies use vague categories like "short-term," "medium-term" or "long-term," and don't measure the actual duration of each asset. Traditional liability-driven strategies are usually limited to fixed income and traditional duration metrics. DDI expands on these approaches by assigning explicit durations to all asset types – including stocks and alternatives. In doing so we create a more quantifiable and precise asset-liability matching strategy.

Recall the chart of diversification from the Essential Principles at the beginning of this book (Figure 0.3). Diversification works because we layer different assets with different return streams. DDI takes this concept a step further by not only incorporating a wide range of assets, but by intentionally layering assets with different *time horizons* into a planning-based framework. For example, when you buy Chevron and Exxon stock you are diversifying by reducing the single entity risk. But you're still invested in corporations, which are inherently long-term entities. But if you add five-year Chevron and Exxon bonds into the mix then you're not only expanding asset diversification, you're also diversifying temporally.

To use a clear example of why this works, you might consider a scenario where stocks are expected to generate 6% per year and bonds are expected to generate 2% per year. These are specifically different temporal instruments because the stocks will reliably generate this average return over a period of 18 years using my methodology, whereas the bonds can reliably generate their 2% return over a five-year time horizon. When you blend these two return streams, you're creating a blended return stream that creates an expected return of 4% per year over 11 years. Figure 20.3 shows how this looks.

Figure 20.3: Why diversification of time works

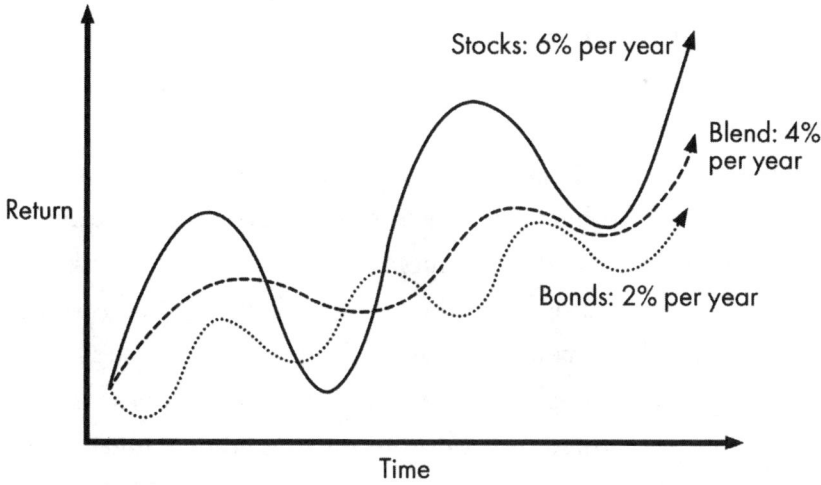

As discussed further below, the strategy "works" because it starts with a financial plan and then matches assets to that financial plan to increase the certainty of cash flows around specific time horizons. The goal is to give the investor a better understanding of the way their assets align with future expected expenses and consumption needs. By quantifying the time horizon of each asset, the strategy aims to improve behavior and provide greater clarity and confidence in the financial planning process.

In my experience it's not only a sound financial planning-based asset management strategy, but it's a powerful behavioral tool. By clearly quantifying each portfolio component and aligning it with specific goals and time horizons, the strategy helps compartmentalize assets in a way that supports both clarity and discipline.

For example, in our exploration of the 60/40 Portfolio I referred to "homogeneous portfolio risk." This happens when a portfolio is structured as one large, aggregated group of assets. While it may be diversified on the surface, it doesn't provide clear visibility or access to each specific asset. So even if the 60/40 Portfolio includes cash or short-term bonds, you can't necessarily access that liquidity when needed – unless you disaggregate the portfolio and isolate the individual components.

I've found that disaggregating portfolios into these very specific temporally defined buckets helps to give an investor more certainty over their portfolio and oftentimes helps them take more risk (and generate higher returns) than they might otherwise. That's because the assets are clearly compartmentalized into specific buckets where, for example, your long-term assets are segmented into a long-term bucket that are allowed to perform in the long-term manner they're intended to. We shouldn't care what the long-term bucket does in the short term because we know our short-term assets are there to meet any potential short-term liquidity needs. As a result of this, if the stock market goes down significantly you can simply ignore that component knowing that you hold some percentage of your assets in T-bills or other short-term buckets that are more than enough to weather a potentially multi-year bear market in stocks.

In short, Defined Duration Investing works because it's a financial planning-based approach to asset management that helps you build a more complete asset ladder using cash, bonds, stocks, and alternatives diversified over specific time horizons. It's not a "beat the market" or "alpha maximizer" portfolio. It's just a sensible asset allocation approach that helps us build temporally diversified portfolios in a quantifiable, planning-based approach.

CHAPTER 20

BUILDING YOUR OWN DEFINED DURATION PORTFOLIO

Most financial planning asset allocation strategies start with an investor risk profile and then allocate assets within a diversified portfolio based primarily on behavioral tendencies and financial goals.

The Defined Duration Strategy is most effective when it begins with a comprehensive financial plan that projects your expenses and liabilities over the course of your life. Unlike traditional approaches that focus on optimizing portfolios for alpha, this strategy is rooted in planning and aims to align assets with the timing of future obligations. By identifying specific future expenses, you gain greater clarity and confidence across your time horizons. From there, you match assets to those time frames – starting with short-term liabilities and methodically building a portfolio that addresses needs across the full spectrum of your financial future.

One way to implement this approach is to think of your portfolio over five specific time horizons. I call these time horizons the five pillars of Defined Duration:

1. **Short-term liquidity needs (0–3 years):** Emergency fund coverage and short-term spending needs.
2. **Intermediate-term liquidity needs (3–7 years):** Expenses like a house down payment, weddings, childcare, or major purchases.
3. **Moderate long-term needs (7–15 years):** Near-retirement expenses, college tuition, and other mid-horizon planning.
4. **Long-term needs (15+ years):** Retirement, healthcare, and multi-generational wealth planning.
5. **Insurance needs (perpetual/unknown):** A flexible allocation for unpredictable risks and extreme scenarios.

Building your financial plan to cover all five of the pillars ensures coverage across every time horizon you might encounter throughout your financial life.

How much to apply to each time horizon?

I always start with short-term planning needs as that's the bucket that we can most accurately predict. As a broad rule, think of it like this:

- **0–3 years**: Allocate enough to cover at least one to three years of emergency expenses and current income gaps.
- **3–7 years**: Fully fund any planned expenses in this window – such as a house down payment, weddings, or planned car purchases.
- **7–15 years**: Allocate roughly 5x your annual expenses or 25% of total financial assets.
- **15+ years**: Allocate about 10x your annual expenses or 50% of total financial assets (or the remaining balance not required by the first three pillars).
- **Insurance**: Consider allocating 5–10% of your total financial assets, depending on your personal situation and risk tolerance. This bucket is often optional, but it can be valuable for hedging extreme outcomes.

I like to think of each of these time horizons as their own organized bucket. Using the average time horizon you can distill each bucket into its own customizable temporal allocation:

- 1.5 year defined duration
- 5 year defined duration
- 10 year defined duration
- 15+ year defined duration
- Perpetual defined duration

CHAPTER 20

Customizing each bucket individually can refine the matching process and further smooth sequence of return risk. The goal is to align each bucket with a specific time horizon – enabling financial plans that more effectively match assets to liabilities and hopefully avoid situations where, such as recently, intermediate bonds have been allowed to drift into longer duration and riskier instruments that create excessive principal instability. As always, if you'd like more details on how I construct and customize these portfolios, feel free to reach out to me directly at cullenroche@disciplinefunds.com.

Continuing our implementation example – if you had a portfolio of $1,000,000, an expected house down payment in the coming five years of $100,000, and annual expenses of $50,000 that were fully covered by Social Security, then you would want the following allocations:

- **0–3 years (short-term needs)**: $100,000 (2x annual expenses) in a custom T-bill ladder and/or cash equivalents.
- **3–7 years (intermediate-term needs)**: $100,000 for the home down payment, matched to a five year defined duration.
- **7–15 years (moderate long-term needs)**: $250,000 (5x annual expenses) matched to a 10 year defined duration.
- **15+ years (long-term growth)**: $450,000 or 45% (the remaining balance) of the portfolio matched to a 15+ year defined duration.
- **Insurance needs (unknown time horizon)**: $100,000 or 10% in instruments that behave like long-term hedges – such as long-term TIPS, Treasuries, managed futures, gold, or options.

If you forgo the insurance bucket (let's say you don't like gold or higher-fee instruments like managed futures), then you could build your own version of a Boglehead Three-Fund Portfolio using three instruments that correspond to the five-, 10- and 15+ year time horizons in addition to a T-bill ladder where the T-bills are operating like your insurance alternative.* Doesn't get much cleaner than that.

But you could also layer in as many time horizons as you wanted to. For example, you could build a T-bill and bond ladder going out five years to cover those two short time horizons. Then layer in a 60/40 Portfolio (or GFAP) for your moderate long-term needs and add the Forward Cap Portfolio for your longest-term bucket. You could then sprinkle in a little bit of Harry Browne and Risk Parity by introducing gold, long-term T-bonds, and managed futures, and you have a temporally diversified portfolio where we're integrating many of the concepts and strategies we've discussed earlier in this book. When you match the assets to your plan's liabilities and expenses you can create asset diversification with temporal diversification. Now we're cooking!

These examples are oversimplified for explanatory purposes and the insurance bucket is optional because it's so dependent on personalization, but I think we're all on the same page here. The primary goal, though, is to build a portfolio that's diversified not just across asset classes, but across *time horizons*, all rooted in your financial planning needs. It's planning-based, simple, highly diversified, low-fee, tax efficient, and most importantly, behaviorally robust. Not bad, huh?

As it pertains to the five pillars, the hope is that our two short-term pillars give us very high certainty of near-term consumption, while pillars three and four generate sequentially higher returns that can be relied on to fund future potential expenses if we should need to draw down pillars one and two. And then our insurance pillar is there to protect the broader plan with longer duration instruments that might protect us during inflation, deflation, or other uncertain events.

---

* I would argue that any time T-bills are generating a real return (current yield > than the current rate of inflation) then they are sufficient insurance alternatives in a portfolio.

Here's how our earlier example might look in a specific asset allocation:

- **0–3 year assets**: 5% custom T-bill ladder over three-, six-, and 12-month bills. 5% BOXX (Alpha Architect 1-3 month T-Bills) for added tax efficiency.
- **3–7 year assets**: 10% across 5 year defined duration instruments such as short-term bonds or multi-asset instruments with a shorter average defined duration.
- **7–15 year assets**: 25% across 10 year defined duration instruments such as 7–10 year bonds, the Countercyclical Rebalancing Portfolio, 60/40, GFAP, Risk Parity, etc.
- **15+ year assets**: 45% across assets with a 15+ year defined duration such as any all stock portfolio in this book or a blend of the Forward Cap Portfolio.
- **Perpetual insurance**: 10% diversified over gold, Trend Following and other insurance-like alternatives.

Figure 20.4: Defined Duration Portfolio

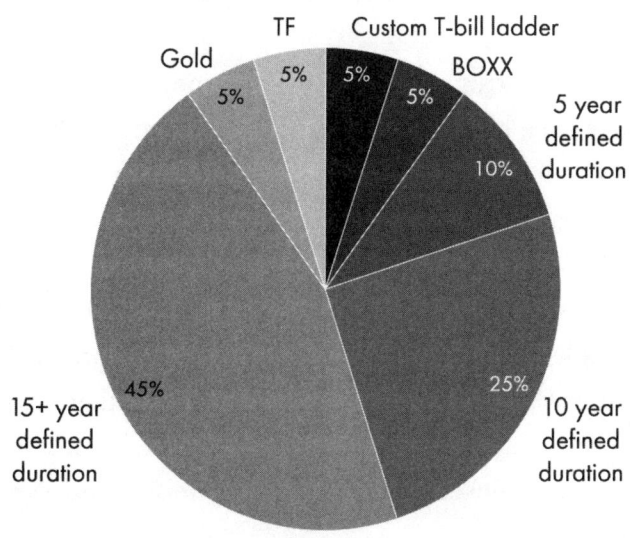

This blends a lot of the concepts we've discussed in this book, but adds a financial planning aspect in the asset-liability matching process that better aligns our portfolio with our actual financial plan.

DEFINED DURATION PORTFOLIO ANALYSIS

This is a uniquely financial planning-based portfolio so it's hard to generalize about the performance since it will always be implemented in a personalized manner. That said, the strategy will end up looking like a custom bond ladder with additional five-, 10- and 15+ year target components. The five-year instrument should look roughly like a three- to five-year bond over time, the 10-year instrument should behave like the GFAP or Countercyclical Portfolio over time and the 15+ year instrument should track closely with a broad stock index over time.

The five-year instrument you utilize should tilt towards something more conservative as you have an inherently short time horizon here. This could be as simple as a mix of intermediate bonds, an aggregate bond index or even a conservative stock/bond blend. But it should be an inherently more bond-like instrument with greater emphasis on principal stability relative to purchasing power protection and/or growth.

Your 10-year instrument is going to be more balanced given the intermediate time horizon it's designed to address. At this range, it's not ideal to be 100% in stocks, but it's also too long a horizon to rely solely on bonds. This is why blending an instrument with a balance of stocks and bonds can work nicely here. As I mentioned before, a 60/40 stock/bond instrument works out to a roughly 12-year instrument so that is a simple piece of the puzzle that can work for many investors. I prefer to throttle the stock market risk a bit by tilting the portfolio more towards bonds using the countercyclical rebalancing strategy.

Your 15+ year bucket is going to be aggressive and can include a single or many aggressive components. I typically like to tilt this bucket in a more growth and momentum-oriented fashion given the inherent riskiness of the allocation. This bucket is where we can take pure stock market risk or even tilt to something that is taking on more risk than the broader market.

And if you include the insurance component, the portfolio takes on a distinct profile compared to a traditional stock/bond ladder, as it allows you to layer in a variety of alternative assets.

In total you end up with a portfolio that looks like a bond ladder except instead of using only fixed income instruments, you're diversified specifically across many different types of holdings.

In terms of performance, this is very specifically not a beat-the-market portfolio in its entirety. It is a financial planning-based portfolio that can be customized in any way necessary.

DEFINED DURATION PORTFOLIO PROS AND CONS

This is my personal favorite portfolio so we can't be too critical, right? Wrong. Let's dig into the bad news.

1. The Defined Duration Strategy is not a beat-the-market portfolio so it could test your patience. Further, it is designed to be very broadly diversified so there will always be parts of it that frustrate an investor.
2. The insurance component is optional and might not be applicable to everyone. Instruments like gold, managed futures, TIPS, or long-term T-bonds might not be necessary for all investors.
3. While this portfolio can be implemented using a DIY approach, it's ultimately designed as a financial planning strategy. For that reason, it's wise to either work with a financial advisor or build a solid DIY financial plan as the foundation.

4. The strategy ultimately ends up looking a lot like a value and momentum strategy where the shorter-duration instruments are tilted slightly to value (and quality) and the longer-duration instruments are tilted towards growth and momentum. This creates diversification, but will also create higher volatility in the long duration bucket that will test your patience at times.

And what about the good news?

1. This is a unique, planning-based asset allocation approach that prioritizes your actual expenses – rather than relying on vague risk profiling or beat-the-market strategies. Because it's built using a framework of clearly defined temporal buckets aligned to specific financial needs, it creates a behaviorally robust portfolio – one that's easier to stick with through market ups and downs.
2. The portfolio can be incredibly simple, almost as simple as the Three-Fund Portfolio, but much more customized and much more diversified.
3. The portfolio is low-cost, tax efficient, and highly diversified.

SUITORS FOR THE DEFINED DURATION STRATEGY

The Defined Duration Strategy is ideal for investors who value structure and seek greater certainty around their financial plan. While it can benefit anyone, it's especially well-suited for those nearing or already in retirement – periods of life where the uncertainty around time and future expenses is often at its highest.

This approach could also be used in a simple format within retirement plans and 401(k)s for investors seeking a more disaggregated option relative to instruments like target date funds.

It's also a great tool for financial advisors who are looking to give their clients more clarity around their financial plans.

If you have questions about the approach, feel free to shoot me a note. If you have criticisms, you know who to contact (not me).

FINAL THOUGHTS

You might be thinking we're wrapping things up – but not quite yet. Hang in there; we've got a few more loose ends to tie up and some important ideas still worth exploring.

In the next chapter, we'll take a look at a few additional strategies and asset classes that may be worth considering. You know, just in case you haven't quite found what you're looking for….

21

POLYGAMOUS PORTFOLIOS

THERE'S a chance that none of the potential portfolios is exactly right for you. You might prefer to dabble in a number of them across different accounts. There's nothing wrong with that.

This chapter discusses different assets and strategies that are blends or different styles of many of the previously mentioned approaches. I picked them because they're all worthy of honorable mention. I won't dive into each one in great detail, but they are assets, funds, or strategies that are worthy of more research if you should choose.

BITCOIN

How could you write an investment book that doesn't discuss the hottest asset of the last 15 years? Bitcoin returned 68% per year from 2014 to 2025. $1,000 invested in Bitcoin at the beginning of 2014 would be worth $189,522 as of 2025. These eye-popping numbers aren't likely to repeat, but what's driving this incredible performance?

Bitcoin is a fully decentralized digital currency with a fixed supply

CHAPTER 21

of 21 million Bitcoins, built on an immutable blockchain ledger. In English, this means that it's a purely digital form of money that cannot be manipulated by a central bank or other currency issuer. It is accessible to anyone with an internet connection and can be used to transact anywhere in the world that accepts it.

Figure 21.1: Bitcoin total real return

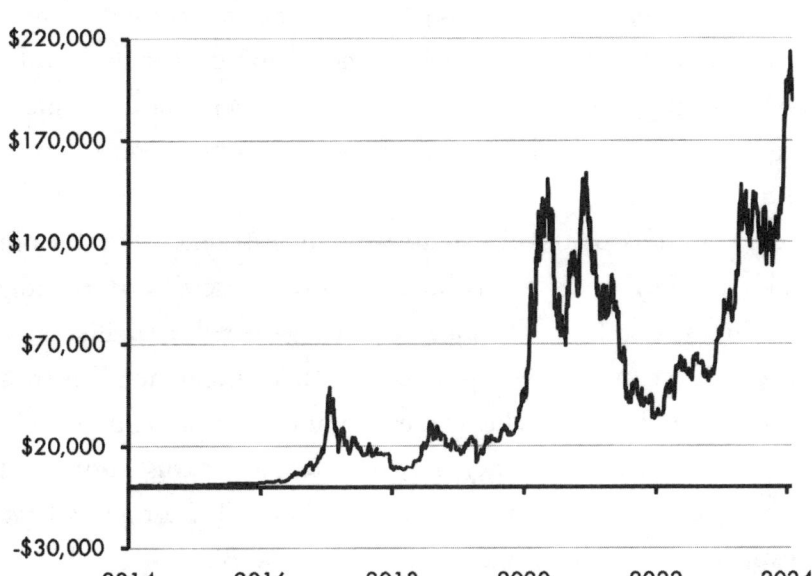

A common question I get is: "What are the use cases for Bitcoin?" On its face Bitcoin seems like an instrument that people mostly just speculate with. It's not like trillions of dollars of commerce is being transacted in Bitcoin. At least we're not there yet.

The use case that I've always found compelling is fiat currency insurance. For example, if you live in Zimbabwe or any authoritarian regime or country with a history of currency collapse, you might consider diversifying into other currencies or assets that protect you from domestic currency risk. You might not be able to own dollar-denominated hedges like US stocks because the intermediaries often have strict requirements. And you probably don't even want to own gold because then you have to store the gold and figure out a way to sell it when the currency collapses (and everyone is chasing you around with a gun). Bitcoin gives these people access to an inflation hedge that anyone with a phone or internet connection can buy and sell.

It's interesting that Bitcoin is popular in the US because I'd argue the dollar is one of the few fiat currencies that doesn't need to be heavily hedged against currency collapse, but when you put yourself in the shoes of any foreign economy the story becomes much more compelling.

There are lots of theories as to why an instrument like Bitcoin would have any value, but I think it's rather basic. It's trustworthy as an immutable form of money and it's garnered a large enough network effect that enough people deem it to be money. This was the theory of monetary value that economist Hal Varian put forth in 2004.[43] He argued that money is used so long as it's trustworthy and gains a network effect. This makes sense. After all, trust and a large network effect are what make money useful. And Bitcoin has achieved these two essential properties, thereby making it a viable currency alternative.

As I've already alluded to, I think of Bitcoin as fiat currency insurance. Insurance is inherently a satellite asset around a core of your financial plan. It's not the central piece of a portfolio and it's way too volatile to comprise a majority of someone's assets, but using it as another form of insurance makes a lot of sense in my view.

Figure 21.2: Bitcoin drawdowns (%)

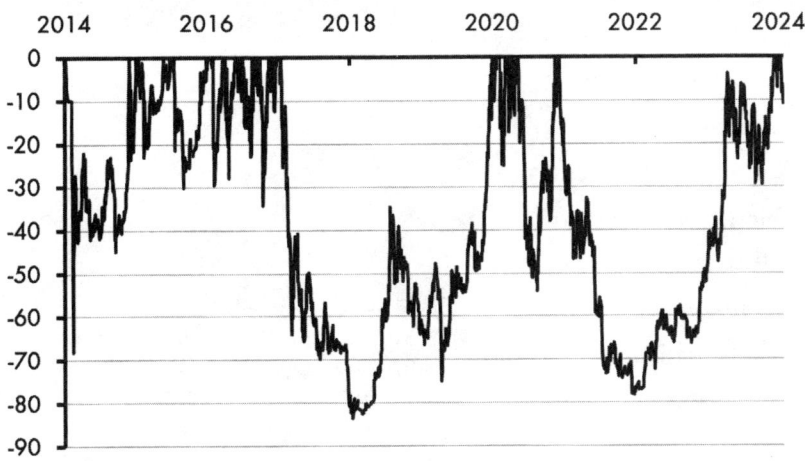

The volatility aspect is important because Bitcoin's huge returns (and drawdowns) could result in a significant amount of portfolio skew as your allocations become unbalanced due to extreme moves. This is one reason to maintain a strict rebalancing strategy around how you utilize Bitcoin.

HEDGE FUND STRATEGIES

Low-cost indexing can be thought of as the Toyota Camry of the portfolio world. Index funds aren't especially beautiful looking, but are low-cost, safe, and will efficiently get you from point A to point B. Hedge funds are your Ferraris. These are the strategies that look sexy, cost a lot, and can *sometimes* get you from point A to point B much faster. Other times they get you there in the same time but end up costing a lot more in the process. These are the strategies you probably don't need, but might want.

"Hedge fund" is a broad term that covers several different types of strategies including:

- Long/short equity
- Short-biased
- Equity market neutral
- Merger arbitrage
- Distressed securities
- Global macro
- Managed futures
- Fund of funds

These strategies are typically difficult to access and as a rule hedge funds should only be employed when you can invest with a top tier fund with a strong track record. But if you're looking for some publicly available funds that replicate some of these strategies you might consider doing more research on some of the following:

- First Trust Long/Short Equity ETF (ticker: FTLS)
- AQR Long-Short Equity Fund (ticker: QLEIX)
- Invenomic Fund (ticker: BIVIX)
- PIMCO StockPLUS Absolute Return Fund (ticker: PSPTX)
- Abbey Capital Multi-Asset Fund (ticker: MAFIX)
- AQR Diversifying Strategies Fund (ticker: QDSIX)
- Stone Ridge Diversified Alternatives (ticker: SRDAX)
- AQR Macro Opportunities Fund (ticker: QGMIX)

A newer firm called Unlimited Funds (unlimitedetfs.com) also offers a number of different hedge fund replicator strategies. Bob Elliott, the founder of the firm, is a former Bridgewater employee and very sharp guy.

CHAPTER 21

RETURN STACKED ETFS AND PORTABLE ALPHA STRATEGIES

In the last few years, portable alpha strategies have made a big resurgence. These are strategies that utilize leverage to construct a beta core with an alpha satellite.

The basic theory is that you can build a beta index as your core holding and then add an alpha overlay using leverage to try to enhance the beta component. As long as the alpha overlay outperforms the cash borrowing rate then you'll have "ported" some alpha on top of a beta position.

These funds are also commonly referred to as capital-efficient funds as they utilize the same basic thinking as someone who takes out a mortgage on their home. Consider a scenario where you have $1,000,000 in cash and are looking to buy a $1,000,000 home. If you expect real estate to generate 0% real returns over the next 30 years, but believe stocks will return 10% per year, allocating all your capital to the home may not be the most efficient use of funds. Instead, you could put 20% down ($200,000) and take out an $800,000 mortgage at a 5% interest rate. This allows you to keep $800,000 invested in the stock market, potentially earning 10% per year. By using leverage, you're effectively substituting a 0% return on housing for the opportunity to earn a 10% return on investments while paying 5% interest, capturing a 5% annual spread on that $800,000 over time. You're essentially stacking the return of stocks on top of the house by using leverage to purchase the home.

Of course, that sounds easier than it really is, but that's the basic gist. Below is a list of funds that implement something similar to this that you might consider.

I would also suggest looking at the Return Stacked products from Corey Hoffstein of Newfound Research and Adam Butler, Rodrigo

Gordillo, and Mike Philbrick of Resolve Asset Management. These are all very smart guys who are worth paying attention to.

Some other funds worth researching include:

- Pimco StocksPLUS Long Duration Fund (ticker: PSLDX)
- PIMCO StocksPLUS Small Fund (ticker: PSCSX)
- PIMCO StocksPLUS International Fund (ticker: PISIX)
- WisdomTree US Efficient Core Fund (ticker: NTSX)
- WisdomTree International Efficient Core (ticker: NTSI)
- WisdomTree Emerging Markets Efficient Core (ticker: NTSE)
- WisdomTree Efficient Gold Plus Equity (ticker: GDE)
- ReturnStacked Bonds and Trend (ticker: RSBT)
- ReturnStacked Stocks and Bonds (ticker: RSSB)
- ReturnStacked Stocks and Trend (ticker: RSST)
- ReturnStacked Stocks and Futures Yield (ticker: RSSY)
- Standpoint Multi-Asset Fud (ticker: BLNDX)
- DoubleLine Shiller Enhance CAPE (ticker: DSNEX)

VANGUARD LIFE STRATEGY FUNDS

Vanguard's Life Strategy funds provide an all-in-one option for investors who want the leanest possible portfolio. They come in various risk profiles as well as income-oriented options. This includes:

- LifeStrategy Income Fund (ticker: VASIX)
- LifeStrategy Conservative Growth Fund (ticker: VSCGX)
- LifeStrategy Moderate Growth Fund (ticker: VSMGX)
- LifeStrategy Growth Fund (ticker: VASGX)

This is as straightforward as it gets. And while they might be great for a core component of a broader portfolio I do think these sorts of funds need complementary components, especially if you need liquidity. But in general, these are the sorts of funds that make investing about as simple as possible.[44]

OPTION-BASED INCOME STRATEGIES

Option-based strategies have also grown in popularity due to the turbulence of the markets in the last 20 years and especially the recent poor performance of pure fixed income strategies. These strategies typically have a core beta exposure with a satellite option system. The options are used like insurance to generate income and potentially protect or enhance the exposure of the underlying core position.

We should be super clear about these types of strategies – they are very specifically insurance-style strategies. These kinds of options were historically used to create greater predictability in the price of an underlying asset over a specific time period. During the Dutch tulip mania of the 17th century, traders often entered into informal forward contracts that included optional clauses, allowing one party to cancel the deal for a small fee. While not true options in the modern sense, these agreements functioned similarly providing a form of insurance against adverse price movements. Tulip growers might use them to lock in profits and protect against falling prices, while buyers used them to manage the risk of rising prices. Though speculative in nature, these early contracts reflected the same insurance-like risk-management principles behind today's put and call options.

These strategies give you insurance-like certainty across a specific time horizon, but they aren't a free lunch as the added certainty means added costs and lower expected returns. And that's typically what we see in these income-based strategies or option hedging strategies. A few funds you may want to research include:

- CBOE S&P 500 BuyWrite Index (ticker: BXM)
- CBOE S&P 500 PutWrite Index (ticker: PUT)
- J.P. Morgan Equity Premium Income ETF (ticker: JEPI)

iShares also has a suite of ETFs called outcome ETFs. These are typically buy/write ETFs that buy the underlying asset and then write options to define the outcome of the fund or income over a specific time horizon.

Innovator ETFs has also created a similar line of funds called Buffer ETFs.

I don't have a problem with options-based ETFs, but I do think people can construct high degrees of certainty around stocks and bonds without unnecessary bells and whistles. As I've said throughout this book, there's nothing wrong with insurance, but you also don't want to be over-insured. And you want to be especially careful of the funds in this space that promise eye-wateringly high returns.

VOLATILITY AND TAIL-RISK FUNDS

Morgan Housel once said that risk is what we can't know. Nassim Taleb famously called these unknowable events "black swans" – rare occurrences that aren't supposed to happen, but do. The challenge with black swan events is that, despite their rarity, they can have a disproportionately large impact on your finances.

It's well known that stock bull markets are the norm. But as the saying goes, stocks take the stairs up and the elevator down. This extreme sort of event is the basis for black swan and tail-risk strategies. These strategies operate like insurance in that they're typically buying far out-of-the-money options that will surge in price in the case of an anomalous black swan event. This gives the investor the potential to make huge insurance-like gains.

CHAPTER 21

Some funds that protect against this are listed below. Keep in mind that these are more trading instruments than anything else. Volatility or options funds can have high embedded costs and many of them have futures contract decay risk resulting from constantly rolling the contracts. As a result, they can be at risk of very negative returns in the long run, or high relative costs that result in asset decay over time. They should be utilized like term insurance to cover you in a specific period of uncertainty where you believe some insurance makes sense.

- Cambria Tail Risk ETF (ticker: TAIL)
- Alpha Architect Tail Risk ETF (ticker: CAOS)
- Amplify BlackSwan Growth and Treasury Core ETF (ticker: SWAN)
- Barclays VIX ETN (ticker: VXX)

CONCLUSION

I hope this gives you a few more interesting ideas to explore. There are countless investment options out there, and I've only scratched the surface. New ETFs and strategies are being launched every year, often with increasingly creative twists. If you've come across a fund or approach that you think deserves a mention, feel free to send me a note – I'm always interested in learning what others are exploring.

22

ODDS AND ENDS

As you pursue your perfect portfolio you'll encounter numerous competing narratives that will influence your decisions. In this chapter I am going to provide some clarity on many of these narratives to help you further narrow down your search.

IS THE PURSUIT OF ALPHA BAD?

We now know that beating the market is really hard. Then again, if we're all active to some degree then we're all implicitly trying to optimize our portfolios for the amount of return we generate per unit of risk. In other words, we're all aiming for alpha, even if it's not an explicit goal. The key difference lies in how we pursue that alpha. As I've mentioned before, there are smart ways to be active – and not-so-smart ones.

There's a popular joke in financial circles that says you can't eat risk-adjusted returns. In other words, while it might be interesting mental gymnastics to calculate metrics like a Sharpe ratio, the statistical output isn't something you can eat. For example, if a hedge fund is touting a 9% return with 10% volatility versus a 10% return in the S&P

CHAPTER 22

500 with 20% volatility, the thinking says that the investor who owned the S&P 500 can eat *more* despite the fact that the S&P 500 had worse risk-adjusted returns. You can eat realized returns because it's actual dollars in your pocket, but you can't eat the Sharpe ratio. While I am a critic of high-fee active strategies, I also think this is wrong.

Let me explain why.

As you know, I like to view everything through very specific time horizons. The financial services industry does a terrible job of explaining time horizons to investors, in part because most of the commentary in the industry is about stocks, and stocks do not have a defined time horizon. That's part of the problem I've tried to solve with the Defined Duration approach by quantifying an implied equity duration and then helping investors understand a reasonable time horizon over which they might expect a certain return.

What we all really want is predictable returns over specific time periods. We want the straight line in Figure 22.1, but what we get is the bumpy outcome. The degree to which you can smooth that ride with various diversifiers will allow you to eat more predictably across time.

So, you might end up diversifying a portfolio and reducing your average returns over time, but if it creates a smoother ride across specific time horizons then you do end up being able to eat the risk-adjusted returns because you can consume more predictably over time.

The real problem with most high-fee stock-picking strategies or multi-asset strategies is they are inherently long-duration buckets in our financial plans. In the Defined Duration model, most homogeneous diversified portfolios end up being 10+ years in duration because they're a blend of stocks or stocks/bonds and other instruments. These investment managers are oftentimes trying to turn water into wine and help you consume out of a long-term bucket. They fail for two reasons:

1. The overwhelming evidence shows that lower-cost alternatives have a strong tendency to outperform over long periods of time.
2. You cannot make an inherently long-term instrument act like a short-term instrument on average.

Figure 22.1: Needs and wants, stock market edition

The result is, when you buy the ABC Multi Asset Stock Bond Hedge Fund with a 1.5% expense ratio, you're probably buying an instrument that has a duration of about 10+ years (because bonds will average five-plus-years duration and stocks are 15+ years). And when you compare that to something like a boring, low-cost 60/40 index fund, you'll find that the funds don't outperform over long periods of time because they cannot outperform in aggregate, and their taxes/fees end up eating too much of the total return to outperform.

CHAPTER 22

But more importantly, you cannot predictably consume out of this bucket because it creates too much short-term uncertainty. That is, after all, why diversified multi-asset funds like a 60/40 Portfolio work in the long run – you have to be willing to sacrifice short-term liquidity to allow long-term cash flows to accrue to the underlying instruments.

None of this means that the pursuit of high risk-adjusted returns is irrational though. It just shows that it's very hard to achieve using inherently long-duration instruments. Still, it does display what we all want – we want stable returns over specific time periods. And we want stable returns because you can eat those returns with greater predictability. In other words, you can plan your life more clearly if you know how much money you'll have at specific times in the future.

Here's the big conclusion – the pursuit of stable and steady returns is a good goal. And you can absolutely eat risk-adjusted returns. You just need to be mindful about the cost of those returns and the specific time periods over which you're trying to achieve them.

YOUR HOUSE AS AN INVESTMENT

Probably the most important asset you'll ever purchase is your house. Houses are basically big blocks of depreciating commodities (wood, cement, etc.) built on top of an appreciating piece of land. That big block of commodities is enormously expensive to maintain and the real returns we generate from this asset are likely to be lower than we think.

I know this all too well as I purchased a fixer-upper in 2017 with zero experience in construction. It took us two years to get a permit (yay, California) and then we found out we were expecting our first child about nine months later. I asked our general contractor how long the project would take and when he told me 15 months, I decided I needed to become a part-time construction worker. I would work my day job from 6 a.m. to 3 p.m. and then become a construction worker every day for nine months from 3 p.m. to 9 p.m. to ensure it was done before my daughter came.

While I can now brag about being proficient in framing, drywalling, and skid steer driving, I also lost about 10 million brain cells and nearly a few limbs along the way. I've slowly acquired the equivalent of a small Home Depot in my house as I regularly repair and update things. While my situation was unique, these are the kind of negative returns a lot of homeowners don't like to tell you about.

Let's talk about the empirical data though. Bob Shiller, the creator of the Case-Shiller Housing Index, has compiled data on the long-term real returns of housing which shows that houses have generated about 0.59% per year in real returns since 1890. The vast majority of these returns came in the run-up to the housing bubble of 2008 and the post-Covid housing euphoria. See Figure 22.2.

Figure 22.2: US house price real returns

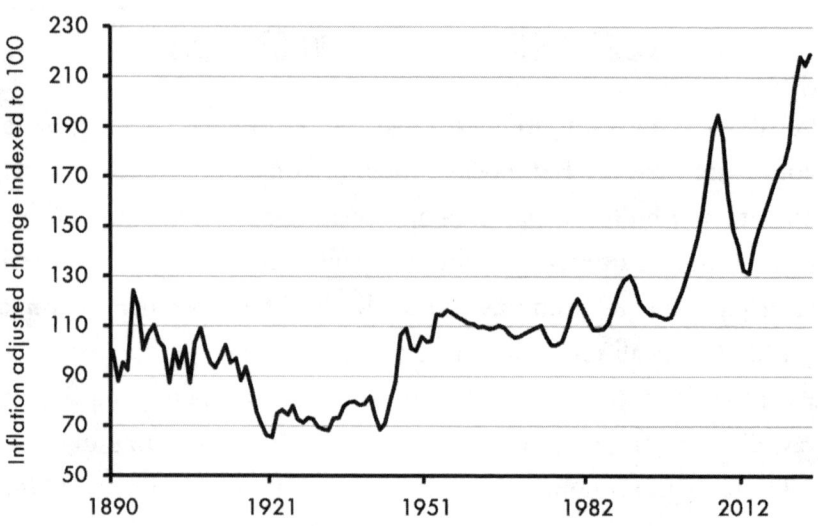

When you back out inflation, maintenance, and transaction costs there's a strong probability that your house will not be a great investment. And unless you operate a real estate business I don't think you should consider your house as an investment at all. It is, first and foremost, a place for you to live and raise a family. It's not a money-making endeavor. Sure, it would be great if you make some money on the house as you're living in it, but you should own it for personal and practical reasons, not pure financial reasons.

All that being said, one consideration in the scope of our discussion that could be very important is whether you own or rent a home. In the same way that your income is like a bond, you can think of your house as a commodity allocation. That is, if you own a house you should consider that you already own a significant commodity allocation. And this might mean you don't need a large commodity allocation in your savings portfolio.

Further, if you have a fixed-rate mortgage then you are effectively short the bond market. That is, your mortgage operates like a hedge against your interest rate risk and this could play a role in how you think about your other bond allocations. I made a lot of dumb decisions while building our house, but the 2.5% mortgage we locked in has turned out to be one of the best investments I've ever made, in large part because it hedged all my other bond positions across my portfolio and has allowed me to earn a hefty excess return on the stocks we maintained (as opposed to buying the house without a mortgage).

When you approach the buy versus rent decision you'll come across a million different opinions and online calculators. None of them can apply your personal circumstances and financial or familial needs and wants. I like to think of a house as a long-duration instrument. And this means your buy versus rent decision is mostly a temporal decision. The odds of you losing money in real estate over a 15-year period is very low. In my Defined Duration model, residential real estate comes out to be a 19-year instrument. If you'd purchased a home at the very peak of the 2006 housing bubble you'd be indifferent to that price change, in real terms, within 15 years. So it's a very long duration instrument and you should go into any buy versus rent analysis with time as an essential consideration.

As a rule of thumb, your buy versus rent decision comes down primarily to how long you plan on being in a particular location. If you're planning to be in a certain area for 15+ years and you can afford the mortgage and down payment then you should probably consider buying. If you're planning to be somewhere temporarily then it's probably wiser to rent.

In short, don't pursue the purchase of a home primarily based on financial returns. Purchase a home that you can afford and makes sense for your family over certain time horizons. If it turns out to be a sound financial investment then that's just icing on your cake.

LET'S TALK ABOUT INSURANCE

I've spent a lot of time in this book talking about the various ways to insure your portfolio. But I would be remiss if I didn't briefly talk about insurance more generally as well. I have a mixed experience with the insurance industry and while a younger Cullen would have been more critical of most forms of insurance, I've come to appreciate it thanks to getting older (and hopefully wiser) and realizing the value of certainty across time. And that's what insurance is designed to do – protect certain assets across certain time horizons to give you peace of mind. Your perfect portfolio might just end up working better because it's better insured.

My first job out of college was selling variable annuities and long-term care insurance. Every morning I would walk into a room filled

CHAPTER 22

with 50 other recent college graduates where each of us was making cold calls from a copy of the *White Pages*.* I had a real problem with this job because I was bad at selling stuff and I was interested in analyzing the product we were selling. I once walked into my boss's office and said, "Terry, I've run some numbers on this product and it doesn't do what the sales material claims it does, can you help me understand this so I can explain it to potential customers?" He took the paper, looked at it, looked at me and threw it in the trash. He said, "Cullen, you don't get paid to analyze the products, you get paid to sell the products." Let's just say I didn't last long at that job.

I often joke that the investment management business has mastered the art of selling the hope of market-beating returns in exchange for the guarantee of high fees. There's an uncomfortable amount of truth to this – there are a lot of financial products that I personally believe should not exist. In the last 30 years the industry has created numerous forms of "alternative" investments that masquerade as alternatives to a 60/40 Portfolio but are largely high-fee products that don't add much value over the core assets in our economy.

At the same time, many of these products are perfectly fine. For example, I've never been a big fan of whole life insurance, but a product like term life insurance is a very practical part of any financial plan. A term life insurance policy is a financial asset that has a negative expected future real return over a specific term. But in the off chance that the policy is needed it can provide a very large asymmetric real return that insures someone in case of death. This could provide life-changing support for the dependents of the insured person.

If we think of stocks and bonds as the center of our financial asset ecosystem then we can look at many of the satellite instruments as forms of insurance. After all, the main argument in favor of portfolio

---

* For the kids in the crowd – the White Pages was a book filled with people's phone numbers.

insurance and many alternative asset classes is that stocks and bonds will not always be sufficient diversifiers on their own. That's because these instruments very often become correlated. Bonds don't always zig when stocks zag. And in periods where they both zig at the same time, it can be helpful to own something that is more likely to zag at that time. More broadly speaking, from a financial planning perspective insurance should always be a consideration in the context of our total portfolio.

So, as we've seen with many of the previous portfolios in this book, it can make a lot of sense to add something that is completely different.

Term life insurance

Buy term and invest the difference. That's the old saying that term life insurance advocates would use and it's exactly right. Term insurance should be used to cover you during a period where your dependents would be devastated by a loss of income. For example, a 35-year-old father who's the sole income earner should consider a 20–30-year term life insurance policy so that his wife and children are covered in case of untimely death. There's no need to overthink this sort of stuff. Buy term and invest the difference.

Whole life insurance*

---

* This section is left blank because there's nothing to say about these things since they're terrible.

CHAPTER 22

HOME BIAS VERSUS GLOBAL BIAS

This is a never-ending debate in financial circles. Especially for Americans. Should we own foreign stocks or does owning US stocks give you enough foreign exposure?

Companies included in the S&P 500 generate about 40% of their revenue from abroad. Some people will argue that this is sufficient to hedge foreign exposure, which means you don't need any foreign stock exposure. This is partially true, but it doesn't change the fact that foreign stocks beat the pants off US stocks during periods of US dollar depreciation.

In the last 50+ years there have been three major USD depreciation events: 1970–1980, 1985–1990, and 2001–2008. During each of these periods foreign stocks more than doubled S&P 500 returns and did so with significantly uncorrelated returns. Table 22.1 shows the difference in performance across these environments.

Table 22.1: USD depreciation = foreign stock outperformance

USD Depreciation	1970–1980 (CAGR)	1985–1995 (CAGR)	2001–2008 (CAGR)
US stocks	5.86%	19.22%	4.97%
Foreign stocks	9.49% (Beta 59%)	34.83% (Beta 37%)	10.28% (Beta 65%)

In short, the main benefit of owning foreign stocks is that you're hedging your domestic currency risk. Yes, this hasn't often been a significant problem for Americans and the US's global reserve currency status, but it's a very significant risk for foreign investors and could potentially become a problem for Americans. As I write this in 2025 it appears that we could be on the verge of the fourth major USD devaluation and foreign stocks are outperforming US stocks in 2025, as expected.

When I consider this issue I view the domestic currency risk as something that is very easily hedged away. And while currency devaluation isn't a huge risk for the global reserve currency issuer, it's also not a zero-probability risk. So I kind of look at this as a situation where the outcomes are potentially asymmetric and given the historical ebb and flow of global returns I say why wouldn't you hedge this risk by owning global stocks?

GLOBAL BONDS VERSUS DOMESTIC BONDS

When it comes to stocks, the argument for home bias is less convincing for me. But when it comes to bonds I don't think this one is really in question.

Bonds are nominal principal stabilizing instruments. They don't beat inflation over time and they don't need to be utilized to protect you from inflation. While stocks and other instruments are your inflation hedges, bonds are your principal hedges over specific time periods. This means that your bonds should be especially safe instruments. And when it comes to safe bonds there's just nothing that comes close to US government bonds in the present environment.

The problem with owning foreign bonds and even corporate bonds is that they often behave a lot like stocks at the same time stocks are behaving badly. For example, in 2008 investment-grade corporate bonds fell 22%. High-yield corporate bonds fell 33%. These instruments did not protect you from volatility at a time when you most needed them to. Intermediate US government bonds, on the other hand, were up over 15% in 2008 as investors reached for the safest instruments in the world. This is what we want from our bonds. We want them to be stable at times when everything else is unstable

CHAPTER 22

and in the world of dirty fiat currencies we want to own the cleanest dirty shirt in the closet.

Speaking of being the cleanest dirty shirt in the fiat closet, it's worth putting some figures on this data for emphasis as people are constantly questioning the quality of the US government's liabilities. The US economy is the largest in the world with over $30 trillion of GDP. The net worth of the US private sector is an astounding $200 trillion. The reason the US government issues the most reliable and stable liabilities is because they are the entity that can tax the wealthiest private sector that has ever existed. The US doesn't have a better printing press than Argentina. It has a better private sector, and that means the money printer in the US is less damaging, in inflationary terms, because the US economy has so much more capacity to absorb.

I mentioned earlier that the US is likely to see a decline in its relative reserve currency status, but we're still talking about a wide gulf between the US and the rest of the world. As of 2025, the euro is the second most widely held reserve currency at 18% of foreign reserves, and the yen accounts for just 5%. The dollar's 50%+ share may decline, but even if it were to fall meaningfully to, say, 30% it would *still* be the most dominant liability issuer by a large margin.

This dominance is also reflected in global tax revenues as the US generates an astounding $5 trillion in federal tax revenue while the second closest liability issuer is Japan at just $1.5 trillion. When we compare the relative safety of different liabilities there is just nothing that comes close to the income generation, wealth, and overall market share of the US. And by virtue of this, it makes the US government's liabilities uniquely special.

As Bill Bernstein emphasized, we want to own bonds for principal stability and that means we need to own the right kinds of bonds. In a world of dirty fiat shirts, the US is the cleanest shirt and likely will be for a very long time.

ASSET LOCATION AND TAXES

I used to spend an excessive amount of time trying to optimize everything for taxes. When structuring a portfolio financial advisors refer to this as "asset location." That is, placing assets in the most optimal tax-efficient location. And yes, there are certain cases where taxes make a huge difference, but it shouldn't be the primary reason you own something or the primary determinant for why you place an asset in a certain location.

For example, many people will tell you that bonds are not tax efficient and should therefore be placed in tax-deferred or tax-free accounts. But this ignores the fact that your tax-deferred accounts are most likely to be your more aggressive long-term accounts. It might be totally inappropriate to hold short-term instruments like bonds in there. In fact, the place where you most likely need liquidity is in a taxable account, so even though it might not be the most tax-optimized place to hold bonds, it is the most practical liquidity pool.

I typically think of taxes as a secondary factor when considering asset location. In other words, if you need liquidity in a taxable account then don't be afraid to place short-term fixed income instruments in there. And absolutely don't place all your bonds in a long-term account like an IRA just because that's the most tax-efficient bucket. After all, that's the place where you likely have the longest time horizon and the most flexibility so in most cases it's the place where you can afford to be the most aggressive.

In short, taxes matter, but don't always let the tax man be the primary determinant over your asset allocation.

CHAPTER 22

GOOD DEBT AND BAD DEBT

We've talked a lot about managing your assets over time, but your liabilities will often fund your ability to afford certain assets or expenses. There's nothing inherently good nor bad about debt, but it can be extremely destructive when it's not used wisely.

One way to assess good debt and bad debt is to consider the likely rate of return on assets. For example, if you are renting a home and believe you can earn 10% returns using cash to invest in the stock market then there's no sense in taking that cash and purchasing a house with a 10% mortgage (unless, as we noted, it makes personal sense). In other words, when the cost of debt is higher than the potential return you can earn elsewhere then we can immediately assess that as bad debt. This is why credit card debt is so destructive. When you're paying 20% interest rates it's virtually certain that you are earning a worse relative return compared to alternative return streams.

This is also why paying down high-interest debts is oftentimes a superior option to owning other assets. When you pay off a 20% credit card loan you can think of that as guaranteeing a 20% return compared to other alternatives. Paying down or avoiding high debts can often be the best investment option you ever make.

Additionally, some people will swear by the peace of mind of having no debt. While most financial nerds will tell you that low-interest debt allows you to reinvest cash at a higher return, there is a reasonable behavioral aspect to the idea that you should pay down debt in order to create peace of mind and guaranteed returns. As we've noted over and over again in this book, you need to do what's good for you behaviorally and not what's good for you in theory.

TIPS VERSUS PLAIN VANILLA TREASURY BONDS

I go back and forth on this debate. Many famous investors discussed in this book prefer TIPS for their embedded inflation protection. On the other hand, several others favor Treasury bonds because of their deflation protection.

I don't have a strong opinion on this one to be honest. The types of bonds and the maturities you buy will always end up being an inflation bet of some sort. That is, if inflation is very high then TIPS will typically beat your vanilla bonds. And if we get deflation, or even disinflation, then TIPS will likely lose to vanilla bonds.

The good news is that we don't have to pick just one. You can hedge your bets and own both TIPS and plain vanilla T-bonds. Or, if you have a strong feeling on which direction inflation will go, you know what to choose.

INDIVIDUAL BONDS VERSUS BOND FUNDS

This is something I've done a 360 on during my career. I used to buy nothing but individual bonds when I was a broker at Merrill Lynch. And then as I became an indexing advocate I deferred towards simplicity and owning bond funds only.

But there's a nasty behavioral quirk in bond funds that I didn't appreciate. Because investors can't see the bonds maturing they can create a lot of uncertainty. This is why I said I don't always love constant maturity bond funds. Their constant maturity doesn't create the kind of certainty that people really desire from bonds, especially short-term bonds. So, I like to buy individual bonds where certainty is needed; for instance, in portfolios with a short-term bond ladder bucket. A constant maturity bond fund can work for longer time horizons, assuming the investor understands the principal risk they're taking in the intermediate term.

ALL YOUR BENCHMARKS ARE WRONG

There, I said it. I know, we need some general benchmark to assess whether certain things are good or bad, but you also need to be careful when benchmarking. I've employed benchmarking throughout this book, but none of those benchmarks are perfect apples-to-apples comparisons.

Once you realize that the GFAP is the one true global financial asset benchmark and that we all deviate from this portfolio then you need to assess your asset allocation in the context of why *you* deviated, not whether it performs better than something like the S&P 500. The thing is, benchmarks will so often look superior to real-life implementations because benchmarks, by definition, do not incur the real-life frictions we all incur across time. As a result they can create a false impression of what your targets and expectations should be.

Remember, you are not in a sprint against the greenest grass in the neighborhood. You're running in a marathon toward your own financial goals – and the only benchmark that truly matters is your personal set of financial needs.

23

PORTFOLIO MANAGEMENT

LET'S discuss a few important things to consider so you can optimize the way you implement your plan and maintain it over time.

1. YOUR RISK PROFILE

One of the most important decisions you'll make as an investor is defining your risk profile. There are countless definitions of what a risk profile is – and even more methods for determining yours. The most common approach is to go through some sort of profiling questionnaire. This is how most advisors and firms perform risk profiles and I have to admit that I don't love that process because it generally involves a bunch of generic, cookie-cutter questions that everyone knows the "right" answers to.

For example, I used to send clients a question about how they might respond to a large market downturn. Predictably, everyone gave the textbook answer – you're supposed to buy during a downturn, right? But the problem is when the stock market falls 30% during something like Covid, most of us will be fearful and assume that the downturn is not over yet. We get frozen by fear because we assume the 30% downturn is the start of a 50% downturn. We hesitate, we wait, and then we miss the recovery. In practice, the emotions don't match the survey responses. So these questionnaires end up being useless because they measure theory, and not realistic behavior.

Another approach is to use something more systematic like the age-in-bonds rule or a target date fund approach. Those are fine options, but very general. As I've already noted, something like the age-in-bonds rule could serve you broadly well, but in certain circumstances, like retirement, could also serve you precisely wrong.

I prefer to use the aforementioned asset-liability matching approach. As I noted in the Defined Duration chapter, your risk profile is really a function of any asset-liability mismatch. People say they sell stocks during a bear market because they're scared – but what they're really craving is the certainty that cash provides across time. The root of the problem isn't just fear; it's the uncertainty baked into a misaligned asset allocation. The solution is to increase certainty in your portfolio. And you do that by building a sound financial plan and understanding how your assets are designed to protect you over time. In the context of the Five Pillars of Defined Duration – if you knew you had two years' worth of cash set aside to cover near-term expenses in Pillar One and then another 20% of your portfolio in safe short-term instruments in Pillar Two, you'd be far less likely to panic and sell stocks during a downturn because you have so much embedded certainty over your ability to ride out a stock market downturn.

We created a quant-based risk profiling tool at Discipline Funds to help investors obtain a better understanding of their risk profile by implementing an asset-liability matching profile. Instead of assigning assets based on vague behavioral assumptions, the tool matches your assets based on a specific financial plan and then fills in the blanks.

You can find the Portfolio Builder, Risk Profiling tool, and much more at www.ria.disciplinefunds.com/tool-suite.

2. INVESTMENT VEHICLES

As you know by now, I am a big fan of ETFs. There are a few unique cases here where I am open-minded to mutual funds (like interval funds or hedge fund replicators, which wouldn't work well as ETFs), but in general I think you should adhere to a mostly ETF strategy. The one major exception is owning individual government bonds, which are functionally diverse in that they're liabilities of the biggest income-generating entity in human history. The other obvious exception is when a product cannot be replicated using liquid underlying instruments.

The secret sauce of ETFs is that they provide a very tight correlation between the actual ETF and the underlying instruments the ETF is designed to track. But the underlying instruments need to be somewhat liquid. They have to be traded actively enough to give us a reasonably real-time pricing structure to allow the market makers to make the ETF work well in the first place. This is why mutual funds and private label funds can sometimes be better wrappers for less liquid strategies.

3. INVESTMENT ACCOUNTS

As we noted earlier, the way you house your investments can make a big difference. You should always aim to optimize the use of vehicles like Health Savings Accounts, IRAs, 401(k)s, LLCs, and Trusts to help protect and efficiently structure your assets.

Further, be mindful of the way you allocate your assets across specific account types. Many of these accounts, such as IRAs, are specifically designed to be longer-term investments and therefore give you the flexibility to be much more aggressive there.

4. REBALANCING

There isn't strong empirical evidence about the optimal way to rebalance, except that less is often more. In general, I lean toward rebalancing annually or less frequently, both to reduce unnecessary trading and to take advantage of lower long-term capital gains tax rates when possible.

Your plan will evolve over time, and rebalancing is a necessary part of the process. To avoid triggering huge costs along the way I think a once-a-year rebalancing rule is just fine. Then again, it very much depends on the asset and the portfolio or strategy you choose to employ. A more active strategy may require more active management. But all else being equal, less is usually more when it comes to rebalancing. Of course, there are always exceptions. As I've noted, I am very hands-on with cash, oftentimes rolling T-bills every quarter. So, it depends.

5. ACTIVITY

I've made it clear that we're all active investors, and there's nothing wrong with that. But beware of being *overly* active, which can lead to excessive taxes and fees. Taxes are the biggie here, and it's always smart to limit unnecessary tinkering that might trigger short-term capital gains.

At the same time, don't be afraid to scratch an itch if it helps you stay disciplined more generally. If keeping 5% of your portfolio in individual stocks that you actively trade makes it easier to stick with a 95% indexing core, that's a perfectly reasonable trade-off.

6. FINANCIAL MEDIA

Don't be afraid to consume financial media, but keep it in the right perspective. Consuming financial news is mostly about staying informed and not so you can jump on the latest investment craze. There are millions of people trying to get your attention and hoping you'll react to their narratives. Financial media is especially hopeful that they can grab your attention, oftentimes preying on your emotions in the process. It's their job to generate eyeballs, not to give you sound advice. After all, if the financial media was accurate they'd write the same thing 95% of all days of the week and it would sound something like this:

> The markets went up and down, nothing much interesting happened, and people mostly went about their lives in a disinteresting manner.

Instead, they'll focus on exciting short-term market moves and whatever fearful narrative is consuming the markets at present. And look, there's nothing wrong with focusing on big risks out there and staying informed. I watch financial TV every day and consume an egregious amount of financial news. But just be sure to consume financial media with the right perspective and a critical eye so you don't overreact.

7. FEED THE BEAST

The secret sauce to any good relationship is to keep feeding it and reinvesting in it. Buffett's secret wasn't just great stock picking. It was consistently contributing to a disciplined plan regardless of what was going on.

As Nick Maggiulli, an advisor and author of a fantastic book by the same name, would say, "JUST KEEP BUYING." You need that Buffett cash-flow machine to keep feeding the beast over time. This not only helps you dollar cost average (unemotionally buying in a consistent manner over time), but it helps consistently take low or zero interest-bearing instruments (your cash income) and reallocate them to higher return-generating instruments. This is an essential piece to keeping your plan healthy.

8. WITHDRAWAL RATES

When you enter retirement, you'll inevitably go down a number of rabbit holes about optimal withdrawal rates. The general rule is something like the 4% rule, but I believe you need to go into excruciating personal detail to quantify this concept. General rules will never apply to you at a personal level.

When you're navigating the lifetime of your perfect portfolio it's going to be important to remember that we cannot control the return of the markets, but we can control our spending. You may not know what stocks will do, but your expenses are far more predictable and manageable. In retirement especially, it's important to have a clear understanding of your liabilities and how they align with your expected asset returns.

Generic rules will be good for general guidance, but you'll need to get down and dirty with the specific details to assess this properly.

9. RETIREMENT PLANNING

As I discussed in multiple chapters, retirement is likely to be the most difficult financial transition you undergo. This is going to be the period in your life where having a plan and certainty will be most important.

The one big key here is to plan ahead. The transition into retirement is difficult for many people because they didn't properly prepare for it. But when you have a plan, like a bond tent or similar approach, then you can better process the difficult transition periods of early retirement.

So don't wait. The earlier you start building a plan, the better. It's important to have a general plan or direction in your early investing journey, and when you reach your 40s or 50s you want to further refine and organize your retirement strategy so you can reach your 60s and ultimate retirement with comfort and confidence.

10. ESTATE PLANNING

A perfect portfolio is optimized when it's most useful for its beneficiaries. And for some of us, our portfolios are likely to become someone else's portfolios at some point in time. Your spouse, children, and other beneficiaries need to be considered in the scope of creating your perfect portfolio because they could ultimately be the ones relying on that portfolio. And this is where sound estate planning comes into play.

Good estate planning means working with an estate planning attorney or financial planner to help you tie up any loose ends in a broader plan. This includes tax planning, trusts, wills, and ensuring that you have beneficiaries assigned on the proper accounts. Your perfect portfolio will appear highly imperfect if your beneficiaries end up having to go through the court system just to get access to it.

Speaking of spouses and estate planning – I deal with this problem far too often so I'll just say it – talk to your spouse about money. Far too many couples let one spouse handle all the finances only to confront an environment in the future where the other spouse now has the responsibility and is in the dark and unprepared. Don't be those people. Perhaps the most important part of your perfect portfolio is making sure you and your spouse both understand it.

11. PATIENCE AND DISCIPLINE

It's only appropriate to finish this book with a note about patience and discipline. If I had to pick the most essential element of investment success it would be understanding time. Patience and discipline are the essential ingredients to navigating time in the investment landscape.

Patience and discipline aren't just virtues – they're the foundation of lasting investment success. Markets will rise and fall. Strategies will come in and out of favor. But if you've built a plan rooted in your personal goals and grounded in time, your most powerful move is to stay the course. The investors who succeed aren't the ones who chase every market move – they're the ones who understand that real progress comes quietly, over years, through steady commitment. Build a plan you can live with, and then give it the one thing it truly needs: time.

★★★

Gosh. I guess that's all I've got to say. I hope you learned something interesting at the very least – and maybe, just maybe, found *your* perfect portfolio along the way.

If you'd like to talk more about your own search for the right plan, feel free to reach out at cullenroche@disciplinefunds.com. I would love to help however I can.

Thanks for reading – and as always, stay disciplined… and don't skip leg day.

ACKNOWLEDGMENTS

A very special thanks is in order for Craig Pearce and the whole team at Harriman House who made this book possible. I am also grateful for feedback from Wesley Gray, Mebane Faber, Cliff Asness, Corey Hoffstein, Morgan Housel, William Bernstein, Michael Covel, Taylor Larimore, and my mom and dad. I owe a special thanks to the online creators I've researched and talked to in the process of considering these portfolios including John Williamson's Optimized Portfolios, Ben Felix's YouTube channel and Rob Berger's YouTube channel.

And most importantly, thanks to my wife Erica and daughters Della and Liv – you all are my real Perfect Portfolio.

ENDNOTES

1   *See* Bradley C. Johnston et al., "Comparison of Weight Loss Among Named Diet Programs in Overweight and Obese Adults," *JAMA* (September 3, 2014), and Christopher D. Gardner et al., "Effect of Low-Fat vs Low-Carbohydrate Diet on 12-Month Weight Loss in Overweight Adults and the Association with Genotype Pattern or Insulin Secretion," *JAMA* (February 20, 2018).

2   www.spglobal.com.

3   William F. Sharpe, "The Arithmetic of Active Management," *The Financial Analysts' Journal* (February 1991), stanford.edu.

4   Michael Cembalest, "The Agony & The Ecstasy," J.P. Morgan Private Bank (November 30, 2022), www.privatebank.jpmorgan.com.

5   Azra Zaimovic et al., "How Many Stocks Are Sufficient for Equity Portfolio Diversification? A Review of the Literature," *Journal of Risk and Financial Management* (November 15, 2021).

6   Stéphane Garelli, "Why you will probably live longer than most big companies," IMD (December 2016) www.imd.org.

7   Warren Buffett, "Buffett: How inflation swindles the equity investor," *Fortune* (May 1, 1977).

8   Barry Ritholtz, "Barry Ritholtz, Everyone Loves a Good Story," *The Washington Post* (July 26, 2013), www.washingtonpost.com.

9   Morgan Housel, *The Psychology of Money* (Harriman House, 2020).

10   Andrea Frazzini et al., "Buffett's Alpha," National Bureau of Economic Research (November, 2013), www.nber.org.

11   Aizhan Anarkulova, Scott Cederburg, and Michael S. O'Doherty, "Beyond the Status Quo: A Critical Assessment of Lifecycle Investment Advice," ssrn.com (March 3, 2025).

12   Cliff Asness, "Why Not 100% Equities," aqr.com (February 12, 2024).

13   Hendrik Bessembinder, "Do Stocks Outperform Treasury Bills?" ssrn.com (May 28, 2018).

14   Jason Zweig, "What Harry Markowitz Meant," Jason Zweig (July 7, 2025), www.jasonzweig.com.

15   Benjamin Graham, *The Intelligent Investor* (Harper Business, 2006).

16   "Capital Markets Fact Book," SIFMA Research (July 30, 2024), www.sifma.org.

17   The WFE Statistics Team, "Market Statistics – December 2024," Focus (November, 2024), www.focus.world-exchanges.org.

18   Richard C. Koo, *The Holy Grail of Macroeconomics: Lessons from Japan's Great Recession* (Wiley, 2009).

19   Joseph A. Schumpeter, *Capitalism, Socialism, And Democracy: Third Edition* (HarperCollins, 2008), Chapters 7–8.

20   Cliff Asness, "There Is No Size Effect: Daily Edition," AQR (September 18, 2020), www.aqr.com.

21   "Fact, Fiction, and Momentum Investing," *The Journal of Portfolio Management*, www.aqr.com.

22   "The All Weather Story," Bridgewater (January, 2012), www.bridgewater.com.

23   "Ray Dalio Breaks Down His 'Holy Grail'," YouTube (April 27, 2019).

24   *Leatherneck Magazine*, April 2018.

25   Christine Benz, "Simplify Your Investment Plan," *Morningstar* (October 9, 2017), www.morningstar.com.

26   Taylor Larimore, "The Three-fund Portfolio," Bogleheads.org (January 1, 2012). www.bogleheads.org.

27   "John Bogle on how to create perfect asset allocation," YouTube (June 24, 2018).

28   William F. Sharpe, "Adaptive Asset Allocation Policies," (November, 2009), stanford.edu.

29   William Bernstein, "Riskless at Age 104," Advisor Perspectives (March 20, 2023), www.advisorperspectives.com.

30   Matthijs de Jongh, "Shareholder Activism at the Dutch East India Company 1622–1625," *Origins of Shareholder Advocacy* (Palgrave Macmillan, 2011), www.papers.ssrn.com.

31 Berkshire's Corporate Performance vs. the S&P 500, www.berkshirehathaway.com/letters/2012ltr.pdf.

32 Ken Fisher, "Chapter 8: High Dividends for Sure Income," *The Little Book of Market Myths* (John Wiley & Sons, Inc., 2013), www.kenfisher.com.

33 **Disclosure**: I serve as an independent trustee for Cambria ETFs mentioned in this chapter and elsewhere in this book. My role is fiduciary in nature and I do not receive compensation from the fund sponsor or advisor, related to the fund's sales and/or performance. This discussion is intended for educational purposes and should not be interpreted as a recommendation or endorsement of any specific investment product.

34 Jesse Livermore, *How to Trade in Stocks* (New York, 1940), p. 20.

35 Brian K. Hurst et al., "A Century of Evidence on Trend-Following Investing," AQR (November 1, 2017), www.aqr.com.

36 Cliff Asness, "Virtue is its Own Reward or One Man's Ceiling is Another Man's Floor," AQR (May 18, 2017), www.aqr.com.

37 Elroy Dimson and David Chambers, "Keynes' asset management: King's College, 1921–1946: The British origins of the US endowment model," VoxEU (October 20, 2014).

38 David Chambers et al., "Keynes, King's and Endowment Asset Management," in *How the Financial Crisis and Great Recession Affected Higher Education* (University of Chicago Press, 2015).

39 David Chambers et al., "Seventy-Five Years of Investing for Future Generations," *Financial Analysts Journal* (September 27, 2020).

40 "How David Swensen Made Yale Fabulously Rich and Changed Endowments," Bloomberg UK.

41 Jamil Baz and Christian Stracke, "Liquidity, Complexity and Scale in Private Markets," Pimco (March 19, 2019), www.pimco.com.

42 Michael Kitces, "The Portfolio Size Effect and Using a Bond Tent to Navigate the Retirement Danger Zone," Nerd's Eye View (October 5, 2016), www.kitces.com.

43 Hal R. Varian, "Why Is That Dollar Bill in Your Pocket Worth Anything?" *The New York Times* (January 15, 2004).

44 "Vanguard LifeStrategy Funds," www.investor.vanguard.com/investment-products/mutual-funds/life-strategy-funds.

ABOUT THE AUTHOR

Cullen Roche is the Founder and CIO of Discipline Funds where he oversees portfolio management and product development. He is a member of the Board of ETF Trustees at Cambria Investments and a graduate of Georgetown University. He started his career at Merrill Lynch Global Wealth Management and has founded several of his own financial firms since setting out on his own in 2005. He wrote the popular book *Pragmatic Capitalism* and manages the website of the same name. His papers "Understanding the Modern Monetary System" and "Understanding Modern Portfolio Construction" are some of the most popular research papers in the SSRN database. He grew up in Washington DC with seven brothers and sisters before moving to San Diego, CA with his wife Erica and daughters Della and Liv.

DISCLAIMER

The information in this book is provided for educational and informational purposes only and does not constitute investment, financial, legal, or tax advice. The views expressed are solely those of the author and do not reflect the opinions of any organization with which the author is affiliated. Readers are encouraged to consult a qualified professional before making any investment decisions. Investments involve risk, including the potential loss of principal. Past performance is not indicative of future results.

The author serves as an independent trustee for the board that oversees certain exchange-traded funds (ETFs) mentioned in this book. This role is fiduciary in nature and does not involve any affiliation with the fund sponsor or advisor beyond oversight responsibilities on behalf of fund shareholders. The author does not receive compensation from any ETF sponsor discussed herein as it pertains to fund sales or performance. Any mention of specific ETFs is incidental and for illustrative or educational purposes only, and should not be interpreted as an endorsement or recommendation.

The author and creators of the strategies discussed in this text do not necessarily endorse any specific implementation within this text. This book is for educational purposes only and the strategies should be implemented with the help of a qualified financial professional.

Another great title
from Harriman House

Have you always followed the rules? Do you believe that beating the stock market is just luck? Learn how to pick the best stocks of the future from The Motley Fool's Chief Rule Breaker.

Available from all good book stores

Another great title
from Harriman House

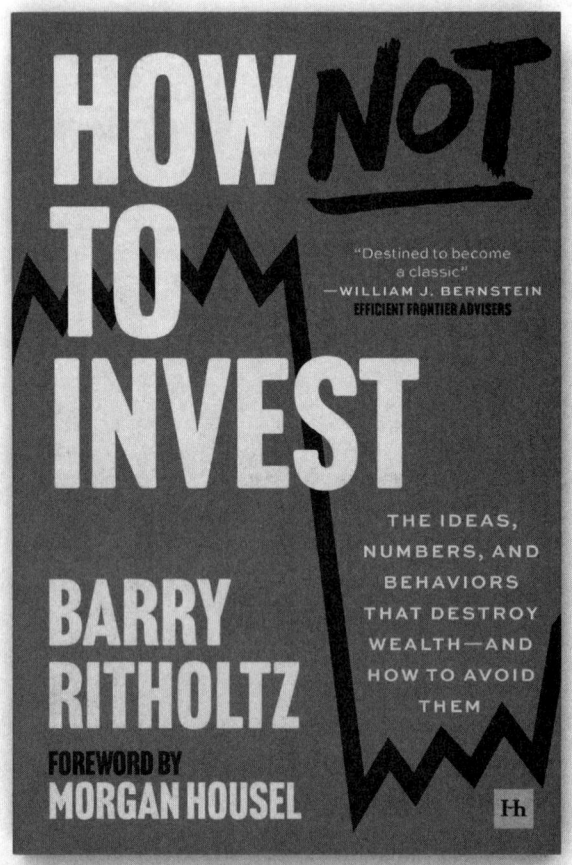

Avoiding errors is much more important than scoring wins. *How Not To Invest* shows you a few simple tools to help you avoid the most common mistakes people make with their money.

Available from all good book stores

Another great title *from* Harriman House

The *Sunday Times* Number One Bestseller.
Morgan Housel explores the strange ways people think about money and teaches you how to make better sense of one of life's most important topics.

Available from all good book stores

Another great title
from Harriman House

Act smarter, live richer by learning why you need to save less than you think, why saving up cash to buy market dips isn't a good idea, and how to survive and thrive during a market crash.

Available from all good book stores